THE SICILIAN KITCHEN

For my parents, who are perfect.
For my brother, who keeps it funny.
For my family, who provides the material.
And for all those who got on the boat.

Thank you.

THE SICILIAN KITCHEN

MICHELE DI'BARTOLO

LANTERN
an imprint of
PENGUIN BOOKS

CONTENTS

WEST END

This is where I grew up
Surrounded on all sides
By the immigrants of Greece
And Vietnam

By the age of ten I had heard
Marital disputes
In almost every language
Learnt an army of
Greek swear words
And could barter
With the 100-year-old
Vietnamese owner
Of the Vulture Street bakery.

We start at the beginning

One day is all it takes to change the destiny of an entire family, both for those present and for those yet to come. Sometimes I wonder what would have become of me if my grandfather was a stronger man, and when his domineering wife said, "Melo, we must leave this place,' he had stood up for himself and said no.

21 April 1959: the birth of my family in its new land.

21 April 1959: the day they arrived in Australia.

On this one day my family stepped from the boat, off the worn track of their history, and made a turn for the unknown.

Nonna Anna is sitting at her kitchen table in her West End home and inner-city Brisbane is buzzing around her. I am sitting directly across the table from her and I watch carefully as she wipes a broad palm across her face and slowly shakes her head.

'Today, forty-seven years ago, we came here,' she says. 'I swear it was only yesterday.'

I look up over the top of her head to the high VJ walls, the panels of timber locking tongue-in-groove and keeping this Queenslander together. This house has stood twice as long as the years Nonna has lived in it, and the smells and sounds of forty-seven years of Sicilian life have been absorbed into its timber walls. Maybe if you chip down far enough you will uncover the smells and sounds of those who lived here before the Sicilians came. Before the whispered kitchen conversations late into the night while everyone else was asleep; the screaming over the sound of plates shattering against the walls; and the roar of laughter coupled with the beating of feet to a frantic tarantella.

My eyes drift down from the timber-slatted walls and back to Nonna's face. Time, it seems, has moved too fast. Her face is that of an eighty-year-old woman, but her soul is still aged forty, and her will is still that of a twenty-year-old girl. Now she finds herself trapped, so suddenly, in a body that won't move.

'Ah,' she says, and mutters the word 'time' under her breath, as if it's become a concept she can't quite comprehend.

Forty-seven years is less than a lifetime. For me, immigration is not a distant memory or something that happened so long ago I repeat it like a worn piece of family history. The people who walked off that boat can still recount in living colour everything they left behind.

'I promised never to return,' Nonna says to me.

'What do you mean?'

'When I left I was happy that I was leaving. When the boat pulled away I promised never to return. I even said it out loud.' She looks past me, out her kitchen window and into her West End backyard. In her small brown eyes I can see the past return and the coast of Sicily reappear. Sadness flares on her face, then just as quickly fades away. I understand in that moment how brave you have to be to look on something you love with the knowledge that you will never see it again. I understand how Sicilian you have to be to know pain like that, but for the sake of pride pretend you are pleased it is happening to you.

'Don't you want to see your home again?' I ask.

'What for?' she replies. 'I have everything here. Family and food. Besides, you can breathe in Australia. Sicily is a prison.'

Nonna stops and again gazes out of the long window and into her backyard. Two pigeons have landed on her clothesline and they make her smile.

'But Sicily is so beautiful,' she breathes.

'Tell me what it was like, leaving.'

Nonna shakes her head slowly from side to side, with her brown eyes closed and her small mouth pinched shut. Her hand reaches up and softly touches the top of her head, as if a point of pain is piercing her skull.

'I've never heard screaming like that,' she shakes her head again and one of the brown curls on her head slowly unfolds. 'Carmelina was leaving that day as well and her sister was on the wharf watching the boat pull away. I've never seen or heard anything like it.'

Her brown eyes open wide.

'With her body she was going like this,' Nonna rocks forward and back in her chair. 'They had to hold her back from throwing herself into the sea.'

I look out of the window and into the concrete backyard. The pigeons have left now: there's only a bare clothesline and the overhang of the ancient macadamia nut tree from the house behind. Like Nonna, I close my eyes and hear 47-year-old screams ringing in my ears.

'Ahhhhhhhh!' the wailing echoes along the length of the Messina wharf. Flanking the Sicilian coast is a passenger ship already loaded with its human cargo. Beyond the ship, the heavy coast of Calabria can be seen through the early morning shadows. Two men in dusty suits and *coppole* take the screaming woman by the elbows. Desperate emotion has given her unnatural strength and the men have to struggle to hold her back.

'You are going to another world!' she screams at the boat, her black dress ruffling in the wind like Nonna's brown curl unfolding. 'We will never see you again!'

Her palms are open to the sky. Bending over at the waist, her black-scarved head dangles between her knees and she's dragging the two men forward with her.

'Ahhhhhhhh,' she wails again as her head comes shooting back up and her body bends back the opposite way, her face now thrown up to the Sicilian sky. The men at her elbows keep tightening their grip but she continues to jerk towards the boat and they shuffle along behind her.

Above them, high in the air, dark heads cluster along the side of the boat and look down onto the wharf. One man takes his brown suit-jacket off and waves it back and forth in the still air as if fanning the screaming woman below. But he is really saying farewell to the crowd and to his island, *la Sicilia*. The screaming continues and the faces of those on the boat crease deeply with anxiety. To some this wailing echoes what they are feeling in their own hearts but are too afraid to express. 'I've never seen anything like that,' says a robust woman on the deck of the ship.

By wrapping their short, strong arms around the woman on the wharf, the men have begun to contain her jerking motion towards the sea.

'My sister will miss me,' says a small woman standing nearby on the deck, and as she grips the ship's railing her wedding band rings on the metal.

'You will never see this land again!' wails the woman below.

'She should stop,' the robust woman says as she turns and looks down crossly at the smaller one, 'she's cursing us.'

Something twitches in the smaller woman's face and fear makes her grip the railing with both hands now, and lean her body over the side of the boat.

'Rosaria!' she yells, and waves a threatening hand at her sister below, 'stop it with this *mal'augurio*.'

'*Sorella mia!* I will never see you again, you will never see this *terra* again. They are taking you to another world and you will never return.'

'Rosaria, if you don't stop it you will bring misfortune to this boat.'

Rosaria takes a deep breath and her small black eyes harden. 'Better to die, Carmelina, than to leave your land and family and never see them again.'

'Ooohhhh,' the robust woman pushes the smaller one aside, 'will someone take her away before I come down there and throw her into the sea myself!' In short, sharp motions she points a finger from the woman below to the sea and cocks her other hand fiercely on a rounded hip.

'And you Anna!' the screaming woman below goes on, her black eyes now turning to pinpricks, 'how dare you leave your parents and your sisters! How dare you send your husband away, never to return to his island and his brothers! Who do you think you are?'

A sharp smile breaks across Anna's face, her teeth grit against each other and her hisses rain down on the wharf of Messina. 'Rosaria, I send all your curses back on you and your children. I am happy to be leaving this island!' She turns and looks at the group of passengers who are staring back at her with blank, frightened faces. She looks back out to Sicily defiantly. 'I promise never to return!'

A breeze picks up off the Strait of Messina and winds itself through Anna's fine brown hair as the boat rumbles to life and slowly peels away from the coast of Sicily. I can see her in my mind's eye, her dark hair flying in the breeze, one hand on her hip and the other waving at the object of her venom, the Sicilian coast. There would have been steel in her eyes, a dead conviction in her voice and a ferocity that would make people back slowly away from her.

At least that's how she would have done it if the story were true.

But I don't believe her.

I don't believe that you can vow never to return to the place where your life began, the place where you lived and loved for your first thirty-three years on earth. Maybe forty-seven years later it's a little false bravado, but whether by choice or by circumstance, she kept her vow. She would never return.

A child appears at Anna's side as the boat enters the Suez Canal.

'Salvatore, have you been taking care of your sister?' Anna asks her eldest son. He's a tall, skinny boy with knobbly knees and a big head. His jet-black hair is parted, sweeping to one side, and his dark eyes are perfectly round. A slight boy, he squints up in awe at his imposing mother and rearranges his three-year-old sister on his hip. The little girl is clutching an old doll made out of scraps of cloth.

'Yes Mamma, but I think she's hungry.'

'Give her to me,' Anna reaches out for the little girl and brushes the fair hair away from her chubby, rosy face. Anna still can't understand where the blonde hair came from. On the day this little girl was born the town of Fiumefreddo was blanketed in snow. From the top of the mountain all the way out to sea, the East Sicilian coast was shrouded in white.

'You should call her *Bianca Neve*,' the midwife said to Anna, 'it's a sign. It hasn't snowed here in decades.'

For a blonde Sicilian baby born in a snowstorm, Snow White would have been an apt name, but Anna did not agree. It was rare that she took advice from others.

'No,' Anna said, 'I'm calling her Rosetta.' Little Rose. Anna's small brown eyes turn to scan the deck of the ship like she's looking for something she's lost.

'Where's your brother? Giuseppe!' she calls out for him.

'I don't know,' Salvatore says, 'he took off when we got on board and I haven't seen him since.'

'You'd better find him. I'm sure he's up to something by now,' Anna says.

Salvatore turns on his heel and scoots off in search of his younger brother, a rotund and mischievous little package of energy. The last time he had been seen, Giuseppe had waved five chubby fingers at Sicily and disappeared below deck. That morning, Anna had poured him into his best suit, the seams straining around his chunky five-year-old form. She knew that by now the suit would be a ruin, but at least they had left looking decent; at least they had left making a *bella figura*.

This little band of immigrants, the woman with the furious heart, the skinny ten-year-old boy, the cheeky five-year-old boy and the blonde Snow White, had packed up a branch of the family tree and were moving it to the other side of the world. They had just taken the detour of a lifetime, leaving one island for another. Waiting for them in Australia was the husband Anna hadn't seen in three years, and the father little Snow White, my mother, had yet to meet. Travelling with them were all their worldly possessions, stuffed into one wooden chest, and all the traditions and recipes of old-world Sicily, locked in Anna's heart. She turns out to see the coast of North Africa sliding by and bounces her daughter on her hip.

'Look, look at that,' she hums but the little girl is too entranced with her rag doll to take note of the majestic continent passing before them.

'Rosetta,' Anna sighs, 'Rosetta, look over there.' She turns so the little girl is facing out to Africa.

Rosetta's hazel eyes look up and in that moment her little fingers loosen their grasp, and her doll bounces onto the ship's railing and sails out into the air.

'You dropped your doll!' Anna cries, her eyes following the little figure into the water as the doll's head dips beneath the whitewash created by the ship's passing. This is my mother's only memory of the voyage to Australia – the moment she dropped her favourite (and only) doll into the Suez Canal. I don't know why, but I often think about that doll, bobbing up and down and knocking against the hulls of passing ships. I wonder where she washed up, and how her immigration story ended?

I open my eyes.

'And now you want to go back,' Nonna says, wiping her face with her palm again and quickly tucking in the loose curl. 'I don't understand. We came here.'

'I don't want to go back forever,' I sigh.

The beginning
Sarsa semplice (Sicilian for simple sauce)

This is where you start. This is the core of Sicilian food, and from this fundamental sauce the soul of Sicilian cooking radiates. Apart from the lemon, no ingredient is more prized to the Sicilian than the tomato. Serve with the pasta of your choice and grated parmesan or pecorino pepato.

olive oil, for cooking
1 clove garlic, finely diced
½ white or brown onion, finely diced
4–5 fresh basil leaves
¼ cup frozen peas
2 × 400 g cans crushed, peeled tomatoes
salt and pepper

Heat some olive oil in a large pan, then add the garlic and onion and sauté until the onion is translucent. Add the basil leaves and the frozen peas, and cook for about a minute, then add the tomatoes. Season with salt and pepper to taste, then simmer on low heat for 30 minutes, stirring frequently.

Serves 4

DESTINY'S DECISIONS

If they look back, can most people pinpoint the moment that their life changes forever? Or the series of events that coincide to achieve an outcome that they would never have dreamt of? For me, it was a rare moment of acting without thinking. A moment when I said yes instead of no that changed everything for me from that point forward. These moments can happen at any time to anyone, and I am sure that even now, all over the world, these moments are bursting unsuspectingly upon ordinary lives.

It is July 2005, and I am in my office when my moment of destiny arrives. The harsh fluorescent light is bouncing off the shiny surface of my desk and piercing my sight. Piles of paper sit all around awaiting my attention but I only have eyes for one thing. There, on my screen, is a snow-capped volcano rising out of the ground, with tiny towns dotted around it that cling to its side. She has captured my attention, this massive mountain. She starts with low sloping hills and a gradual incline that fills the entire screen. This is the mountain that makes my grandmother clasp her hands together and raise her eyes to the sky when it's mentioned. The mountain my father talks of in stories of his childhood. She draws me in. And holds me. Until someone in the doorway coughs and drops a bundle of papers on the desk in front of me.

I look from the papers, to the face of the man standing in my doorway, then back to the shape of Etna blinking in front of me. There's a crackle of something in the back of my mind. A fierce fire takes hold of me from the inside out, and for the first time in my life I understand what it means to see red. A film descends over my eyes so that the image of Etna floats in a haze of lava and the room closes in around me.

'You know what?' I say slowly, alarming myself with my calmness, given how I am feeling inside.

'What?' His face has started to turn a dark shade of crimson. It begins at the collar of his shirt and is slowly sweeping upwards in long ragged lines.

'You can do it yourself.' I bend down and pick up my bag.

His eyes dart from me to the door; I can see that he wants to block my path.

'You're leaving?' he asks.

'Yes.' I rearrange my bag on my shoulder. 'I'm leaving. I may be back on Monday. I may not.' And I walk.

Never before in my life have I walked.

This time I walk.

I've just become my own version of a bubbling volcano. In my stomach the frustration loosens and is swept away by sheer adrenaline, the rush of grabbing hold of your life with both hands and giving it a good shake.

I hit the down button for the elevator.

I turn, expecting someone to be following me, but it's just me and the receptionist in the white, clinical foyer.

'You on your way out?' she asks brightly.

I smile at her as the light for the down elevator blinks on.

'Yes, and I may not be coming back.' I step in and ride the elevator down to my new and unknown life.

By the time I hit the ground floor I'm high and flustered and I break out of the building with legs pumping and arms striding, seemingly without any input from my brain. I fly around the block and find that my mad emotional rush gets me as far as the corner of Adelaide and Edward streets, where I come to a sudden and unexpected stop. Across from me is the Embassy Pub, where I have spent many a Friday night trying to forget yet another week from hell. It makes me smile. It seems so appropriate that I should come to a stop here, staring at the place where I have tried in vain to drown my career sorrows. But I have a more urgent reason for stopping. The heel of my shoe is stuck in the footpath, wedged so tight I'll have to bend down and pull it out with both hands. I look down to inspect the damage but I'm secretly happy that I've come to a standstill. My heart is beating somewhere in my throat and the past few minutes already feel like a lifetime ago. This is what it feels like, I realise, to be pushed one step too far. What it feels like, after years of overwork and stress, to finally snap.

I feel a vibration coming from my bag and reach in for my mobile phone.

'Hi Ma,' I answer.

'Hi! So have you decided?' My mother's brisk voice comes down the line.

I suck my bottom lip into my mouth.

'I'm not sure.'

'What do you mean you're not sure?'

I hold the phone away from my ear for a few seconds' rest. Are all mothers' voices so unnecessarily strident, even in the course of ordinary conversation?

'It's going to cost me a fortune. I should pay off my car. I have a mortgage. And oh, yeah, I just quit my job.' I pause, and feel the wave of panic rise and my own face turn crimson. I pull on my heel but I'm jammed tight – I can't move forward or back.

'You quit your job?' she asks slowly.

'Yes, I quit my job.'

'Well, then you can definitely come!'

I blink. It isn't exactly the answer I'm expecting.

'Did you hear what I said?'

'Yes, you quit your job.' I can hear her talking and chewing on something at the same time.

'But I've got a mortgage, I've got a car loan and I have no job!'

'So?' is my mother's eternally optimistic reply, and I hear her teeth grate mid-chew.

'So? What do you mean so? And what are you eating?' I bark.

'Piece of Italian bread and olives,' she says as I hear the sound of bread tearing between her teeth.

'Black olives?'

'No, the green ones your Nonna makes.'

'Is the bread soft or really crunchy?'

'It's soft in the middle and crunchy on the outside the way you like it. So you're coming, right?'

I bite my bottom lip again. I'm thinking a lot about the decision I have to make. But for some reason I'm also thinking a lot about olives and bread. Maybe a slice of *galbanino* and a sliver of *cacciatore* salami as well. It's early July and at the end of the month my parents and brother are going to Sicily for two months, both for a holiday and so that my parents can reclaim what is their birthright but what immigration took away from them – Italian citizenship. It has been decades since my father saw the town of his birth and the place where he spent the first eighteen years of his life. My mother, Snow White, left the same town at the age of three as a little blonde girl in her older brother's arms, and has only returned once, in 1974. My brother has never set foot outside Australia.

'What am I going to do for money?' I worry some more.

'Oh will you stop worrying about it and come with us. You don't have to worry about the money!'

I click my tongue against the roof of my mouth. I'll be turning twenty-nine this year and it really is time that I stop relying on my parents. Money is communal in most Sicilian families – you do anything for those that share your bloodline, especially opening your wallet. Besides, if I don't say yes right now they'll be going to Sicily and I'll be staying home. In a couple of weeks they'll be eating Sicilian olives with Sicilian bread under the Sicilian sun and where will I be? Banging around an empty house, probably dining on a can of baked beans or driving to Nonna's for a proper meal.

I exhale slowly and shut my eyes against the busy Brisbane street. In my mind I visualise everything I know or have heard about Sicily. I see the little triangular island against the back of my eyelids and imagine Etna rising above Sicily's jagged hills. I feel the crunch of countryside stones beneath my shoes and taste the lava dust on my tongue. My ears hum with the incomprehensible sound of Sicilian traffic, while my nostrils catch the heady mix of vanilla and almonds that infuses every Sicilian bar. I imagine myself walking those ancient streets and feel that strange shift inside of me whenever I hear that magic word.

Sicilia.

It draws something out of me I can't explain. It holds a power over me I can't resist. In that moment I feel that I have no other choice.

'Go,' I whisper to myself.

It seems that it's the smallest things that make the biggest difference. The chance encounter, the decision to go or to stay, the first step onto the boat that will take you away or onto the plane that will bring you back. It's the moments you don't even notice which can start a chain of events that have you suddenly veering off onto the tangent of a lifetime. I pull on my heel one last time and the footpath obliges. Now I am free to continue on my way.

The little things
Nonna's green olives

It's the little things, Nonna says, that make a meal.

It's the type of cheese you sprinkle on your pasta, that little extra bit of fennel you put in the sausage, it's even the type of fork you use to twirl your spaghetti.

It's the little things, like the olives you start with before the meal even arrives.

'Ma,' Uncle Salvatore, or Sam, as we call him, will say to Nonna, 'will we make the olives?' He looks at her the same way he did when he was ten, standing on the deck of the ship. Part respectful, part awestruck. She'll just nod and smile. Later on he will place a large rectangular cardboard box on her kitchen table. He'll whip off the lid and inside will be hundreds of raw green olives, perfectly round and smooth and as hard as little rocks. Mother and middle-aged son will spend an afternoon washing them and preserving them in wide glass jars filled with salted water and topped with thick fronds of fennel. When they're done, Uncle Sam will load his car with the jars and drop a couple off at our house, the first stop on his olive delivery run.

These olives are hard and salty, and their piquancy goes perfectly with a piece of hard cheese like pecorino pepato. *Eat them with a piece of crusty Italian bread and a glass of strong red wine. If you were in Sicily, you would eat them sitting under a tree in the rocky countryside, and after a good glass of wine you'd lie down in the shade and fall asleep.*

½ kg raw green olives
handful table salt
dried fennel fronds or olive sprigs

Wash the olives well under cold water. Fill a 750 ml-capacity preserving jar with water to measure out the liquid, then transfer the water to a large stockpot and throw in the table salt. Stir over medium heat until the salt has dissolved, then remove from the heat and let the water cool. Put the olives in the jar and pour the salted water over, covering the olives and filling the jar almost to the top. Place the fennel fronds or olive sprigs on top and push down gently (these will help keep the olives completely submerged in the water). Seal the jar and store in a cool, dark place. The olives will be ready to eat in 2–3 weeks.

Makes enough to fill one 750 ml-capacity preserving jar

HOME

The No. 200 bus takes me from inner-city Brisbane to the dream suburb of Italian homemaking: Carindale. Even the name rolls easily off the Italian tongue. It's a place of housing estates and impressive constructions with Doric columns and concrete drives. When the Sicilian immigrants of the fifties had saved up enough money to get out of inner-city West End, New Farm and Lutwyche, this is where they fled to. A place where they could finally build their dream Roman villas.

'Guess how much I bought my house for?' Nonna asked me one day. I was sitting, as always, in the kitchen of her eight-bedroom Queenslander.

'I don't know Nonna.'

'It was so long ago we were still using the old money,' she said, and shook her head quickly.

'How much?' I asked, and she popped her small brown eyes wide open and looked quickly over her shoulder as if she was worried someone was eavesdropping on her.

'Three thousand pounds,' she smiled dryly.

Three thousand pounds had turned into over a million dollars, I thought to myself. Not a bad return for one good decision, and forty-seven years of waiting.

When the Sicilians came to town, they moved to the centre of it. Then, when all those locals who had looked down their noses at the inner city decided it was suddenly fashionable to live there again, the Sicilians sold up for a small fortune and bought themselves a slice of suburbia. Their version of *la campagna*.

'You should sell,' I suggested to Nonna, but she shook her head violently.

'Never!' She brought her hand down on the kitchen table with a crash. 'One day when I die you will buy out your mother, aunt and uncles. None of them want this house, but this is the family home and it must stay in the family!' Her palm came up and crashed back on the table again, and I wondered how I was ever going to afford this place.

'You're going to have to live long enough to for me to save up, Nonna. At least another forty years,' I grinned.

Contrary to the Italo-Australian ideal, my parents' house at Carindale is a sprawling replica Queenslander built by them in 1992, with lawn front and back. Where Nonna's Queenslander is made of slats of timber and creaks in the wind, my parents' house is double brick, wrapped firmly all the way round with a broad timber veranda. The kitchen, family and dining room are all part of one enormous open-plan space at the heart of the house. In the centre of this open space is a working fireplace which my father proudly uses on the one night a year that Brisbane's tropical climate drops to a chilly 8°C.

'Where are the listings for firewood?' he'll say as he flips through the local paper, as though he's going to need a trailer-load of it to get through a harsh winter. We all smirk but let him romanticise about lighting the fire and tending to it for an entire evening. In his mind, he'll see himself in front of the blaze with a glass of wine and a bowl of hot roasted chestnuts. More often though, we'll wake to the voices of Martin Tyler and, until recently, Johnny Warren, on the TV, and the smell of a burnt-down fire. My usually composed father will be found perched on the couch, buried under a blanket or standing by the TV gripping the fireplace poker in one hand with the anxiety of it all.

These are the thoughts that scatter through my mind as I ride the bus to my parents' place. Nonna's house, my parents' house, and the meaning of home. In the darkness, I step up onto the front veranda and my feet get tangled in something blocking my path. I bend down and my hands make out the shape of a box. The smell of the earth lifts gently off its contents. I heave it up and feel the thud of fleshy tomatoes bang against the side.

'Hello!' I call out as I walk through the front door.

'Hello!' comes the usual chorus from inside.

I walk through the foyer and turn into the family-room-cum-kitchen to find my father sitting in his usual serene manner at the dining table. Before him lie trails of salami skin, the crumbs of a bread roll and a handful of olive stones. The remains of a typical quick Sicilian meal. At his side is a glass half-full with strong red wine. My papà is gazing quietly into the distance, thinking his own tranquil thoughts, occasionally letting his fingertips caress the outside of his glass and bring it dreamily to his lips.

My louder and far more imposing mother is fussing around the sink and haranguing my brother.

'What do you want for dinner?' she asks him.

'I don't know,' my brother Ross mumbles as his eyes follow cartoon characters on the TV.

'Here,' I say, and put the box down on the granite kitchen bench, 'someone left this at the door.'

My mother leans across the counter and takes a peek. 'It must have been your Uncle Sam. Nonna sent him to pick up some vegetables from Mrs C.'

Mrs C is a worn and ancient Italian woman who lives in an enormous brick house on a broad patch of earth in the southern suburb of Capalaba. In this patch she grows fruit and vegetables the old-fashioned way, tending to them rain or shine with an old scarf wrapped around her small head. Her face is creased by the sun and her hands are stained with dirt, but she grows the largest and most intensely-flavoured tomatoes to be had in Brisbane. When Mr C was alive, the two of them would fill their garage with all the produce from their backyard, throw up the garage door and sell to passing motorists lured by the boxes upon boxes of home-grown tomatoes, beans and strawberries. Back then, on Sunday afternoon we'd collect Nonna from West End and make the forty-minute trip to Capalaba, where Mr and Mrs C would have a box of vegetables ready for us to collect. Nonna would slowly get out of our car parked on Mrs C's drive, and the two old ladies would grasp each other by the sides of the head and shoot quick kisses across each other's cheeks in greeting. Although Nonna is Sicilian and Mrs C is Roman, they would greet each other as if they were both from the same town and hadn't seen each other in decades. Week after week they'd go through the same ritual. Although Mr C is dead now, Mrs C goes on with what she's always known – tending the earth and growing her tomatoes. Sometime during the week she'll call Nonna to tell her what she's grown, then Nonna will place an order which Uncle Sam will be directed to pick up and distribute.

My mother runs her hand over the large tomatoes and the green snake beans then picks up a zucchini for closer inspection. She sniffs the zucchini then drops it back in the box and turns back to my brother.

'What do you mean, you don't know?' She puts a hand on her hip, a Sicilian woman's warning sign that things are about to get a bit more intense.

'I don't know. I don't even know if I'm hungry,' my brother replies.

My mother sighs out some hot air that she keeps stored up for just these occasions, and her head cocks sharply to one side.

None of us can understand Ross' attitude to food and eating. While my mother and I are cuddly and round at the edges, Ross is rail-thin and bony sharp. Worse still, if no-one cooks for him, he'll languish and starve just two metres from a fully-stocked kitchen. On the rare occasions he is hungry and takes time to eat with us, he has a strict eating ritual that mustn't be violated, although invariably it is.

'Watch my plate,' he'll say to me, as he gets up from the dining table in search of tomato sauce.

I keep an eagle eye on his plate, waiting for the juices of the various food groups to start trickling towards each other. He'll come running back and try to stem the tide with his fork, but the invasion is inevitable.

'I can't eat this now! Everything's touching!' he'll cry, and throw his fork down in disgust. I'm sure that somewhere his problem would be declared a disorder, but in our family these things are dealt with efficiently by my mother. From across the dining table, she'll arch an eyebrow and say, 'Get over it.'

He was genetically blessed, my brother, to take after my father's side of the family. All of them are straight up and down and run on the most spectacular metabolism. They are in stark contrast to those on my mother's side, who are all round and plump and cheery. I look at my brother, hip bones protruding, and wonder why, on the way to conception, I didn't make a grab for some of those fashionable Di'Bartolo skinny genes. My mother is at my side, and I suddenly realise that looking at her now is like looking at myself in twenty years' time.

'Well, are you hungry or not?' my mother tries Ross one more time.

He runs a hand through his black hair and screws up his green eyes and dark olive-skinned face. 'I don't know.' He kicks out one of his flat feet in desperation and sends a tower of yellow sofa cushions tumbling to the floor.

'I don't understand why you just can't eat,' I say, pulling open the fridge door.

My mother nods in agreement. 'Like you have to be hungry to eat something,' she rationalises.

'What did you have for dinner?' I ask while I cast my eye over the contents of the fridge. I'm not really that hungry but I need something to do, anything that will help me avoid explaining, at least for a little while, why I quit my job. Why it was that in that moment, the colour red and the sight of Etna made me get up and walk.

Last night's *pasta e piselli* is sitting in a large white bowl in the fridge. The *cacciatore* salami is snuggled in a tea towel next to a wedge of yellow Swiss cheese. Little bowls of olives, and grilled capsicum and eggplant in oil, are dotted like satellites among the shelves. Towards the back, sweating honey, is a plate of Greek sweets courtesy of Ross' Greek girlfriend's mother. Almost every night platters of Greek food arrive fresh from the inner-city suburb of Dutton Park,

and it gets me thinking about Greeks bearing gifts and if the wedding plans have already been put in motion without my brother knowing it. Even so, I have never been able to resist a piece of baklava, so I reach out for the sweet stuff, but my hand strays as I spot Nonna's green olives.

'Your father had salami, cheese, olives and tomato salad. Ross!' my mother switches her attention between her two children and her voice arcs to screaming pitch but Ross barely blinks. He's used to it. We're all used to it. Screaming is just how Sicilians communicate. A concerned next-door neighbour once asked me, 'Is everything alright at your house?'

'Sorry?' I replied.

'Is everything ok? I mean, I hear a lot of screaming

coming from your place sometimes.' She looked worried, not sure if she was touching on something sensitive.

I just smiled and clarified, 'It's not screaming. It's just the way we talk.'

'Rosetta!' My father, who is usually a quiet, reserved man, snaps out of his reverie and joins the goings-on in the kitchen. 'If he doesn't want to eat then let him starve,' he says. 'And don't you think that at twenty-one years of age it's time you stopped watching cartoons?' My father points a finger at my brother who ignores all of us and coughs in reply.

'I give up!' My father slaps his thighs in desperation, as if the worst thing that could happen in today's world is my brother missing a meal.

I look at them all. My mother, standing behind the kitchen bench, hands on hips and bristling with tension. My father, running a hand across his forehead and looking at my brother as if he's wondering where he went wrong. And Ross, beleaguered by two sets of Sicilian eyes boring into him while he gets thinner by the second. Where else do people get so enraged and passionate about something as mundane as dinner?

'I give up!' my mother proclaims, balling up a tea towel and slamming it down on the granite benchtop for dramatic emphasis. With Ross now abandoned, she turns to me.

'If you're coming to Sicily with us,' she says, 'you'll have to go past Nonna's and say goodbye.'

I close the fridge door and start to sigh but a ringing phone interrupts me.

'Hello,' my mother picks it up. 'Ah, ciao.'

'Nonna!' she mouths at me.

My jaw loosens and drops. 'How does she do that? As soon as she's the topic of conversation, she's on the phone. You don't find that a little strange?' I'm sure voodoo is a Sicilian thing.

'*Si*, aha, *si*, yeah Sam dropped it off. Hmmmm, ok, I'll let her know. She has to come past and say goodbye to you anyway because she's coming with us. Aha, *si* Ma, ok,' she sighs, hangs up and looks at me.

But I already know what's coming.

'What do I have to do?' I ask.

'She wants you to go over there tomorrow to collect the cheese from Giovanni and grate it for her.'

'Uuhhhh,' I groan, and start to slump my shoulders for added effect, but my mother freezes me in her cold gaze.

I'm caught mid-slump.

'She raised you, the least you can do is grate some cheese for her.'

She's right – Nonna did raise me. At the beginning of their marriage, my parents set up home in Nonna's house, so I was with her every day for the first few years of my life. Even after my parents moved into their own home, I still spent every morning before school and every afternoon after school at Nonna's house while my parents were at work. When I think of those days, I always see myself sitting in Nonna's lounge room in front of the TV, and out of the corner of my eye I see her coming in carrying a plate of salami sandwiches. Nonna raised me, her eldest grandchild, and for eight years her only one until my brother came along.

Guilt and olives became my dinner that night.

At home on the back veranda
  Tomato and onion salad

Along the back of my parents' Carindale home runs a timber veranda. On hot days when the sky is that hallucinogenic blue that you only get in Queensland, my mother sets the table for dinner here. The setting is Australian but the food is entirely Sicilian. A hunk of pecorino pepato sits pale yellow and crumbling next to the salami, Nonna's olives, tuna in olive oil and the most classic of all Sicilian salads: tomato and onion.

I break a piece of crusty Italian bread and run it through the little river of olive oil on my plate. It's coming from the salad on one side and meeting the stream from the golden tuna on the other. A bite of cheese; a slice of salami; the pop of an olive; and a sip of red wine. This is what Sicilian food is all about. The blending of simple ingredients, eaten with a slow languidness, framed against the backdrop of a magnificent view.

1 onion (white, brown or red)
6–8 tomatoes
generous drizzle olive oil
large pinch salt
large pinch dried oregano

Chop the onion into quarters and then slice. If you are using white or brown onions put the slices in a bowl of cold water while you cut the tomatoes.

Sicilians aren't as methodical about cutting a tomato as other people are. They will hold it whole and carve triangular-shaped pieces out with a knife and a flick of the wrist. Cut the tomatoes this way, then combine with the onion slices (drained, if soaking in water) in a salad bowl. Dress with olive oil, then add the salt and oregano and toss together.

Serves 4

Cameron Street, West End

West End is one of those suburbs to which immigrants instinctively gravitate. It sits almost directly across the river from the CBD, and in ten minutes you can walk from your front door to the middle of the city. The houses in West End sit side by side, so close they are almost touching, much like they do in the old country, and in some parts the suburb shows its age by the curve of hidden laneways and traffic-choked narrow streets. When I was a child, it sang with the sounds of voices in a trio of languages: Vietnamese, Italian and Greek. People walked up and down Boundary Street, West End's major thoroughfare, and each knew everyone else. The bakery was Vietnamese, the fruit shop Greek, the linen shop Turkish and the shoe shop Australian. When she was younger, Nonna would go shopping along Boundary Street armed only with a smile and a sweet incline of the head. She could walk away with half the contents of any shop on credit because back then everyone knew where everyone else lived.

I drive down Melbourne Street heading towards West End with the tall buildings of the CBD behind me. This street has narrowed over time from a four lane thoroughfare to a jumbled mass of traffic lights, traffic islands and traffic gridlock. It used to be striped with enormous zebra crossings that you had to hold your breath to get across. Every afternoon after school, my cousin Gracie and I would walk from Brisbane State High School back to Nonna's house in Cameron Street. Gracie lived one street over in Norfolk Road. But before we could make it safely home we had to brave Melbourne Street, and the only way to stop the traffic was to step out in front of it. It wasn't until you were at least four stripes out into the middle of the road that anyone even noticed you.

'Don't look, just walk and concentrate on the other side,' Gracie and I would say to each other as we stepped out from the safety of the footpath and onto the first of the giant stripes.

I brake at the traffic lights where one of the zebra crossings used to be and watch as people walk calmly across the road with the flashing green man assuring them safety. Now where's the fun in that? I turn right into Edmonstone Street and try to shoot straight over Boundary Street, but a newly-installed traffic island stops me from getting across into Norfolk Road.

'On you and all your children!' I curse at whoever thought to put it there. Instead I take the street parallel to Norfolk Road, and crawl over three speed bumps at the newly-regulated 40 kilometres per hour. At the end of the street I turn left into Montague Road and drive past Norfolk Road on one side, and on the other the old bottle factory that sent plumes of smoke into the air every day of my childhood. Finally, I make the left hand turn into Cameron Street, crawl over another speed bump and park in my usual space beneath the paper-barked tree in front of Nonna's house. Inner-city driving has become a slow and tedious affair in this part of Brisbane.

I step out of the car and take a breath. This is the little quarter of my childhood. This street, Norfolk Road and Boundary Street beyond were the perimeters of my life for so long. Carindale is lovely and quiet the way suburbia is meant to be, but West End is where I slide into my own skin. It's now choked with noise and traffic and smog but to me it will always be home. I look up and see Helen and George, Nonna's neighbours from across the street, sitting out on their front balcony. George is a tiny Greek man, perfectly-put-together and impeccably neat. His hair resembles a jet black helmet and he sports a tiny black moustache. Helen is tall for a Mediterranean woman, with a dark, heavy-featured face and a head of coarse bristly hair now almost completely grey. They have known Nonna for almost forty years, and when they were young women Nonna and Helen worked side by side at the South Brisbane Fish Board, shelling prawns for hours on end.

'Hello Helen! Hello George!' I call out to them.

Helen leans forward. 'Rosetta?' she calls out, confusing me with my mother. 'No, Michele,' I call back.

'Oh, hello darlink!' she cries in her heavy Greek accent, while George just raises a hand in greeting.

The residents of this broad street have remained unchanged for the best part of thirty years, and it is a street peppered with Georges. Helen and George live across the street from Nonna, another George and his wife live next to them. On Nonna's side of the street, Georgina and her husband live between Nonna and Great Uncle Charlie's house, and a decade ago Old Man George bordered Great Uncle Charlie's house on the other side. I look up and see the latest development of pigeon-hole-sized apartments rising into the sky from the street behind and looking down onto Cameron Street. Pretty soon these oppressive developments will crowd around and block out the sun.

Looking back at Nonna's house, I see that the curtains of Uncle Joe's downstairs flat are pulled shut.

'Hello,' I knock on the window, 'Zio, are you in there?' I call and tap on the glass of the aluminium sliding door but get no response. I hear it then, a low growl, a throbbing from somewhere distant, getting closer. The sound turns off Montague Road and into the bottom of Cameron Street with a throaty roar and rips apart the quiet that existed only moments before. I turn slowly to face the street and I see Helen across the road toss an idle hand in the air and smile as if to say, 'Here we go again.'

A battered red Fiat comes screaming up the street, becomes airborne over the speed bump, and comes to a screeching halt in Nonna's driveway. As Uncle Joe slams on the brakes I see his little body pitch forward and then back into his seat with the force of the Fiat stopping.

'Yello!' he calls from his car.

'Hi,' I say slowly, and raise a hand.

The Fiat is bellowing smoke from its muffler which is creating a hazy cloud over this side of Cameron Street. One of the headlights has got a hole in it that looks suspiciously like a shotgun blast, and if you look really closely you can see that the driver's seatbelt is held together with a giant safety pin.

I choose not to ride in Uncle Joe's car when he's driving. After the first few minutes of tailgating, speeding and sharp corners, you lose all feeling in your lower body and it takes you half an hour and a stiff drink to unclench your fingers again.

Uncle Joe snaps off his safety pin-secured seatbelt and jumps out. He's a short man with skin blackened by the sun. He's round in the middle and held up by little stubby legs – his physique unchanged since the age of five.

'Michele, how ya goin'?' he rattles at me in a harsh Australian accent. He may have been born in Sicily, but a lifetime of working at construction sites has turned him into a regular Aussie Joe.

'Good Zio, how are you?' I ask as he comes around the car.

'Yeah good,' he grins.

'Is Nonna in?'

'Yeah, I think so. She got home late last night though,' Uncle Joe replies.

'Late? Where did she go?'

'Where do you think she went?' he looks at me blankly. I smile.

'You coming up?' I ask.

'Yeah, I'll be up soon,' he says, and lets himself into his downstairs flat. This

is where he has lived his whole Australian life, in this house, in West End. A steep incline of steps rises up the front of Nonna's house, but only strangers and hawkers climb the two dozen steps to the little-used, cold front door. Everyone else goes to the back, because this Sicilian woman always holds court in her kitchen.

Nonna's house is timber yet surrounded by concrete. To one side is a long and crooked concrete driveway that separates her house from the one next door, where a tiny Greek lady used to live before she was claimed by a nursing home. Nonna would stand on her concrete drive wrapped in an apron and, for four decades, they would chat over the chicken-wire fence in a language of odd words drawn from Greek, Sicilian, Italian and English.

'All Greeks understand Italian,' Nonna says, 'a lot of them learnt it during the war.'

Like Old Man George, who spoke perfect Italian, and when I was a child would constantly bail me up to correct my Italian grammar and rattle his worry beads at me.

'Oh no, it's Old Man George,' I'd whisper to Gracie if we saw him on our way home from school. Almost every afternoon we'd find him sitting on the low brick wall that curved around the flats on the corner of Norfolk Road and Boundary Street. He'd sit and sun the mushy white skin on his face while he counted on his rattling wooden beads.

'What are we going to do?' she'd ask as we walked up Edmonstone Street and crossed Boundary Street without even looking out for traffic, because there was hardly any back then.

'Nothing. He's seen us now.'

He'd raise a hand in greeting and grin with mushy white dentures. Everything about his face was mushy and white. His long worry beads were wrapped around the palm of one hand and his cane was clutched in the other. I could see his white singlet through his long-sleeved white shirt.

'*Buongiorno*,' he'd say as we passed.

'*Buongiorno*,' we'd chime back in unison.

'*Come state?*' he'd ask to our quickly-retreating backs.

'*Buoni*,' we'd reply in Sicilian.

'Bene! Bene!' he'd cry after us in proper Italian, banging his cane on the concrete footpath.

'Si, bene!' we'd call back over our shoulders, *'Bene, bene!'*

Proper Italian was the entry fee we had to pay almost every afternoon to get into Cameron Street.

I'm still on Nonna's driveway. The chicken-wire fence running down the side has turned a rusty brown over time, and the modern-day hippies who now live next door have let the grass flourish. I look down and a plump hen waddles up to the fence and clucks at me. I can't help but smile. Here I am, surrounded on all sides by concrete and steel, with a city that everyone in the country seems to be flocking to only a stone's throw away. But here, in Cameron Street, I can happily step back in time.

Backyard chicken
Pollo con sarsa

Before my time, when my mother was a girl, Nonna kept chickens in her backyard as well. Fat, overfed hens in the middle of the city. Nonna would hand raise them and then, when the time was right, she would set aside an entire day for their demise. Nonna and Great Aunt Rosa, with their aprons firmly tied around their ample waists, would get up early and give chase around Nonna's West End backyard, stretching the necks of the chickens they caught. With string, Nonna would tie them to the clothes line and the two women would get gossiping and plucking. Towards midday they would start pulling the carcasses apart, taking care not to waste a single piece, because everything had a purpose and a place.

To this day my mother prizes the parson's nose because Nonna would make sure, when the chicken was roasted, that it was set aside just for her Little Rose.

2 × 400 g cans crushed, peeled tomatoes
salt
2 tablespoons olive oil
1 clove garlic, finely diced
2 tablespoons finely chopped flat-leaf parsley
1 whole chicken (about 1½ kg), cut into eight pieces
4 medium-sized potatoes, cut into halves or quarters
1 small butternut pumpkin, cut into small chunks
1 cup frozen peas
4 small or 2 medium-sized brown or red onions, cut into halves
pepper

Preheat the oven to 250°C. In a large baking tray, mix together the tomatoes, one teaspoon of salt, the olive oil, garlic and parsley. Place the chicken, potato, pumpkin, peas and onion pieces in the sauce. Add some more salt and pepper to taste, then cover with foil or a lid and bake for one hour, turning the chicken and vegetables halfway through the cooking time. Remove the foil or lid and continue cooking for half an hour more, or until the chicken and vegetables are cooked through.

Serves 4–6

SICILY IN WEST END

The long concrete driveway leads to a concrete backyard, out of which rises a set of squat and functional concrete steps that stop at a steel security door. This sea of cement is Uncle Joe's handiwork, a concreter by trade who likes to bring his work home with him. The back steps are studded with sharp-edged stones that add traction beneath elderly feet, but can rip through flesh if you are unfortunate enough, like me, to go sliding down them on your shins. My right leg still bears the long, jagged scar of the day I tripped over my school bag and out Nonna's back door. If I close my eyes I can still see my grandfather Nonno's anxious face when my blood started to flow out onto the hot concrete.

I look past Nonna's towering chilli plants, thumb-sized peppers glowing red and green in the mid-morning sun. Her backyard is a solid square of concrete bordered by flower beds, but no flowers have ever grown in this Sicilian garden. Here only chillies, parsley and mint are allowed to flourish. In the front are the lemons which occasionally Aborigines will wander past and pick. To the Sicilians, lemons are the very essence of their island: to the Aborigines, they are prized bush lemons in the middle of the city.

'Ciao Zio!' I call out to my Great Uncle Charlie who is sitting in the middle of his backyard two doors down. The yards on this side of Cameron Street face those from the houses along Norfolk Road behind. The fences dividing these yards are made from waist-high chicken wire, and you can either climb over them or pass between the gaps that have been created for that purpose.

'Ciao!' he calls back across the fences with a raised hand. Behind him, like the backdrop of some inner-city industrial landscape, are the smoke stacks from the old bottle factory down on Montague Road.

'Ciao Zia!' I call out to my Great Aunt Rosa as she appears at her back door and steps down to sit with her husband in their backyard.

'Ciao!' she calls and waves back.

These are my father's aunt and uncle. Completely by twist of fate, when my Great Uncle Charlie married Great Aunt Rosa they set up home two doors down from Nonna's house. Perhaps it wasn't entirely the hand of fate though, because these two families came from the same Sicilian town, so it seems only right that in their new country they should find themselves together again. When my father came to Australia aged eighteen (to conveniently avoid compulsory Italian military service), he came to stay at his Uncle Charlie's house. One day he strolled out into the backyard and looked to his right, over the tops of the fences and into Nonna's backyard. My mother was there hanging out the washing, and he promptly fell in love. Two *innamorati* from the same Sicilian town found each other in a West End quarter on the other side of the world. Fate indeed.

The smell of eggplants frying in olive oil floats out of Nonna's kitchen window and snaps me back into the present. My sense of smell tells me that good things are afoot here, and I can already feel the texture of the pasta as it slides between my teeth with the resistance of perfect al dente. The heat of the kitchen and the volcanic Sicilian temperament living here rises to flush my cheeks and warm my blood. The smell of danger and garlic flash through the air.

'Nonnina,' I call out my diminutive and affectionate form of Nonna and knock on the steel security door. After a few moments I start to hear her slow, creaking progress towards the back door.

'Ahhh, Anna, Anna, look how you've ended up,' she mutters to herself. Even from outside I can hear the tortured click of her knees as she makes the turn into the hallway from the kitchen.

She's a small woman now with dark brown hair she still has set in a forties style, and an impossibly straight nose with delicately flared nostrils. Now that she's eighty she's lost some height and a lot of weight, but as a young woman she was legendary in her strength. Her force of character remains, however, and I'm certain that her art of manipulation grows keener with the years. But I think it's her Sicilian pride that keeps her upright and she refuses to use her walking cane in public because *la bella figura* is more important than anything else.

'Ahh,' she laments again when she sees me, and fumbles for the door key in the pocket of her housedress.

'In the old days,' she starts, and I wish she'd hurry up because I've been standing on the back step for almost ten minutes now, 'you should have seen me,' she goes on. 'People would hear me coming by the sound my heels would make on the stone streets. They'd stop and say "Hear that? That's Anna coming". Now look at me.' She smiles slowly and her eyes glaze over as she looks back fifty years. In my mind I can see her strong hips sway down stony Sicilian streets while dark eyes follow every move.

'Nonna, can you let me in please?' I tap my foot on the concrete step. She slides the key into the lock and leans heavily on the cane that used to belong to her husband. Judging by how much I remember of Nonna and her figure, I assume she was a voluptuous woman in her day. Tanned from working in the Sicilian fields, strong and always laughing. Robust, friendly and formidable all at the same time. I've only seen one photo of Nonna as a young woman, and she stands at an angle to the camera with a hand sitting on a jutted hip. A half-smile plays cheekily across her face and her eyes are flirtatious but strong. There are six other people in that photo but your eyes go straight to her. I wonder if that's what happened to my grandfather when he first saw her, as he rode his bicycle past my grandmother's family's property. She would have been working in the fields, and as he pedalled lazily past he was thrown off balance by her very presence.

'Ciao Nonnina,' I grin as the door finally opens.

'Ciao *bella, quant'ave che non ti veddu?*'

How long has it been since I've seen you, she says in the rough Sicilian dialect of fifty years ago. When she got on the boat in Messina, Nonna took Sicily with her wrapped in a bubble of time. I am the only one of her six grandchildren who knows this ancient language, the only one she can converse freely with. After I am gone no-one in my family will remember how to speak it.

The Sicilian dialect has a rapid sound, flecked with the clipped words of Ancient Greece and the exotic words of Arabia. It's a language that comes from the back of the throat, the syllables rubbing against each other in a lovely grating sound that makes the words roll and rumble together. I find ease in its pronunciation and comfort in its sound because my first hesitant words were spoken in this ancient tongue.

'Where's your father?' my mother had asked me in English. We were in Nonna's backyard and I could see my father across the fences sitting with Great Uncle Charlie.

'*Da banna*,' I tossed my very first words back at her in Sicilian. Over there.

I take a step up into Nonna's house and draw a deep breath. This is more my home than the place where I sleep every night. This is where I shed my shell – it's here that my shoulders relax and my tongue loosens around the Sicilian words I always long to speak when I am away from here. But then Nonna's house is like that for everyone. Through these doors a stream of Sicilian boarders has passed, fresh from the long voyage. Families just arrived from Sicily with dark, brooding sons. (I remember, as a ten-year-old, locking eyes with one of those gorgeous creatures over Nonna's dinner table and feeling thoroughly shaken to the core.) Old men looking for a nation untouched by war, and young women shipped over after their photos had been approved by their future husbands. There was the Sicilian butcher who made his fortune in Australia and then returned to Sicily where he bought half a town's worth of real estate. Or the impoverished Mr Pippo, the communist who couldn't read but would help me with my maths homework every afternoon while my grandfather looked on, baffled by the long division.

A lot of Sicilians started their Australian lives by passing through or passing time at Nonna's house. Its eight bedrooms would swell with the chatter of the old country and fill with the smell of garlic, hot olive oil and tomatoes when Nonna cooked for them all. This mishmash of people, all speaking my beloved tongue and all eating Nonna's Sicilian cooking, created for me, in this house in West End, the Sicily of my childhood. If I close my eyes and press my hands to the timber walls I can still see their young faces, the awe at being so far from home and the joy that only the feeling of such possibility can bring. More than that though, I used to love their amazement at a house made entirely from timber.

The Arabian Sicily
Eggplant parmigiana

The pounding of Arabian blood is strong in every Sicilian. Sometimes you see it in the eyes or the nose or the hue of the skin. But nothing feels more like Arabia to me than the pale flesh of an eggplant. Like the cupolas and palm trees left by the Arabs in Sicily, the eggplant stalks many a Sicilian dish.

There's a quiet danger and sense of strength about the eggplant. It carries a mystique that elevates it above that of any other ordinary vegetable – perhaps because it is also a symbol of history. Sicily may be part of Italy and modern-day Europe, but its people have adopted the best of every marauding cuisine.

3 large eggplants
1 quantity *sarsa semplice* (see page 11), warmed
olive oil, for cooking
2 cups grated mozzarella cheese
1 cup grated parmesan cheese
1 cup grated *pecorino pepato* cheese
salt

Cut the tops off the eggplants. Standing the eggplants upright, and without slicing all the way through, cut into slices about ½ cm thick. Sprinkle salt over each slice, front and back, and then press together. Salting them this way draws out their bitterness. Leave the eggplants to one side for 30 minutes, then slice all the way through, rinse thoroughly and pat dry with kitchen paper.

Preheat the oven to 200°C. Heat a 1 cm layer of olive oil in the bottom of a frying pan, and fry the eggplant slices in batches until golden brown, then drain on kitchen paper. Coat the bottom and sides of a large rectangular baking dish with olive oil. Add a layer of sauce, then a layer of eggplant slices. Mix the grated cheeses together and sprinkle a layer of cheese over the eggplant, using roughly ⅓ of the total amount. Continue adding layers in this order until all ingredients are used up (you should get 3 layers of each), making sure that the top layer is a good helping of cheese. Bake for 20 minutes, then remove from the oven and set aside to rest for 5 minutes before serving.

Serves 6–8

COFFEE AND BISCUITS — THE UNDOING OF
CHARLIE THE COCKATOO

I bend down to give Nonna a kiss on the cheek. I'm only five foot one, but I still have to bend down to her. She presses one broad palm to each side of my face, draws each cheek to her mouth and delivers a rapid succession of tiny kisses. It's like puckering machine-gun fire against my face.

'*Mangiasti?*' she asks. In Sicilian culture, the basic question, 'How are you?' is replaced with 'Have you eaten?'

My face is still in her vice-like grip. Strength of this kind is impressive in an eighty-year-old woman, and I remember how as a child I would watch fascinated as she cracked walnuts in the palm of her hand.

'Yes Nonna,' I mumble through a mashed-up face.

'*Che mangiasti?*' What have you eaten?

Her dark little eyes bore into mine.

It doesn't really matter what I've eaten, there's always room for a little something more at Nonna's house. I don't know why, maybe it's because I grew up here and spent every morning and every afternoon after school here, but everything tastes better at Nonna's house.

Finally she releases me and starts to move back into the kitchen.

'Do you want a cup of coffee?' she asks and takes a seat at the kitchen table. Behind her big, sliding aluminium windows look into her Greek neighbour's house.

I let out a deep breath. Here in Nonna's kitchen is where everything about me begins. It is here that I've eaten food cooked from recipes that have remained unchanged since my grandmother was a girl; that I've listened to stories of how she and her sisters worked the Sicilian soil; and it's here that I've been taught the values of a culture steeped in tradition and the darkest of superstitions. It was in this room that I first heard about the *mal'occhio,* or evil eye, and how to have it removed.

'With water, olive oil and a special prayer,' Nonna said, 'but I can only teach you the words in church on Christmas Eve during midnight mass after you've taken communion, otherwise it won't work.' In Nonna's kitchen Sicily came to life, a world away in space and time.

Straight from the hospital, it was in Nonna's kitchen that I was fed for the first time and where my love of everything sugar-coated began. When my mother wasn't looking, Nonna would slip a teaspoon of sugar into my milk bottle.

I reply to Nonna's offer of coffee with a firm, 'No thanks, Nonna.'

'I've got those biscuits you like,' she smiles her beguiling half-smile.

'No thanks,' I say as I pull out a chair from under Nonna's kitchen table and take a seat. You have to be firm here. A visit to Nonna's might evoke the romanticism of ancient Sicily, but it's also a dieter's obstacle course strewn with biscuits and salami and a hundred other delights. You can't say no, because here eating equals happiness and if you refuse to eat offence will be taken. You may start with a firm resolve, but with her half-smiles Nonna will always break you in the end – it's only a matter of time, and the right food group.

'Gooooooo,' she draws the word out, 'have a look, the biscuits are in the fridge.' She waves a strong hand in the direction of the two fridges. There's only Nonna and Uncle Joe left in this enormous house but they still run two fridges and a thirty-year-old chest freezer. I'm sure Nonna's need to stockpile food in the land of plenty must have something to do with years of going without in the old country. The new millennium had a cataclysmic effect on Nonna, and I remember bending into her chest freezer stacking tubs of pasta sauce in preparation for the end of the world.

'Someone's going to be eating a lot of pasta after New Year's Eve,' I had mumbled.

'Do you think we have enough?' Nonna asked, wringing her hands as she peered over my shoulder at about a hundred Chinese-takeaway containers full of red pasta sauce.

'No, I don't want any coffee,' I start to say, but I'm stopped by a mad rush of air and frantic flapping behind my head. 'What the . . . !' I jump up out of my chair.

A black and white long-legged bird lands on the kitchen table and stares at Nonna with tiny black eyes. It emits two short squawks at her and flaps its wings once. Nonna just shakes her head, chuckles and reaches for a loaf of bread hidden under a corner of the tablecloth.

'What's this?' I'm stunned that there's a bird in the house. I'm even more shocked that it knew to fly through the bars of the security door, down the hall and take the first right-hand turn into the kitchen.

Nonna calmly drops little crumbs at its clawed feet.

'He's taken to coming in for breakfast every morning at ten o'clock. I started by throwing him crumbs out the window every morning and now he comes straight into the kitchen. He's so smart, he even knows what time it is,' she smiles at him proudly.

'He's a bird! In the house!'

'They get hungry too you know,' she says archly. 'My father always said that we are like God to the animals and we have to look after them. He was a strong man my father, but he always looked after the animals.'

When she's sitting in her kitchen and looking out to her backyard, Nonna often monitors the birds that come throughout the day to sit on her clothes line. The very same clothes line where she used to hang the chickens with freshly-stretched necks, ready for plucking. I've seen her smile slowly at the doves that fly in pairs and sit for hours cuddling each other. She'll smile mournfully when one flies in without the other. 'He's lost his wife,' she'll say, 'he's been pacing in the parsley bushes all day.'

The bird on Nonna's table eats its fill, squawks a thank-you, then turns and flies out of the kitchen. I follow him out the kitchen door and watch as he makes a neat left-hand turn into the hall and cruises back out between the bars of the security door.

I shake my head and smile at her. 'At least you didn't offer him a coffee.'

'Ha!' she slaps the kitchen table with a broad hand, 'I won't be doing that again after what happened to Charlie.'

'I wish I'd been around to see Charlie.'

'Ahhh,' Nonna sighs over the bird that has become somewhat of a family legend, 'now there was a good Sicilian bird. He was this big,' she spreads her hands to show the height of a fully-grown cockatoo. 'Every morning I'd take him a little cup of espresso and two milk-coffee biscuits. Every morning at eleven a.m., and he'd drink the whole cup, the *bastardo*,' she says affectionately, 'but if I was running one minute late, the whole street would hear him!'

Charlie the cockatoo died an old, cosmopolitan bird long before I was born, but I like the image of my Sicilian nonna serving tiny cups of black espresso on her front veranda to the birds of West End.

'So,' she drops her voice and a twinkle flares in her eyes, 'you no fu-coffey?'

She knows perfectly well what it means when she slurs those words together; that's why she always delivers them with a cheeky smile.

'No, Nonna, I'm not for coffee, thank you.'

The black stuff
A Sicilian cup of coffee

A Sicilian cup of coffee begins and ends on the stove. Nonna has a stovetop espresso maker that sits about a foot high and makes close to twenty-four shots of viscous, black coffee. When they were strong middle-aged women raising young families, Nonna and Great Aunt Rosa would meet each other between chores and drink two of these pots a day. 'You wouldn't believe how much work we'd get done,' Nonna says, shaking her head. I believe it, Nonna.

She only takes the espresso maker out at Christmas time now, and when it's on the stove we all watch it out of the corners of our eyes. When the coffee hits its gurgling peak, Nonna starts waving an anxious hand towards the stove and my mother or Auntie Gina get up and run to it. If you sit in Uncle Joe's spot at Nonna's kitchen table and look up at the timber ceiling, you can still see the dent left there by The Coffee Incident one Christmas Day ten years ago.

Making the mistake of grinding the coffee too finely and then packing it in too tight, Nonna created the espresso version of a homemade rocket that sent everyone running for cover. With the pressure of boiling water that had nowhere to go, the pot took off with a burst of gas flame beneath it and went crashing into the ceiling above. We all watched it go up, then quickly realised that it had to come down. 'Bloody hell!' yelled Uncle Joe who was directly under the descent. He grabbed me by the arm and combat-rolled me out the door, while a mass of Sicilians dove for cover.

The real secret to a great cup of coffee is to make a pot when you first buy the espresso maker and throw it out. This lines the interior with coffee. After this, never wash the pot with detergent – just rinse it out with water to clean, and occasionally wipe out the inside with a dry cloth.

a 3-cup capacity stovetop espresso maker
3 heaped teaspoons ground coffee

Fill the bottom of the espresso maker with cold water and place the filter on top. There should be enough water in the bottom section to come up a little through the holes in the filter. Fill the filter with ground coffee, but don't pack it in too tight. Screw the top on and heat it over a medium flame on the stove. You will hear the coffee gurgle, and then reach a gurgling peak. When it starts to quieten down, it's ready. Lift the lid and stir the contents with a spoon, then pour.

Store any leftover coffee in the fridge and drink it later on as iced coffee. Or in summer, take a scoop of vanilla ice cream and pour a shot of cold espresso over for a simple but buzzing dessert.

Makes 3 cups

BOILED TOMATOES

I hear Uncle Joe slam a door closed downstairs. Further away I hear Great Uncle Charlie laughing and Great Aunt Rosa's clothes line turning. Someone next door starts running the shower, and out on the street a car starts up. In the background I can hear the faint gurgling of the chickens next door, blending into the Saturday morning sounds of this little piece of West End.

'Where were you last night?' I ask Nonna, and raise an eyebrow in her direction.

'Ah!' she slaps another hand on the kitchen table, 'that bloody dealer!'

'So you lost?'

'Doesn't everyone?' she asks, lifting her shoulder in enquiry.

'What time did you get home?'

Nonna presses her lips together and raises both eyebrows. Her dark eyes open wide and she holds up four fingers.

'Four a.m.!'

'But in there you lose track of time!' She waves a dismissive hand through the air and shrugs the same shoulder again. 'By the time you find a good table, have a coffee and play a little, time passes like that,' she snaps her fingers.

'Do you think it's safe going there on your own and coming out at four a.m.?'

'Carmelina waits for me, and there are no stairs where we go to play.'

They braved a sea voyage to the other side of the world so they could spend their old age together at the casino playing blackjack. A journey well worth it, I think.

'You want to come with me next weekend?' Nonna asks.

I look at her blankly. I can see a tight squadron of eighty-year-old Sicilian women, sucking on lemon squashes and tepid cappuccinos, their jet-black hair awash with the harsh neon lights of the casino, while they cruise through looking for a lucky table. They mumble and gossip amongst themselves in Sicilian, holding their purses tight to their bodies. Occasionally one will dash to the ladies' room to pull wads of cash out of crevices where pickpockets would never dare to venture. When things go bad they'll curse the dealer and shoot him the evil eye, making the sign of the devil's horns under the table to protect themselves from the curse rebounding on them.

I'd love to go. But these ladies are too rich for my blood. The minimum bet for a Sicilian grandmother is $25 per hand.

'I don't think so.'

'You should go out more,' she says.

'Nonna, I go out all the time.'

'You should go out more. Men won't knock on your door you know.'

'Nonna!'

She raises one eyebrow and zeroes in on me with a beady eye. Her gaze holds me for one penetrating second in which I'm sure she can read my mind. The art of the Sicilian grandmother is their ability to be kind, generous and thoroughly dangerous in equal measure.

'Ah, if only I were young now', she sighs, 'you know, I probably wouldn't get married at all.'

'No?'

'No. The world is a completely different place now.' Down the street, Great Uncle Charlie laughs again and Nonna's ears perk up. 'Who's that?'

'Zio Charlie.'

'What's he doing?'

'I don't know, he was just sitting in the backyard when I saw him.'

'On his own?'

'With Zia Rosa.'

'What are they doing?'

'I don't know! Sitting outside I guess.'

'On their own?'

'I suppose so, you want to call them and ask? What's with all the questions?'

'You want a cup of coffee?'

'No!'

Nonna picks up her previous thread of conversation and continues, 'The problem with today is that people have too much money.'

I just nod and look out the window.

'No-one appreciates the simple things. People don't even cook at home these days, they go out for dinner every night of the week.'

'That's true for some,' I say.

'When I was growing up we ate simple things. We'd go out and gather vegetables then come home and cook them. If we were walking into town we'd pick fruit right off the tree and eat it on the way. Now people wouldn't know a green bean if you slapped them in the face with it.'

I just nod and we fall into a long silence, both contemplating how the world has changed since my grandmother was a girl.

'I don't wish it,' Nonna starts again, 'but sometimes I think the youth of today need to be taken back to live through the war years to know how good they have it. We ate bread that was more stone than bread. *Miseria*,' she goes on, 'there was complete *miseria*. Then, as if it wasn't enough that we were starving to death, we had the Americans bombing us as well.'

'Really?'

'Of course! Look at this,' she turns her leg slightly and pulls the flesh on her calf, 'this is where I was wounded. We were out in the countryside picking *verdura* when they came. Tut-tut-tut-tut, their guns sounded like, and we had to throw ourselves into a ditch for cover. They got me here,' she taps the faint outline of a scar on the back of her leg, much like the one on my shin from my fall down Nonna's back steps.

'I didn't know you were wounded during the war!'

'My sister Adele held me up by the waist and we hopped all the way back home. My mother made me lie down on my stomach and eat boiled tomatoes while my father went into town for the doctor.'

'Boiled tomatoes?'

Nonna nods her small head quickly. 'They're good for the blood.'

'Oh,' my mouth goes round, 'Then what happened?'

I'm enthralled. I had no idea Nonna had been wounded in the war. I knew that my grandfather had signed up to fight but never made it to the front. Three days into his first tour of duty he came down with chronic back pain, and spent the entire war laid up in bed. He never shot a bullet or even raised a gun in the direction of the enemy, but after he migrated to Australia he was always one of the first spectators to line up in Adelaide Street for the Anzac Day parade. Nonno loved watching the old soldiers march. I wonder if he realised the irony that if he had gone to war, the Anzacs, at least for a couple of years, would have been his sworn enemy. It makes me think of my father and how he opted to immigrate to the other side of the world to avoid military service. Seems like the men in my family are more lovers than fighters.

Nonna, on the other hand, found herself in the direct line of American fire. It's so like her to be the one shot at, while her husband, my nonno, was at home recuperating.

'Then the doctor came but he told my father he couldn't operate because there wasn't any anaesthetic.'

'None?'

'Of course not, this was the war! But my father said, "We can't just leave her like that, you have to do something". So the doctor did what he had to do.'

'He operated on you without anaesthetic?'

'He had no choice,' she turns her palms up and shrugs her shoulders in resignation.

A horn blasts from the street and breaks the spell that Nonna's story has cast over me.

'Thank God!' she says. 'That's Giovanni. I never know anymore if he's going to turn up or not. He's old and some Saturdays he can't make it. Can you go down for me?'

I nod vacantly and only faintly hear Nonna tell me that downstairs Giovanni has a wheel of cheese awaiting collection. I'm seeing my Nonna in a Sicilian field picking vegetables when the American planes fly in low and start peppering every-thing with machine-gun fire. I can see her and Adele limping home with a trail of blood behind them, and the look on their parents' faces when they came crashing through the door of their stone house. Laid flat on her stomach, with a blade slic-ing through her leg, she would have screamed, but she would have taken it.

PARTITO COMUNISTA

NE

81

Australian

BY L'ALPINA

Verðura from the fields
   Fried spinach with garlic and chilli

Sicilian food is about taking things straight from the earth or the sea and doing very little to them before they get to your plate. If you go out into your Australian backyard you are sure to find some peculiar little weeds growing on your lawn. They lie flat, with long leaves growing from their centres. Cosce vecchie, *they're called in Sicilian. Old women's legs.*

'When I come over tomorrow, we'll collect some cosce vecchie,*' Nonna will say. We'll start at one end of my parents' front yard, Nonna taking the lead with a small brown-handled knife in one hand and a plastic bag in the other. She'll bend over directly from the waist because her knees no longer work, and start pulling the plants out of the earth. 'Is this the right type, Nonna?' I'll ask, holding up a plant roughly the same shape as the one we're looking for. Nonna will shake her head quickly. 'Their leaves are jagged,' she'll say and tap her knee with the end of her knife, 'like* cosce vecchie.*' Old women's legs.*

In our own way, even if it was just in the front yard of my parents' house, we were gathering verdura *from the fields just like Nonna did when she was young. Just like she was doing when the Americans took a shot at her.*

2 bunches fresh spinach, leaves picked
salt
2 cloves garlic, finely chopped
1 fresh red chilli, deseeded and finely chopped
⅓ cup olive oil

Blanch the spinach by plunging it momentarily in just-boiled, salted water, then drain. Sauté the garlic and chilli in the olive oil for a couple of minutes, then add the spinach and a pinch or two of salt and fry until the spinach is well coated. Serve with crusty Italian bread.   *Serves 4 as a side dish*

SWINGING SALAMIS OVERHEAD

'Ciao Giovanni,' I call as I come down Nonna's driveway and out onto the street. Giovanni's white truck is parked behind my red hatchback.

'Ciao Mischella,' he says, converting my name to a more Sicilian sound, 'your Nonna not coming down this morning?'

'No, it's just me today.'

'Ah,' he sighs quickly and wipes his forehead. His relief is palpable.

With the slow motions of a man whose bones and joints aren't cooperating as well as they used to, he releases the latches on the back doors of his truck and throws them open. Inside it's an Aladdin's cave of cheeses, breads and tinned meats. Giovanni is a deli on wheels. There are wheels of *pecorino*, *provolone* and Swiss cheese, knobs of mozzarella and logs of *galbanino*. He has towers of canned tuna in olive oil, stacked to the ceiling and loaves and *mezze lune* of golden Italian bread piled thigh-high. In my favourite corner of the truck, closest to the right-hand door, he hides piles of miniature chocolate cakes shipped straight from Italy, and a pile of assorted Nutella products.

When she could walk down the stairs with ease, Nonna would stand out here in this West End street with Great Aunt Rosa and the other Sicilian and Greek women who lived in the surrounds. Every Saturday morning they'd crowd around the back of Giovanni's truck while he ran around inside putting orders together and trying to avoid the swinging salamis overhead. As kids, my cousin Gracie and I would love to go out and watch the action at the back of Giovanni's truck. Mostly though, we'd enjoy the chance to choose something from his stockpile of sweets. We'd be hoisted up to sit on the edge of his mobile deli with our legs dangling off the side and swinging in the air.

'Is the bread fresh?' Nonna would always ask Giovanni.

The women arrayed behind her would either have one or both hands cocked on their hips, their aprons fluttering in the breeze and their dark eyebrows delicately arched.

Giovanni would always start the dance with a roll of the eyes, then raise both hands, palms up, out from his waist.

'*Signoraaaaa*,' he'd wail, 'of course it's fresh. It's fresh every week and every week you ask me the same question!'

'And every week the bread seems a little tough, so every week I ask!' Nonna would throw back at him.

'Here! Take a look!' Giovanni would yell and thrust a *mezza luna* into Nonna's hands. 'Go on, call me a liar!' he'd dare.

From my vantage point sitting on the edge of the mobile deli I would always see little beads of sweat break out across Giovanni's forehead. Sometimes he would shoot me or Gracie a desperate look but there was nothing we could do to save him.

'Hmmm,' Nonna would turn the half-moon-shaped bread in her strong hands.

'*Signoraaaaa*,' he'd wail again, 'it's fresh! Believe me, I picked it up fresh this morning!'

Nonna would sigh again and draw Giovanni's desperation out like a thin, tenuous thread. She'd eyeball him with a pair of cold dark eyes. 'If you say so,' she'd drawl as if she didn't quite believe him. 'What's the salami like?'

And it would start again. Every product inspected, examined and sometimes even tasted before purchase. In the middle of the street Giovanni would hand out shards of cheese and slices of salami. The women would huddle and confer in Greek and Sicilian over the samples, umming and ahhhing before finally, to Giovanni's relief, purchasing.

'This is for your Nonna,' Giovanni says, passing me an entire wheel of *pecorino pepato* cheese. He's looking over the top of my head and I turn to follow his eyes but there's no-one there. The days of a crowd forming at the back of his truck are long gone. Nonna can't get down the stairs by herself anymore and a lot of the other women have died or moved away. I look back at Giovanni and our eyes meet – his old hazel ones and my young brown ones – and we both know that those days are not coming back.

'Eh,' he sighs, 'things change,' he shrugs his shoulders. 'Do you want anything else?'

I look to the right and he smiles. 'And some things never do,' he says. Reaching over, he pulls out a chocolate cake in plastic wrapping. It's a snack-size cake made of two pieces of sponge dipped in liqueur and held together by chocolate icing.

'Gratis,' he says handing it to me and smiling slowly.

'Thanks Giovanni.' I shift the heavy cheese in my hands, 'I'll see you next week,' I say as I step off the street and onto the footpath.

He waves goodbye but doesn't answer me.

It seems like it's a day of goodbyes. I can't help but feel, as I watch Giovanni's truck drive to the end of Cameron Street and turn into Montague Road, that it's dying; my Cameron Street, my old West End. The high-rise apartments are closing in, and the original residents that are left are ageing fast – this cast of characters from my childhood is slowly fading away. In that moment, standing on the footpath of Cameron Street with a wheel of cheese in my arms, it seems that all the joy and fun that used to live here is now in the past.

Nonna's old *mezza luna*
  Pane condito

Sicilians have a use for everything edible, including stale bread, because over the course of their history they have known real hunger.

As is Nonna's way in this land of plenty, she always buys more than she actually needs and always enough to distribute to all her children. One of the mezza luna *loaves from Giovanni's truck will always make its way to my mother's house. If it spends too much time in the pantry my mother won't throw it out, instead she'll transform that stale bread into something aromatic and filling. She'll douse it with olive oil and turn it into a warm, winter meal for us to enjoy in front of my father's one-night-a-year fire.*

1 *mezza luna* or French stick
2 cloves garlic, cut in half
⅓ cup olive oil
150 g black olives, pitted and cut in half
100 g sun-dried tomatoes
50 g anchovy fillets in olive oil (optional)
⅓ cup grated parmesan cheese
1 tablespoon finely chopped flat-leaf parsley

Preheat the oven to 250°C. Cut the bread in half lengthways and rub the insides with a piece of garlic, then chop the garlic pieces finely. Douse each cut side of the bread with 2 tablespoons olive oil then sprinkle the garlic on top. Layer one cut side with the olives, sun-dried tomatoes, anchovies (if using), parmesan and parsley. Place the other side on top and wrap in foil. Bake for about half an hour, or until the cheese has melted. Cut into thick slices and serve warm.

Serves 4

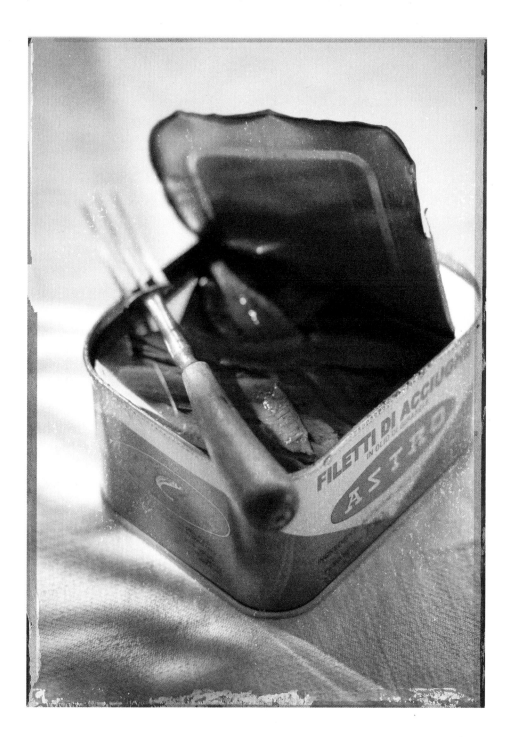

Swinging salamis overhead 61

FOOD AND DEATH – A SICILIAN CONVERSATION

'Did you taste it before you paid for it?' Nonna asks, as I dump the cheese wheel on her kitchen table.

'No Nonna,' I sigh.

She slaps a palm on the table. 'Haven't I taught you anything? You always try before you buy!'

'Nonna, you've been buying from Giovanni for thirty years!'

'Doesn't matter,' she waves a finger at me, 'the best meatballs are usually made by those you trust!'

I furrow my brow. 'What does that mean?'

'It means you don't trust anyone!'

'What has that got to do with meatballs?'

Nonna rolls her eyes at me. 'What sort of Sicilian are you that you can't understand anything I say?'

I sigh and slump my shoulders. 'Are we going to grate this cheese or what?' I ask.

Nonna allocates culinary tasks to female family members according to age and cooking experience. I am the youngest, after my mother and her sister, Auntie Gina, and being single I have the least cooking experience. Therefore, I get the most time-consuming and boring tasks, like grating the cheese, a job I've had for as long as I can remember. I wield a foot-long knife and cut the cheese into pieces small enough to fit into the food processor. After it's been grated, Nonna stuffs freezer bags full of it and distributes these cheese packs to her children. *Pecorino pepato* has a heavy taste and an interesting smell, and every

Sicilian fridge will have a tub of it sitting in the corner, waiting to be dusted over a bowl of pasta. But Nonna always leaves a piece of it ungrated so that it can be eaten with olives and bread or stuffed into the decadent *falso magro* (wide pieces of steak wrapped around meatballs, cheese, salami and eggs, tied with string, and lowered into a vat of red sauce).

The cheese wheel is about fifteen centimetres high and thirty centimetres wide. I've wrapped an apron around me and as I cut into the wheel, I lean all my weight onto the knife, one hand on the handle and the other on the blunt side. I alternate my weight on each end of the knife in a see-saw fashion until I've made it all the way through and the wheel is sitting in two halves.

Nonna looks at me.

With the apron on, and my long dark hair tied up in a bun, I'm gripping the knife hard and the strong scent of the cheese is on my skin.

'You look just like a *Siciliana*,' she says to me.

'I am a *Siciliana*, Nonna,' I smile back.

'So do you think you'll like it there?'

'Where?' I ask, still chopping the cheese.

'Sicily,' she replies slowly.

'Nonna,' I sigh, 'of course I'll like it.'

A sliver of cheese splits away from one of the pieces I've cut. I break it in half, pass a piece to Nonna and slide the other into my mouth. I look at her and see that tears have started to well in her brown eyes. Her chin starts to wobble and she's sucking her bottom lip into her mouth.

'What are you crying for?' I ask, a little harshly.

'Ahhh,' she sighs, 'I just hope I'll be here when you get back.'

Pleadingly she looks up at the ceiling and crosses herself.

'I'm sure you can live another two months,' I say, exasperated by a lifetime of dramatics.

'I don't have long left,' she drops her head slowly. Her eyes drift pitifully to the floor and she shakes her head. 'Look at my feet, see the veins? They're black. That means it's almost time.' This from the woman who only a few hours ago was perched on a stool at a blackjack table.

I'm gripping my knife. 'For what?' I chop another piece of cheese violently in half.

'Ahhh, time for me to go.' Tears are in her eyes again but they don't spill over.

'Go where?'

The tears wobble a bit but stay in. I try grinning but it doesn't seem to work.

'The time is near,' she says with a hushed and theatrical finality.

It's normal, this constant talk of death. It stalks every Sicilian conversation. We're obsessed, frightened and, I think, secretly thrilled by it.

'Listen,' I talk tough and wave my knife a little in the air, 'I'm only going for two months. That's it. It's a holiday, you understand? I'll be back in two months, so just stop it with the dramatics!'

'*Si, si,*' she waves a hand at my knife, 'but do you think you're going to like it there?'

'Ahhh! It's like talking to a brick wall!' I mumble to myself in English.

'*Si, come un muro,*' she replies.

'I like that you understand English when it suits you.'

'*Si, si, Inglese,*' she mutters to herself and looks out the kitchen window to her backyard. 'There's misery in Sicily you know.'

I take a giant breath that fills my chest and squashes my rising temper.

'They can barely afford to eat there, they're all starving. You should see how they live, in tiny houses all made of stone, right on top of each other.'

I look up and see Georgina, Nonna's Greek neighbour, switching on her TV, and I wonder if the houses in Sicily get any closer than this.

'It's not like Australia with all this freedom,' Nonna goes on.

I assemble the food processor and wedge in a piece of cheese. I turn it on to drown Nonna out but she just talks louder.

'Here you can breathe,' she takes a lungful of air for effect, 'Sicily is a prison.'

Finally she is silent and stares out of the window. I turn the food processor off and start sifting grated cheese into the freezer bag Nonna is holding open.

'But it's so beautiful,' she whispers, and our eyes meet.

There's a look of foreboding on her face that makes me shiver.

How to make a meatball
The perfect *polpetta*

The smell of a frying meatball means Sunday lunch to me. And Sunday lunch is Sicilian religion. 'La Domenica è sempre Domenica,' my father says. Sunday is always Sunday. And on Sunday we all have to be together for lunch, which commences at precisely midday. My mother will get up earlier than the rest of us, and at ten a.m. you can hear the sizzle of the first meatball going into the pan. The smell fills the whole house and mingles with the smell of her early-morning espresso.

'Do you want a fried meatball before I put them in the sauce?' she'll ask when the first ones are done. It's hard to say no. When you put your fork through the meatball and the juices blend with the cheese and parsley inside, you know you made the right choice.

½ kg beef mince
2 slices white bread
2 eggs, beaten
½ cup grated parmesan or *pecorino pepato* cheese
2 cloves garlic, finely chopped
½ cup chopped flat-leaf parsley
salt and pepper
olive oil, for cooking

Put the mince in a mixing bowl. Put the slices of bread in a separate bowl and add water until they are soggy, but not falling apart. Squeeze the excess water from the bread, then mix the bread with the mince using your fingers. Add all the other ingredients and mix well. Form into thick, round patties about 2 cm high and 6 cm wide. Fry in batches in olive oil until cooked through.

Serves 4–6

Food and death – a Sicilian conversation

Flying Nuns

'You're staying for lunch, aren't you?'
Nonna asks. She's standing at her freezer door surveying her collection of pasta.
I look at the clock and find that two hours have disappeared in idle chit-chat
and cheese grating.

'What are you having?'

'Pasta with *melanzane*.'

My stomach replies before my mouth has a chance.

'Call your Uncle Joe – tell him I'm putting the pasta on.'

I head down the long central hallway of the house and stop at the front room
that used to be a veranda before Nonna had it enclosed. This room was once fitted out with a kitchen and my parents lived here when they first got married.
Beneath the front window my mother had wedged a little dining table, and the
three of us would eat dinner there together in our little corner of the house. I'd
set the table while my mother finished cooking. Every night my father would
come home smelling of paint from his job, except Fridays, when he'd smell of
custard tarts dusted with cinnamon, our weekly treat that he'd pick up on his
way home. Now the front veranda is just storage space and home to Nonna's
ancient deep freeze. I pick up the broom handle leaning against the wall and
give the floor two sharp taps.

'Comin'!' yells Uncle Joe from downstairs.

'You want spaghetti or penne rigate?' Nonna asks over her shoulder, her
upper body still buried in her freezer.

'I think you have to have spaghetti with *melanzane*, Nonna.'

'She's right you know,' she says to my uncle, who has come up from downstairs and taken his usual seat.

'Doesn't worry me,' he replies. 'So how's work?' he asks, turning to me.

'It's a bit slow at the moment.' So slow I wasn't going anymore, but I wasn't in the mood to answer questions.

Uncle Joe is seated at the end of the long kitchen table closest to the window that looks into the backyard. That's where he's been sitting all his life, with me to his right and Nonna to his left. We've eaten many a meal here, the three of us.

'Pass me the water will ya?' he asks, and I reach to my left for the bottle of water.

He pours half of it onto the tablecloth and the rest in his glass. In the middle of the table, Nonna's put a plate covered in foil. It's warm to the touch and smells of hot olive oil.

Nonna comes slowly around the table and moves to the stove. She picks up a long wooden spoon and starts stirring the water in a tall pot. She puts the spoon down and slides the contents of a packet of spaghetti into the boiling water. Outside the sun's beating down on the concrete and inside Uncle Joe's chugging his glass of water, and I start to realise that you can live some of life's most beautiful moments in just one, simple room. I want to lock this moment up and put it away forever. I want my childhood in this house back. I want my old West End back.

'What was West End like when you were a kid?' I ask Uncle Joe.

'Full of wogs and nuns,' he says, 'that's all I remember.'

I start to laugh.

Nonna turns from stirring the pot. 'What are you laughing at?'

'The wogs and nuns of West End,' I reply.

'Ah, the nuns,' she says, 'of course that's all your Uncle Joe can remember, he used to get a beating from them almost every day.'

'What's the matter, didn't you behave in school?' I ask him smiling.

Uncle Joe has that cheeky twinkle in his middle-aged eyes that some people are born with and never quite goes away.

'I was misunderstood,' he says.

'Oh really?'

'Yeah, well occasionally I'd do things I shouldn't, but that's no reason to beat the life out of a kid.'

'Like what?'

'Oh, there were a few things,' he grins slyly.

'Tell me one!' I cry, because no-one tells a story like Uncle Joe. He's a born showman – the whirling mass of mischief he was as a child is still there, flashing in his wide grin and chocolate, sparkling eyes.

'Best one,' he starts, 'was the day my best mate and I found a box of tomatoes on the side of the road up on Peel Street, must have fallen off the back of a truck or somethin'. So my best mate dares me to throw a tomato at a car.'

Uncle Joe gets out of his chair and plants his feet. Sicilians can't tell a story unless they act it out for you.

'I wait until a car comes, I pick up a tomato and throw it. Except this idiot's got his passenger-side window down. So this tomato goes sailing through the car and explodes all over the inside of the driver's window. Just about wet myself! He gets out of the car and drags me by the ear all the way into Mother Superior's office.'

'Did she call Nonna?'

'Call Nonna?!' he yells. 'She locked all the doors and windows and took out the cane! I was throwing myself over chairs and desks trying to get away and she was coming right after me – I've never seen a nun jump over furniture like that!' Uncle Joe's arms are flapping through the air mimicking a flying nun tossing chairs and tables out of her way.

'I suppose you know you're in trouble when a nun locks the doors and windows.'

'Tell her what I did when you came home,' Nonna says, draining the pasta and stirring in the red sauce.

'Ah, now that's the best part,' smiles Uncle Joe. 'When I came home I told Nonna what happened. She went down the road to her *cummari's* house on Boundary Street and they went straight down to Mother Superior's office.'

'You should have seen that nun's face when she saw me,' Nonna says, picking up the story, 'I said to *cummari* Maria, you have to translate every word I say perfectly to this *butana*. And I said to that nun if you ever touch a hair on my son's head again I'll come down here and beat the life out of you with my bare hands!'

'What did Mother Superior say?'

'Nothing,' Nonna shrugs and puts a white bowl of steaming red spaghetti in the middle of the table, 'she had nothing to say because she knew that if she ever touched my son again I would have killed her.'

'Then what happened?'

'Then,' Uncle Joe grins slowly, 'Nonna came home and I got the life beat out of me again. Pass the cheese will ya,' he finishes off.

'No-one touches my son but me,' Nonna says, and whips the foil off the fried eggplant.

I reach out with my fork and put one of Nonna's stuffed eggplant slices onto my pasta. Uncle Joe slides the cheese in my direction, and I dust my plate all over with the cheese I have just bought fresh off the street and grated myself.

I smile at Nonna. I'm pretty sure she would have killed Mother Superior if she'd gone at my uncle again. And I'm pretty sure she would have killed my uncle if he was caught throwing tomatoes at passing cars again.

'You should come to Sicily with me,' I say to Uncle Joe.

He's midway through slurping his spaghetti and little red freckles splatter his chin.

'What for?'

'To see where you were born. Don't you want to go back and see it?'

'What for?'

'Because you were born there!'

'So what?' he sucks up a strand of spaghetti.

'I don't know. I thought you'd want go back to see where you began,' I sigh and look down into my bowl.

'This is home,' he says stabbing a finger at the table.

Nonna's head goes up and down. 'While I'm still alive, you all have to live here, near me.'

'It's just a holiday Nonna, it's not permanent.'

I twirl my spaghetti, my eyes fixed on the red strands in my bowl. When I look up, Nonna's eyes are wide. 'Let's hope,' she says and touches the top of her head again, 'let's hope.'

Lunch at Nonna's
Melanzane piene

Lunch at Nonna's is about warm food, incessant chatter and stories of the past. It's about eating till you burst and laughing till your sides split. Nonna's cooking is heavy on the Arabic influence and her favourite vegetable, like mine, is the eggplant.

2 large eggplants, trimmed and cut into slices ½ cm thick
1 quantity meatball mix (see page 66)
salt and pepper
olive oil, for cooking
1 quantity *sarsa semplice* (see page 11, add an extra 400 g can of crushed, peeled
    tomatoes), warmed

Salt and rinse the eggplant slices the same way you would for eggplant parmigiana (see page 42). Prepare the meatball mix as described on page 66, but do not divide into patties. Take a slice of eggplant and top with a ½ cm thick layer of the meatball mix, and put a second slice of eggplant on top. Repeat with the remaining eggplant slices, sprinkle with salt and pepper, then fry in batches in oil until the eggplant is golden brown on each side. Then carefully lower them into the pan with the warmed *sarsa semplice* and simmer for 30 minutes until the meat is cooked. Serve one eggplant sandwich per person with a generous amount of sauce spooned over the top.

Serves 4

HERB BALLS AND LEMON WARS

She perplexes me, my nonna. My holiday means something more to her than just a few weeks baking in the sun and discovering my family roots. Maybe it's because she's never been back, or because to her a voyage to the other side of the world is a voyage from which you may never return.

'Ok Nonna, this is it, I'm saying goodbye now.'

Nonna has taken my wrist in her hand and I don't think she realises how much strength she still has left in those old fingers. Someone loosens the strings in her chin and it starts to wobble uncontrollably. This only makes her squeeze my wrist harder, as if she's going to keep me here by pure physical strength alone. I bend down to give her a goodbye kiss and she wraps her strong forearm around my neck and brings my cheek smashing into her mouth. Her kisses smack me with a strong sucking sound and mix with the tears that have finally started to spill down her face.

'Nonna,' I say, 'it's only a holiday. I will be back.'

Her grip tightens and for an instant I can't breathe until finally, after one last squeeze, she releases me. I turn quickly from the tears on her face and walk towards the back door. Nonna gets up slowly from her seat at the kitchen table and follows me. I leave her standing on her back step, her hand outstretched between the steel bars of the security gate in a final, agonising goodbye. Out on Nonna's concrete driveway and out of her sight, I take a deep breath and sigh.

I hate goodbyes but today, there are more to come.

As with Nonna's house, you make your way into Great Uncle Charlie's and

Great Aunt Rosa's West End home up a long and narrow concrete side path leading into their backyard. They were in the same spot I had seen them when I waved to them hours before, sitting on plastic chairs in the middle of their garden – one of only a handful of gardens in this quarter that consists entirely of grass. Seeking refuge from hot concrete in the Brisbane summer, this is where Gracie and I would come as children to turn cartwheels and play ball. When we looked parched, Great Aunt Rosa would appear at our sides with a plate of fresh lemons, cut into quarters and dipped in sugar.

'Ciao Zio, ciao Zia,' I kiss them both on each cheek, 'I've come to say goodbye.'

'Ahhh, you're going to *Sicilia*, your mother told us,' chuckles Great Uncle Charlie. Great Aunt Rosa chuckles along with him, waving at me to sit down. I'm not sure what they're laughing at, unless they know something quirky about Sicily that no-one's told me about yet.

Great Uncle Charlie has, like a lot of men on both sides of my family, a bright pair of blue eyes. They defy the stereotype of the southern Italian male. In his youth, Great Uncle Charlie looked like a shorter version of Paul Newman and Great Aunt Rosa a thinner version of Sophia Loren. Now they have aged, like everyone else around here, and all of a sudden, in my eyes, they look frail and vulnerable.

'Wait until you see Sicily,' Great Aunt Rosa sighs, and then starts to laugh again, 'it's beautiful.'

I look at Great Aunt Rosa and remember someone telling me that her photo was sent from Sicily to Australia with a letter of introduction. Evidently my Great Uncle liked what he saw, and the next thing Great Aunt Rosa knew she was leaving her beautiful island and meeting her husband for the first time.

'Yes, but here's better,' adds Great Uncle Charlie.

Why does everyone keep saying that to me?

'But you always go back,' I say.

'Beautiful for a holiday,' Great Uncle Charlie explains, 'but no-one can live there. Here,' he takes a deep breath and waves a hand in front of him much like Nonna did an hour before, 'you can breathe.'

I take Great Uncle Charlie's word a bit more seriously than Nonna's. She left a war torn, impoverished island forty-six years ago and never saw it again.

Great Uncle Charlie and Great Aunt Rosa make the trip back to Sicily every two years. In the heady days of the 1980s they'd travel every year in the depths of the Brisbane winter and the height of the Sicilian summer. We'd be dragged, my cousin Gracie and I, along to Brisbane Airport to watch Great Aunt Rosa, in stockings and heels, gold jewellery catching the sun, stride out to the waiting TAA jumbo. Great Uncle Charlie would walk casually at her side, suit-jacket slung over his arm, occasionally turning to wave up at us in the viewing gallery, the airport reflected in his dark aviator sunglasses. Once on board Great Aunt Rosa would pull out a white handkerchief and wave it against the window. While the rest of the casually-dressed passengers boarded and the plane got ready for take-off, Gracie and I would take turns riding the mechanical Qantas kangaroo at the end of the viewing gallery. Our parents would yell out for us when the plane started to back out onto the tarmac and we'd go running to our viewing places. With breaths held, we'd watch as the plane taxied into position and took off right in front of us. Great Aunt Rosa would wave her handkerchief against the glass the whole time, and the fluttering would climax as the pilot opened up the engines with that beautiful roar and gunned the plane down the tarmac. Then, when Great Uncle Charlie and Great Aunt Rosa were on their way back, we'd do it all over again. Head up to the viewing gallery, ride the mechanical Qantas kangaroo and watch the white handkerchief wind down to a slow wave as the engines were shut down. I used to think Great Aunt Rosa waved her handkerchief all the way to Sicily and back.

Back in West End, Great Aunt Rosa would open her suitcase and we'd be assaulted by the smell of Sicily. Vanilla and almonds. Tucked beneath a layer of clothing were stashed boxes of *paste di mandorla*. Odd-shaped almond biscuits dusted heavily in icing sugar, crisp on the outside and delicately smooth in the middle. I can smell those biscuits now as I look and smile at my father's aunt and uncle.

A rustling sound comes from somewhere over Great Uncle Charlie's left shoulder. With a swiftness that belies his age, he swings up and out of his plastic chair and runs the two short paces into the garden bed. I see him wade between the parsley, basil and mint plants that he has grown and pruned into massive herby balls. He disappears behind them and rummages around towards the sound while Great Aunt Rosa rises slightly in her chair and calls out, "Melo? 'Melo?'

When my mother runs out of parsley all the way over at Carindale, she sends my father for a drive to West End to collect some from Great Uncle Charlie. Carefully, he'll pick the best of the crop and hand it to Great Aunt Rosa who'll wrap it in foil like a bouquet.

A high-pitched screech rips the air and Great Uncle Charlie swears roughly in Sicilian as a cat comes screaming out from behind the herbs.

'When old Mr Barbi lived behind us there were never any cats in this neighbourhood. Now look!' says Great Aunt Rosa.

'That's because he poisoned them all,' I point out.

She just nods her head and shrugs her shoulders, as if the sacrifice of the neighbourhood's cats was a small price to pay for perfect basil.

Great Uncle Charlie is still up to his shoulders in herb balls. He makes a space with his hands between the mint and parsley and reaches out to his lemon tree. 'Here,' he says when he reappears from his herby forest, 'take this to your father.' He drops a green lemon into my open palm.

'Tell him to try that, and then I dare him to tell me his lemons are better than mine. Tell him that's what a real lemon is meant to taste like!'

'Ok,' I say and sigh.

Some men compare cars, jobs or material wealth in an effort to prove some sort of advantage over the other. The men in my family compare lemons. Whenever my father visits Great Uncle Charlie, or Uncle Mario in Mitchelton, he will be sure to take a bag of his home-grown lemons with him.

'Here,' he'll say, passing his bag of lemons over, 'I've brought you some real lemons.' It's the first shot fired in their cross-suburban lemon war, and the favour is always returned.

I roll the green lemon in my palm and smell its scent mingling with that coming off the disturbed herb bushes. I lift my head and see Georgina's husband next door turning the earth in his flowerbed over some seeds he's just sprinkled. Further up I can see Uncle Joe standing in Nonna's backyard with a tiny, white espresso cup and saucer in his hand.

'Ciao Rosa! Ciao Charlie!' Uncle Joe calls over.

'Ciao!' they reply.

'*Yassou!*' Uncle Joe calls to Georgina's husband next door.

'*Yassou* Joe!' Georgina's husband replies and wipes his brow, smearing brown earth across his face.

Behind Georgina's house Rose, the English neighbour, is hanging out her washing.

'How ya goin' Rose?' Uncle Joe calls to her.

'Good Joe, and you?'

Everything is good, I want to call out to her. Everything in West End is perfect. The sun is out, the lemon in my palm is intoxicating, my stomach is full of spaghetti and eggplant and everyone I love is living happily within calling distance of each other. If only it would just stay this way.

The voices of children float up from the street to the back of the house.

'That sounds like Angelo and the kids,' smiles Great Aunt Rosa, about her son and grandchildren.

'I'll go out and see them, it's time I headed off anyway,' I say, getting out of my plastic chair.

Great Aunt Rosa gives me a kiss on each cheek and I notice that even though she's smiling she's got tears in her eyes. She takes me by the hand and follows me out to the street where her son is getting out of his car.

'Hi Ang,' I say to my cousin Angelo as he bends down to kiss me on each cheek.

'I hear you're going,' he says, 'just be careful over there, ok.'

'Careful of what cuz?'

'Of the boys,' he says and winks.

I look at my cousin Angelo, now in his early forties and a father of two. I have one memory of him that I can never erase – even when he's an old man I think I will remember him the same way. I was thirteen and had just walked out of the gates of Brisbane State High School on Edmonstone Street. Grouped around the gates were all the blonde girls I loved to hate. I shrugged past them and turned to head past Musgrave Park when I heard the sound of thunder rumbling low and fast behind me. With a screech of brakes a red Falcon pulled up to the curb, barely inches away. As if by magic, the passenger door swung open and the sound of eighties pop music blasted from inside. There was cousin Angelo, his dark hair puffy and lacquered, wearing tight blue jeans, a tight white T-shirt and black sunglasses. His car was fire-engine red, the stereo was pumping, and tied around the gearstick was a fistful of red plastic chillies to ward off evil spirits. He was the epitome of cool on that late-eighties day.

He only said two words, 'Get in.'

The faces on those perfect blondes dropped to the ground. 'Who is that?' I heard them whisper.

'He's my cousin,' I said wistfully over my shoulder. It was the best day in grade eight. Thanks cuz.

He's standing here now out the front of his parents' house on Cameron Street with his wife and two children at his side. But for me, he'll always be that cool guy on that very cool day.

I look over to see Helen and George still on their balcony watching us all standing and talking on the street. Over at Nonna's place, Uncle Joe comes down the side driveway and opens the door to his downstairs flat.

'Hi Ang!' Uncle Joe calls out.

'Hi Joe!' Angelo returns.

Nonna's front door swings open and she pulls up a chair so that she can sit and look out onto the street.

'Ciao *cummari!*' Angelo and his wife call up.

'Ciao!' Nonna calls back from two doors up.

Greetings are exchanged back up the road with Helen and George across the street, and Georgina, who briefly puts in an appearance in her front yard. I get in my car and leave them all talking out in the open, in the street.

A green blur
   Potato and herb omelette

When my father gets home with his bouquet of herbs from Great Uncle Charlie, my mother takes the parsley and chops it up into a fine green blur. This is the dish she makes when we've run out of sandwich fillers or if we just want something hot and fast. It's more than just an omelette: it's a parsley, potatoey delight.

2 large potatoes, peeled
olive oil, for cooking
salt and pepper
6 eggs
1 cup chopped flat-leaf parsley
¼ cup grated parmesan cheese

Cut the potatoes into thin rounds and pat each side dry with kitchen paper. Fry the potato slices in olive oil in a large frying pan until cooked through, seasoning on both sides as they cook. Set the fried potato slices aside and mix the eggs, parsley, cheese, salt and pepper together in a bowl. Heat some more olive oil in the frying pan, layer the potato slices in the base of the pan and pour the egg mixture over the top. Cook the omelette for a few minutes on one side, then carefully flip over and cook for a further few minutes on the other side, or until golden brown.

Serves 4

Herb balls and lemon wars 81

PIG TROTTER WALK

I drive up to the top of Cameron
Street where it meets the back of the West End Markets. Before it became home
to hair salons and coffee shops, this was a cavernous shed with a 100-year-old
brick façade. Inside was the only coffee shop in West End, with giant sacks
bursting with coffee beans in a variety of flavours. Wedged into each sack was a
scoop, and hanging above were small paper bags in which you could concoct
your own blends to take home. Past the coffee shop was the Vietnamese fruit
and vegetable shop, the French patisserie and the local supermarket, Jack the
Slasher (named so because apparently, Jack slashed all the prices). He has
been gone for an eon but we still call the supermarket "Jack's" for short. Every
week, when I was a child, Nonna, Great Aunt Rosa, Gracie's mum Auntie
Anna, Gracie and I would all head to Jack's for the big weekly shopping trip.
We'd cross Cameron Street to the boarding house at the top of the street, cut
under the house and pick our way down the slope to the Jack's carpark. At the
beginning there were no ticketed prices on the groceries at Jack's. You had to
collect a black felt pen from the cash registers and make a note of the prices on
each item as you went.

'That price will do,' Nonna would say, slashing her own prices.

The gap in the side fence of the boarding house we used to slide through is all
bricked up now because it's holding back the waves of modern apartments closing in. If you want to head down to Jack's now you have to take the long
circuitous route out to Norfolk Road and down Boundary Street.

I turn left at the top of Cameron Street, and left again, this time into Norfolk

Road. I'm going this way for a reason. Before I see her again, I have to say goodbye to Gracie as I knew her.

I stop outside Gracie's old house. She's not here anymore: she hasn't been here for seven years. When she was eight years old her parents, one of which is my father's sister, decided to leave Sicily and come to Australia. They stayed for close to twenty years in West End, where Gracie and I grew up together like sisters, spending every waking minute at each other's side. We loved and hated each other, drove each other crazy and missed each other desperately when the other was gone. Then seven years ago, Gracie's parents decided that Australia had given them all that they needed, so they packed up and went back to Sicily.

'Do you think you'll like living there?' I'd asked her the day before she left.

'How could I not like living in the country I was born in? Besides, I'll be in the same country as the Colosseum. How could I not like that?' was her reply.

How could you not, I thought. Except that sometimes, home is not the country you were born in but the country you grow to love.

Every morning we'd walk to school together and every afternoon we'd walk back again. As soon as I walked into Nonna's house, I'd have just enough time to drop my bag then I'd be back out the door, on the daily shopping trip that was one of Nonna's unbending habits. Clutching the cobbled-together list of grocery items she needed, I'd head past Norfolk Road where, without fail, I'd find Gracie coming down her front steps clutching her mother's shopping list in her hand. A couple of kilos of tomatoes from the Greek fruit shop on Boundary Street or the Vietnamese one in the West End Markets, whichever Nonna decided on the day. A dozen bread rolls from the Vietnamese bakery at the top of Boundary Street and while we were passing that way could we stop in at Mr Shay's shoe shop to see if there were any slippers on sale for Nonno. On the way back we'd pick up 200 grams of mortadella from Steve the Greek deli guy. All these purchases and most others we could handle as long as we could buy a thickshake along the way. The milk bar in the West End Markets had a giant blackboard suspended along its back wall with what seemed like an endless list of thickshake flavours. Vanilla, chocolate, peppermint, pina colada. All these flavours tumbled through my mind in the ten minutes it used to take me to choose one every day.

'Gracie,' I said to her one afternoon, 'I've got something a bit different to buy today.'

'What?' she said, flicking a long curly piece of black hair from her face.

'Promise you'll come with me.'

'What? No! Tell me what you have to buy first!'

'If I tell you, you won't come in with me. Promise you'll come in with me.'

She stopped at the corner of Norfolk Road and Cameron Street and narrowed her dark eyes at me.

'What is it?' She had both hands on her hips.

I had my hand wrapped around my Brisbane State High tie, subconsciously tugging it.

'We have to go to the butcher.'

'Ok, so let's go to the butcher! But why do I have to promise to come in with you?' she flapped a hand in front of my face.

'As my cousin,' I said, suddenly stamping my foot and pointing an accusing finger at her, 'you could at least be a little supportive!'

'Uhhh, whatever,' she said, waving another hand in the air then spinning on the balls of her feet and walking away from me, 'how bad could it be anyway?' she called over her shoulder.

'It's pretty bad,' I mumbled after her and ran to catch up.

When we got to the butcher's shop, Bruce, the thoroughly Australian butcher, was at the counter assisting about fifteen customers, all of which I wished would just disappear. I loitered, I lingered, I even pretended to be interested in the ox tongue display, until Gracie jabbed me in the back with a taloned finger.

'You gonna get served or what?' she hissed into my ear. 'I want to get out of here and get a thickshake.'

'Alright, alright,' I hissed back and stepped up to the counter.

'What can I do for ya, love?' bellowed Bruce.

'I've come to pick up an order for Anna,' I stood on tippy-toes and whispered while I scanned quickly to my left and right. The old lady to my left was a little too close for comfort.

'For who, love?' boomed Bruce.

'For Anna,' I spoke up and gulped some air at the same time.

I could never understand how Nonna, with her limited English, managed to place orders over the phone to Bruce, who I was pretty certain didn't know a single word of Sicilian.

'Ahhh, Mamma Anna,' he smiled, 'what's the order, love?'

He had to be kidding? He knew exactly who I was talking about – there was only one Mamma Anna in West End – and it wasn't exactly an order that would slip your mind. I looked around at the unsuspecting customers and caught Gracie glaring at me.

'Hurry up!' she mouthed. 'What's the matter with you?'

I coughed and looked into Bruce's ruddy face and warm, friendly, butcher's eyes.

'Pig's feet.'

The lady standing next to me took a step back.

'Oh yeah! Pig's feet!' amplified Bruce for all to hear, 'crazy Mamma Anna,' he chuckled to himself, and shaking his head he disappeared into the back of the shop.

'Are you mad?' Gracie jabbed me in the back again. Her face was flushed a deep scarlet.

'It's not my fault,' I started, but she was already sliding out of the shop door as if someone had greased her.

Bruce reappeared with a plastic bag in each hand and I was sure I could see the imprint of pig trotters through the bag.

'You gonna be alright carrying these home, little one?' he asked as he handed one bag over the counter to me, 'there's fifty pig's feet here.'

I tried to bury my head in my shoulders while Bruce handed me the second bag but they locked with the weight of the bags. When I turned it seemed like all the customers had moved to the fringes of the shop.

'That's a lot of pig's feet, love,' Bruce confirmed, shaking his head and wiping his thick hands on his blood-stained apron.

'Yeah, thanks,' I replied and made a stumbling escape out of the shop.

'My God, that was soooooo embarrassing!' squealed Gracie as I swung one of the bags at her.

'You can at least help me carry them.'

'Eeeewwww, pig's feet, think of all those pigs without feet! How disgusting!

Poor pigs!'

'Hey, I don't eat them ok, Nonna and Uncle Joe do. I've just got to get them home.'

'I'm never coming with you to the butcher ever again by the way,' Gracie said, tossing her curly hair as we headed out of the West End Markets.

'I miss you Gracie,' I say to her old house, 'see you soon.'

I start up the car and after a long morning leave West End behind me.

Short and round
The Sicilian sausage

Pig's feet make a strange little meal that I've never tried and don't really care to. Nonna would boil them in salted water and pile them up in a huge bowl. A feast of feet.

There is one Sicilian meal made out of pork, however, that is a perfect delight – the Sicilian sausage. These sausages resemble human Sicilians in a number of respects. They are, like most Sicilians, a little short, a little round, and bubbling with juice just beneath the surface of the skin. All in all, a package of hot, melting, explosive flavours.

I like the fact that Sicilians are often considered a disorganised, chaotic and time-consuming type of people. Perhaps they are, but when it comes to making sausages, Nonna becomes a German general and her team a well-oiled machine of crack troops. You have to arrive early on Sausage Day, no excuses. They're always made at Nonna's house, no excuses. Everyone has a job depending on their age, size, life experience, and whether or not Nonna considers you a trustworthy cook. The team has remained unchanged for the past twenty-five years, and is as follows:

- mixer of ingredients and taster of sausage mix: Nonna Anna
- person who processes the meat through the machine to ensure even distribution of meat to each sausage: Great Aunt Rosa
- person in charge of buying sausage meat and sausage skins, ensuring the skins are clean and soaking in enough water, and twisting of sausages into individual links: Mamma Rosetta
- person in charge of winding sausage links into wheels for storage and packing: Auntie Gina
- sausage pricker: me.

My mother's sister, my Auntie Gina, is forty-six years old, and I'm almost thirty, but we've had the same sausage job for the past twenty-five years, right at the bottom of the sausage-making hierarchy. We can't move up into a more responsible job until someone ahead of us dies. That's just the way it is. Sausage-making is important work, hence the lifetime positions.

Being the youngest with the least culinary experience, I am cursed with the most annoying and boring job on Sausage Day. But it is the only job that requires the use of a sharp object – a pin. Wrapped in its tight skin, the Sicilian sausage is a chubby, round mass of meat and delicious chunks of fat all churned together with pepper and fennel. Put one on a hot barbecue and the chunks of fat inside will start to melt, and the liquid fat builds up between the meat and the skin. If you haven't pricked holes in the skin to let the fat drain out, those round Sicilians will turn into exploding hunks of meat spraying hot jets of fat. Uncle Joe is the family's official barbecuer and as he's prone to the occasional fiery accident, I have to do my job well.

At the end of the sausage assembly line I await the sausage links and as they come my way I prick them all over. No sausage-making session is complete, however, without Nonna's ominous warning, 'Be careful with that pin, you lose it and we have to throw the whole batch out.'

This recipe may be a little time-consuming, it may be involved and it may take a team of people to put it together, but a few things are guaranteed. You'll have a lot of fun (do it Sicilian-style and finish the day with a family barbecue), and you'll end up with the best sausages you've ever, ever tasted. When the sausages are well cooked, take the time to taste the sweet buried hunks of fat, let the pepper tingle on your tongue and taste the fennel drawing all the flavours together.

This is Nonna's recipe using Nonna's measurements. I would like to give you exact measurements for the fennel, salt and pepper, but there aren't any. Nonna uses her fist as a measurement and she tastes as she goes – it's the only way (although I recommend you fry a small piece of the mixture before tasting it!). This recipe makes a lot of sausages, so just do as much as suits you. You'll need a sausage-maker or a special attachment that fits onto your food processor.

pork skins – your butcher should be able to tell you how many you'll need
    depending on how much mince you've got
2 tablespoons brown vinegar

2 kg shoulder pork – ask your butcher to remove all the skin and outside fat
    and grind the shoulder pork into a coarse mince
500 g coarse beef mince
dried fennel
salt and pepper

Rinse the pork skins well under cold water, inside and out, then place them in a bowl of cold water with the brown vinegar to soak while you make the sausage mix.

Put the pork, beef, fennel, salt and pepper into a large bowl, and mix together. Assemble your sausage-making machine, put the drained skins on one end and push the meat through the other. Alternatively, if you don't have a sausage-making machine or attachment for your food processor, you can fit a 2 cm wide nozzle to a piping bag and hold the skin over the nozzle. Half-fill the bag with sausage mixture and squeeze the mixture through until it is all used up. The sausages should come out plump, well-rounded and about 2 cm in diameter. Their death, as the Sicilians put it, is on a hot barbecue.

THE MAN WHO BELIEVED IN MERMAIDS

I have one more farewell to go. He's no longer here in West End, where he spent thirty-six of his seventy-one years on Earth. I have to drive to Mt Gravatt to see him because that is where he is now.

He was a quiet man. Not a man of great achievement, but a good man. A man often overshadowed by his strong-willed wife, but who, in my eyes, shone more brightly than most. A man who missed his island home, and a man who believed in mermaids.

'I believe in them because I saw one,' he said, taking a long drag on his cigarette. 'Besides, why do you think they put a picture of them on the tuna cans? Because they're real.'

'Carmelo,' laughed Great Uncle Charlie, slapping his thigh and stamping a foot, 'where did you see her?'

'Don't laugh Charlie, I saw her as close as I'm seeing you right now,' Nonno Carmelo tipped the ash from his cigarette into the topless Golden Circle pineapple can they were using as an ashtray. They were sitting in the sun in the middle of Great Uncle Charlie's backyard.

Gracie and I had lost our ball in the vicinity of Great Uncle Charlie's tomato plants, which were meticulously tied to stakes evenly-spaced along the back of the garden. We were thinking hard of ways of getting the ball out without being seen and subsequently throttled. There was no contest between us and the tomatoes – they were far more important.

'I could go around to Norfolk Road, cut through the back neighbour's yard and come at the tomatoes from behind. You keep a watch from this side,' Gracie suggested.

'That's a good idea, but you've got to get in and out without Great Uncle Charlie seeing you, and make sure you don't step on anything.'

'What did she look like?' Great Uncle Charlie was asking. He leaned forward with a smile on his face and an amused spark of interest in his blue eyes. I couldn't tell, sitting on the low brick wall just metres away, whether he could see our predicament from the corner of his eye.

Nonno took another long drag on his cigarette, drawing the moment out like a true Sicilian showman. He was leaning back in his chair with his face tipped back to the sky, his eyes half-closed and his enormous hand playing with his cigarette.

'She was the most beautiful thing I have ever seen. We were fishing off Acitrezza and I heard her before I saw her. The most beautiful sound I've ever heard and then there she was on the rock out there, you know the one. The big one.'

'*Polifermo*,' said Great Uncle Charlie.

'What?'

'*Polifermo*, the Cyclops, he threw that big rock at Ulysses.'

Like most Sicilians, Great Uncle Charlie confuses mythology with historical fact.

'Hmmm, yeah, that one,' nodded Nonno.

I was keeping an ear on the conversation and an eye on the tomato plants. Gracie had been gone for a few minutes now, long enough to walk around the block. I saw her under the back neighbour's house. We never had any qualms about trespassing: here everyone's backyards were a shortcut to somewhere else. If I wanted to get to Great Uncle Charlie's place from Nonna's without walking out to the street, I'd slide through the gap in Nonna's wire fence and scoot across Georgina's concrete backyard. To get to Gracie's place in Norfolk Road from Great Uncle Charlie's house, I'd carefully pick my way through the tomato plants through to the facing backyard, then walk under the neighbour's house and out onto Norfolk Road.

'She was a brunette.'

'A brunette mermaid? I've never heard of such a thing.'

'She was a *Siciliana!*'

'Uh well, you've got a point,' conceded Great Uncle Charlie.

Gracie delicately cleared a space in the foliage with her palms while her eyes scanned for the ball. 'Where is it?' she hissed, 'can you see it from there?'

I was still sitting on the low brick wall that ran along the back of the garden. I shook my head. Nothing could be seen beneath the thick foliage of Great Uncle Charlie's plants.

'She looked like this,' Nonno swept his thick hands into a very generous hourglass shape. Great Uncle Charlie's eyes bulged and he blinked furiously to keep them in his head.

'How big?'

'She was a *Siciliana!*' Nonno threw his hands out, palms up.

'Uh well, I see your point.'

Out of the corner of my eye I saw Great Uncle Charlie's head turn. 'What is that?' he bellowed, and I saw Gracie freeze with one foot hovering between two tomato plants.

'Most beautiful thing I ever saw. Probably would have run away with her if Anna wasn't waiting for me at home, and Anna's the type who would have come looking for me,' Nonno nodded to himself, his mind back in Sicily on his fishing boat, oblivious to everything around him. He kept his blue eyes fixed in the distance.

'What is that in my tomatoes?'

I swallowed hard. Great Uncle Charlie raced across the lawn, heading straight for me. He leapt high into the air and landed expertly in his garden without stepping on anything, as if the plants had cleared a space for him. He bent forward so that he was eyeballing the soil. I could see Gracie slowly backing away from the tomato plants on the other side and trying to slide back under the neighbour's house without being seen.

Great Uncle Charlie's hand closed around something round and shiny. I swallowed again. He pulled hard and came out holding a giant quivering eggplant.

'Carmelo, you ever seen an eggplant like this?' he called out, holding his vegetable triumphantly in the air.

The sound of his name brought Nonno forward thirty years in time and back to West End. He finished the last drag of his cigarette and stubbed it out in the

Golden Circle can. 'No Charlie,' he shook his head, 'I've never seen an eggplant like that.'

'It's a *Siciliana!*'

Nonno was a man who believed in mermaids but refused to believe that man landed on the moon. 'Look,' he said to me, and made me stand at the back door of his house, 'do you see the moon?' He pointed out to the night sky and the full moon. 'How could the Americans have ever gotten there, it's so far away! I don't believe it!'

He was the man who walked me to preschool and primary school every morning and then picked me up every afternoon. On the way home we'd stop at a takeaway shop on the corner of Montague Road and Mollison Street, across the road from the concrete factory, and buy two custard tarts. We'd sit side-by-side on a concrete stoop eating our custard tarts in comfortable silence before dusting off and heading home. These are my favourite memories of Nonno. Of my grandfather.

I realise only now, long after he's gone, that he was a romantic and gentle soul who was sometimes sidelined in life. Sidelined by a dominant wife and by a country he never really felt a part of. For the last five years of his life he spent every day sitting on the back veranda of his Queenslander in Cameron Street, smoking and staring off into the distance.

What were you thinking about Nonno? Were you thinking about your life and how you ended up on the other side of the world?

And every day, sitting on his back veranda, he'd eat the same lunch, day in, day out.

Whiting dusted in flour and fried in olive oil. A wedge of white onion dipped in salt. A piece of crusty Italian bread. A glass of red wine. Were you thinking about your mermaid?

I'd like to think so.

Nonna says she fell in love with his whistle and the way he could make her smile. She was in the fields when she first saw him pedalling past on his bike and whistling a melody to himself. I've seen photos of Nonno when he was a young man and I can understand how he could make you smile. Like so many men in my family he had gorgeous blue eyes and thick wavy hair. He was a movie star masquerading as a Sicilian farmer's son. In Australia he matured into a handsome middle-aged man, who took the time every day to slick back his hair, slip on a sports jacket and a dark pair of sunglasses and ride the old 177 or 178 bus into the Valley. There he would sit with his old Sicilian cronies in the Italian cafe, watching the girls walk by and pretending they were all the way back home.

Nonno lives in the halls of my memory now – the most precious of which I pull out only once in a while, in case it gets used up if I try to remember it too many times. In it I am only five years old and it is one of those insufferably hot Brisbane days. The kind of day when even the bitumen starts to melt in the heat. Everyone I know is crowded out onto the hot concrete of Nonna's backyard. My parents, Uncle Sam, Uncle Joe, Auntie Gina, Great Uncle Charlie, Great Aunt Rosa and all their children. Nonna's turned on the hose and takes turns spraying people with it when they're not looking.

'Anna!' yells Great Aunt Rosa as she cops a face full of cold water.

Nonno appears out of the corner of my eye carrying a giant green- and white-striped watermelon. Its colour and shape have taken on a cartoon quality in my memory. Nonno picks up a big knife and cuts a long seam down the length of the fruit. He puts the knife down and with his strong hands splits the melon apart with an almighty crack. Taking the knife again he cuts the melon halves into long red smiles peppered with black seeds. His blue eyes seek me out and he calls my name, 'Mischella,' in that melding of Sicilian and Australian accents. Nonno holds out a giant red melon smile that takes up my entire field of vision. I look up and see his smile over the top cascading down on me.

I touch my fingers to my lips now, reach up and deposit a kiss on his photograph. He's been put into the top left-hand slot of the family mausoleum.

'Ciao Nonno,' I say to him, and I feel the tears coming from a place that hasn't healed in thirteen years. A place I know never will. There will always be tears in me for him. I wish I could gather him up and take him with me. I wish I could return him to his island, to his sea and to his mermaid.

Nonno's favourite
  Fried whiting

'What did Nonno like to eat the most?' I ask Nonna.

'Don't tell me you don't remember!' she replies and huffs happily. 'Whiting, fried whiting. That man made me clean more fish for him than all the fish I cleaned when I was working at the Fish Board.'

I do remember. I remember it clearly. If I could go back in time, I'd join him, eat whiting at his side and ask him to tell me stories of Sicily.

4 small or 2 large whiting, cleaned but left whole
plain white flour
olive oil, for cooking
salt

Dust the whiting in flour. Heat some olive oil in a frying pan and fry the fish till golden brown on each side. Add salt to taste. A Sicilian would eat this fish with a wedge of raw white onion dipped in salt, a piece of Italian bread and a glass of red wine.

Serves 1–2

FIUMEFREDDO DI SICILIA

SOUTH
A PLACE OF COLOUR
AND CHAOS
WHERE THE SMELL OF FOOD
ASSAULTS YOU
AND THE TASTE OF EVERYTHING
IS INTENSIFIED
IN THE HOT SUN

SOUTH
A PLACE
WHERE SEDUCTION APPEARS
IN THE FORM
OF A RIPE TOMATO.

THE ITALIAN APPROACH

From the sky, the trail of the Aeolian Islands leads you like stepping stones to Sicily. Once you see them emerge from the blue sea you know you are close. Even from the sky, you can sense the pulse of history drawing closer, feel how old the land is and how many souls have lived and died right beneath you.

Our pilot left Rome in a huff, and bad-temperedly dipped and wove his way down the southern Italian coastline – my father cradling his head in his hands the entire way.

'I'd like to see Sicily again,' he mumbles as he throws his hand forward to brace himself against the seat in front. My mother, sitting across the aisle from us, looks over and grins. Upon leaving Brisbane, she had entrusted my brother and I to the care of my father for the entire journey, and on each flight she sat herself across from us, oblivious to all goings-on. As the plane waited on the tarmac at Brisbane airport, my mother had broken the plastic casing on her purple and blue blanket, unfurled it, drew it up to her chin, and promptly fell asleep. That's how she has been for the entire thirty-hour journey so far, waking up only in time for meals and to disembark. My father, brother and I, on the other hand, had stayed awake for every bump and jostle of turbulence and every nail-biting pocket of air. The trek across the Bay of Bengal was, I was sure, among the last moments of my life. At one point, the air hostess came bustling down the aisle, frantically making sure everyone was buckled in tight. The look on her face gave me no comfort, and I was certain she knew something and was not telling us for fear of creating a panic. So, with the exception of my mother, who was being lulled to sleep by the toss of our impending crash, we all sat upright and alert, awaiting our early morning fate off the coast of India. Somehow, by the grace of some deity, we made it through, and on landing in Rome I felt the worst was finally over. Until I entrusted my life to an Italian pilot.

'Enough is enough,' sighs my father as the plane abruptly loses altitude in a steep dive. It's a tight flying circle in this part of the world.

I turn to look at Ross but he's got his nose pressed to the window. I look past him and out to the sky and then, out of nowhere, there she is.

Etna. Towering. Unmistakable. Terrifying.

'Mamma! L'Etna!' cries the little boy sitting behind me.

I look out of the window again to her smoking peak. My heart surges and my soul rises to just beneath the surface of my skin so that all the hairs on my body stand on end. I turn to my father beside me and see tears in his eyes. Home, his expression says. Finally, I am home.

Ross and I crowd closer to the window. Forty-six years ago this is where we came from. If not for a decision made forty-six years ago, this is where we'd still be. If not for Nonna turning to Nonno one day and saying, ''Melo, we must leave this place.'

The plane dives again into a turn that sweeps around the volcano, as if the pilot is making sure we all get a good view of the hidden nooks and crannies of this steaming giant. My father ducks his head down again, his face blanching in terror.

'This man is going to fly us into a ditch. As if I haven't been through enough already,' he says as the plane sweeps out of its turn and plummets a few thousand metres closer to earth.

The city of Catania is below and from up here it looks like the entire city has been carved out of stone. There's no greenery in sight and everything is crammed tightly together, the buildings shoulder to shoulder.

The sound of the landing gear being released hums beneath me. Then stops. Then hums again. Then stops. Hums again. Stops. Hums. It sounds like someone's pressing the landing gear button but getting no response from the equipment. Ross and I eyeball each other.

'That doesn't sound promising,' I say as the island of Sicily gets closer to the belly of the plane.

Hums. Stops. Hums. Stops. I clear my throat. The land approaches.

The pilot tries again. I imagine him in the cockpit pressing a big red button over and over and shaking his head whilst we continue to dive to earth. Agonising seconds pass before finally I hear the long buzzing sound of the landing gear dropping, and within seconds it hits the tarmac of Catania's Fontanarossa Airport.

We're hurtled headlong down the stretch of bitumen, the terminal building passing as a streak on our right. Our arms are outstretched to the seats in front to stop us from flying out of our seatbelts.

'What's he doing now?' Ross asks, looking alarmed as the plane veers off the tarmac and onto the grass.

'I don't know,' I say, 'but it looks a lot like he's doing a three-point turn: he's overshot the terminal.'

The plane turns neatly around and parks near an oversized shed that is Catania's one and only airport terminal. From the back passengers start clapping and the euphoria of being alive sweeps up the length of the plane. One of the air stewards strolls down the aisle accepting the applause with a small wave of his hand and a half grin.

Welcome to Sicily.

We disembark the plane down steps that lead straight on to the tarmac like in some old Hollywood movie. I take my first breath of Sicilian air and find that the dust of it gently coats the inside of my mouth. Inside the terminal there is only confusion and the throbbing sound of full-speed Sicilian chatter. For some unknown reason there are close to two hundred people standing around a luggage carousel that's not moving. There are another few hundred grouped at the lost luggage counter, waving their hands, rolling their eyes and wiping their brows in a frantic attempt to attract the attention of a sole attendant who's tapping away at his computer as if there's no-one there. What started as confusion is now starting to look more like chaos, and we stand there for a moment, lost amidst it all.

'Signora,' an anonymous woman in uniform comes up to my mother, 'if you have come off an international flight then you must pick up your luggage through there,' she points in the direction of an unmarked door.

My mother turns and heads for the door, 'And how were we meant to know that if she didn't tell us?'

I shrug. 'I suppose we should just be happy she did.'

Airports are interesting places. They're like miniature-sized versions of your destination, and everything that is good and bad about a place is condensed and squeezed between the airport walls. It seems that at Catania's airport you have to chance upon your luggage. It makes me wonder what sort of state the real Sicily is in if this is its gateway.

'How long have we been waiting now?' my mother asks, impatiently tapping her foot on the linoleum. We're standing near a conveyor belt that's delivering up the same three pieces of luggage over and over again.

'This is ridiculous!' she huffs.

The belt goes around again with the same three pieces, as yet unclaimed by any of the one hundred people waiting.

'It's been about forty minutes,' my brother says.

'At least!' sighs my mother.

'Will you calm down!' I say to her. 'It'll happen, just relax.'

The belt stops.

Another ten minutes pass before it comes to life again and another three pieces of luggage appear, sparking intense interest and speculation from the waiting passengers.

'How come no-one's collected the first three pieces?' Ross asks as we watch them go around again.

'Maybe they're dummy pieces. They send them around to make you think they're doing something back there,' I ponder.

'We're going to be here forever,' my mother rolls her eyes, and I can see my father itching to get out and away.

An unexpected gust of air and burst of sunshine at one end of the conveyor belt heralds the long-awaited arrival of our suitcases.

'Now what?' my father asks. 'We have to go through Customs, don't we? We didn't go through any in Rome.'

'Well, it doesn't look like there's Customs here,' I say, as my eyes roam over the cavernous interior of the shed terminal. I head towards a little paper sign that reads 'Exit'. It's stuck to a pillar with a glob of Blu Tack. Almost on my way out I stumble across a diminutive dark-haired lady sitting behind a steel desk.

Perched in front of her is what looks like a computer monitor, hooked up to a giant box and a conveyor belt. Standing a few metres away, chatting to an airport employee, is a heavily-armed Customs official who's completely ignoring us. His head is turned to his companion and his arms are flapping around him in conversation – the gun at his waist is within easy reach of any casual passer-by.

'Do we have to put our bags through the X-ray?' I ask the woman.

She just raises an eyebrow in reply. I take it as a yes.

'I think this is Customs,' I say to my father, and heap my luggage onto yet another conveyor belt. It goes through without a word, sigh or gesture from the woman, so I pick it up at the other end and, finally, head out to Sicily.

Nonno's Sicilian packed lunch
Cotolette and roasted capsicum

Although Nonna never returned to Sicily, Nonno did go back once for a holiday in 1974, taking my mother and her younger sister, Auntie Gina, with him.

Knowing Nonno would never be able to eat the plane food, Nonna prepared him a special meal for the flight. She took a hunk of Italian bread and sliced it down the middle. Along the length of it she laid crispy brown cotolette *and on top mounded a heap of roasted capsicum dressed in olive oil. With a broad palm she pressed the top of the bread down, wrapped the whole thing in aluminium foil and stuffed it into his hand luggage.*

'We got on board,' my mother said, 'and as soon as we were in the air your grandfather took out this giant panino *with* cotolette *and capsicum. He made the whole plane smell like garlic and olive oil. And that's all he ate, all the way to Sicily.'*

4 red capsicums
2 cloves garlic, finely chopped
olive oil, for cooking
salt and pepper
4 veal steaks
½ cup plain flour
2 eggs
½ cup breadcrumbs
¼ cup grated parmesan cheese
¼ cup finely chopped flat-leaf parsley
1 loaf Italian bread

Roast the capsicums whole on the barbecue, turning them often to ensure they cook evenly. Once the skins turn black they're ready. Carefully peel the skin from the soft capsicum flesh whilst they are still warm. Remove the white insides and seeds and tear the flesh into strips with your fingers. Season the capsicum with salt and dress with the finely chopped garlic and plenty of olive oil in a serving bowl, and set aside.

Pound the veal steaks with a meat mallet or an empty wine bottle to about a ½-cm thickness. Take three large plates and lay them out on your benchtop. Scatter the plain flour onto the first plate. Beat the eggs in a small bowl with a pinch of salt and pepper and pour onto the second plate, and combine the bread-crumbs, grated cheese and parsley on the third plate. Coat each veal steak in flour, then dip in the egg and finally coat in the breadcrumb mix. Heat some olive oil in a pan, and fry the steaks until golden brown on both sides, seasoning to taste.

Cut the bread in half lengthways and generously fill with the *cotolette* and roasted capsicum, then cut into portions and serve.

Serves 4

Via Ferrara

Without even knowing it, I am holding my breath. On the other side of the facing opaque glass doors is the place I have heard about my entire life. Since I was born I have been force-fed other people's experiences, thoughts and views of this island, but finally I am going to see it for myself. And I am going to make up my own mind.

The exit doors slide open in front of me and I am hit by an exuberance that fills the air, and my ears, with noise. Hundreds of anxious, smiling faces appear – people line the doorway and almost spill over the side of a nearby staircase awaiting the arrival of relatives. It's infectious. One family group grab hold of a loved one ahead of me. There are shouts of joy and hugs and kisses and it seems that the whole airport joins in and erupts in communal happiness. Even the police officers standing either side of the exit doors can't help but smile.

'Ciao!' people call down from the staircase.

'Angelo!' someone close to me yells, but all I see is an arm waving frantically from the crowd, the body swallowed up by the people in front.

It's absolute chaos, but everyone is smiling and I can't help but grin ear to ear myself.

I make my way into the crowd and instantly lose my parents and my brother in the crush. I see everyone and no-one at the same time. I am only standing there disoriented for a few seconds before I am hit sideways by a flap of curly black hair and entwining arms.

'Michele!' screams an Australian voice into my ear.

I have black curls in my mouth and a set of fingernails tearing into the flesh of my upper arm.

'Gracie?' I cough.

'Michele!' she screams back.

'Gracie!' I smile and look at her.

It is her. Exactly the same, completely unchanged. A riot of black, curly hair, a voluptuous figure enhanced by tight, light-blue jeans and a strappy coloured top. A proud glaze to her dark eyes and a cheeky grin. I hug her back and we smack a kiss on each other's cheeks, at a complete loss for what to say after so long apart.

Another set of fingernails dig into my arm and I'm torn away from my cousin Gracie and flung into the arms of another relative. I'm kissed, poked, manhandled and pinched, and looked over by set after set of inquisitive eyes. I lose track of their names and how they're related to me. They're all rushing to tell me that they're my father's aunt or my mother's second cousin, but it all means nothing to me right now. There's so many of them and their eyes are eating me up. But I can tell by their hip bones and the sweep of their hairlines who belongs to my father's side and who to my mother's.

'You're coming in my car,' Gracie says, taking me by the hand.

I look at her bright, tight top and the way the rhinestones along the side of her jeans sweep over the curve of her hips. A pair of enormous black Guccis slide down to cover up half her face and stop just above her brilliant grin.

The airport exit doors slide open and we step outside.

The heat of the Sicilian summer comes over me and sucks the oxygen out of my lungs. It's a dry, parched heat that draws the moisture from my skin. I feel like I'm baking, hot and slow.

'Uhhh,' I sigh like someone's punched me in the stomach.

'It's hot,' Gracie says, 'but you'll like this heat, there's no humidity.'

'I can't believe I'm here,' Ross says at my side and it makes me look around. But there's nothing to see except a car park. The people look different here though, dark and brown, and the cars have different licence plates, but that's about it.

'I can't believe it's you,' I say, as Gracie stops near a car and I walk around to get in.

'You gonna drive or you want me to?' she asks, and puts her hands on her hips.

I look down into the window I'm standing in front of and see the steering wheel.

How I've missed her special brand of smugness.

There is nothing but highway from the airport. Gracie has the accelerator almost down to the floor, and trees and signs for beautiful-sounding towns fly past us.

'Zia Maria will have the pasta on by now,' she says, explaining the mad rush. 'This is us,' she says and points upwards. An enormous green sign suspended over the highway announces the birthplace of my family tree.

Fiumefreddo di Sicilia. Coldriver of Sicily.

Somewhere else in Italy there must be another Coldriver that required our town to be proclaimed 'of Sicily'. Our Coldriver takes its name from the fresh-water river that dives beneath the town and comes out at the Ionian Sea.

'Welcome to Fiumefreddo!' Gracie sighs and takes a hand off the wheel to wave a curvy arm through the air. She plunges headlong off the highway much the same way our Italian pilot had landed at Catania's airport. The car flies into a tight curve at alarming speed, like a racing car tucking into a bend. We emerge flying into the straight, my fingers like claws against the armrest.

Everything is happening so fast that I feel like I'm being swept up in some-one else's dream. Ross is quiet in the back seat, his face turned to look out of the window.

'Are those eucalyptus trees?' he asks.

Gracie looks up into the rear-view mirror, her eyes off the road and on my brother, the car not slowing down. 'Yep,' she says, 'Mussolini planted them here. They're strong and hold the earth. Good for when the volcano tries to shift things around.'

I see them buzzing past, tree after tree, and find myself strangely happy and comforted to find this iconic piece of Australia so far from home. Do these trees know they're meant to be somewhere else, or have they just happily integrated into their new home, I wonder.

I reach out and touch Gracie on the arm. She takes her eyes off the road again and looks at me.

'Just checking that you're real,' I say.

That's the strange thing about travelling, I am slowly discovering. The time you spend in flight is like being in a tunnel. You leave one place and pop out the other end somewhere else completely, without comprehending the distance you've crossed to get there. It's different to travelling by boat like Nonna did. On the water you get a sense of time, space and the enormity of your voyage.

The town of Fiumefreddo starts as plots of earth, with trees tied to stakes in the same technique Great Uncle Charlie uses in his backyard. Then come rundown farmhouses and old multi-storey houses slowly crumbling to the ground and giving way to new apartment blocks. Gracie makes a sharp turn and we're onto the main thoroughfare of this town of ten thousand people. The *centro* is a one-way, single lane street bordered on both sides by shops, houses and apartments, and with an enormous church taking pride of place. There's no sense of zoning here, no order, just a jumbled mass of human existence finding space where it can. And everything is made out of stone.

All I can see is stone. The street, the footpaths and the buildings are all carved out of this ancient building block.

The traffic is moving slowly and inside the car we're quiet. My brother and I are looking out on the street where once our family walked. People stand on street corners and watch the cars go by. Old men sit in groups outside the bars and watch the women go by. Young boys call out to their friends on the other side of the street while young girls check their reflections in the shop windows. Car horns beep incessantly.

We inch forward a little then stop.

'What's all the beeping for?' I ask.

'People beep for a lot of reasons,' Gracie starts, 'to say hello, to say goodbye, to say get out of my way, go faster, go slower, to tell you your lights are on,' Gracie tosses her hair, 'and sometimes just because they feel like it.' She giggles and blasts her horn at nothing in particular.

At the intersection ahead a car waiting to cross over the main road blows its horn and the male driver waves in our direction.

'Do you know him?' I ask.

Gracie leans over to my side to see if she can get a better look.

'Nah, don't think so. Can you get a good look at him from here? Is he cute?'

Someone behind us toots their horn in a rapid two-beat rhythm.

The guy at the crossroads mimics this, and Gracie chimes in with two long blasts. The centre of Coldriver of Sicily turns into a cacophony of horns blaring. An old man sitting outside a bar raises a hand and yells at the traffic but that only makes everyone beep louder. He shakes his head at the youth of today and goes back to smoking his cigarette. He looks strangely familiar. I stretch back to get a better look at him but as the traffic moves forward his face disappears from view.

'Ok, now coming up on your left,' Gracie says in her best tour guide voice as she gestures gracefully, 'is Fiumefreddo's famous landmark fountain, I Dui Scricci,' she says in Sicilian. Both of her hands have now left the steering wheel: one is shifting gear and the other is pointing out the window.

Ross and I turn, hoping to see something important, a miniature fountain of Trevi or something left behind by one of Sicily's conquerors. As the car creeps forward we stretch our necks around the corner and I see Gracie smiling to herself.

'It's coming up, don't miss it,' she says.

We watch and wait, willing the traffic to move forward.

'Very impressive,' I mumble to Gracie as it comes into view. It's a drinking fountain that looks like a marble bathroom sink with two jets of water spurting straight up into the air. Gracie erupts into a peal of giggles but I'm just happy to see both her hands on the wheel again.

'You haven't changed,' I sigh and smile at her.

'There used to be water fountains like that all over the town once,' she says once she's composed herself. 'You won't get water out of the tap colder than you do here.'

'Ah, this,' she goes on, waving her hand up and over her head so I assume she means the area we're passing through, 'is Putieddi or, in proper Italian, Botteghelle. This is the upmarket part of town,' she shakes her head, 'not where we come from.'

By 'we', I assume she means the family we have in common, the Di'Bartolos.

'We're from Castello, or in Sicilian, Casteddu, the more, shall we say, downmarket part of town,' she adds.

Gracie makes another turn and narrowly misses an oncoming car: they pass within centimetres of each other without slowing down or flinching. We find ourselves on a long street surrounded on both sides by two-storey houses joined side by side. Now I see in real life Nonna's memory of tiny stone houses and people living in each other's pockets. Every house along this street has a common wall and the front doors open directly onto the footpath. Two middle-aged women have balanced folding chairs on the narrow footpath outside their front doors and are sitting in their aprons gossiping and watching the traffic roll past.

'This is Via Marina. If you follow it all the way down you get to the beach. And this,' Gracie puts her indicator on and waits for the oncoming traffic to get out of her way, 'is the famous Via Ferrara.'

How many times have I seen my father write this address on envelopes to be sent overseas? How many times have I heard this street mentioned in countless stories of his childhood reminiscences?

In this street my father's parents and grandparents lived and died, as did their parents before them. This street is the genesis of my family. I come from this one stone street.

Now Gracie and her mother Anna live in the very house where generation after generation of Di'Bartolos were born, raised and died. In the front room of this house, generations of our family have laid the bodies of our dead, awaiting their funeral and burial in the town cemetery.

Every day my cousin Gracie wakes up and walks through the halls where generations of our family walked before.

There is no need for us to retrace our family tree because here in Via Ferrara, at No. 7, we can press our hands to the stone walls and feel their very presence.

An age-old dish
Caponatina

There's something very classic about this dish. Maybe it's because the ingredients inspire a lesson in history – the eggplant and the potato. Or maybe it's because I know that when I eat this dish I am eating one of the most iconic of all Sicilian dishes.

As with many Sicilian meals, it's made from fresh vegetables and it's eaten with a piece of crusty bread.

2 potatoes
2 red capsicums, seeds and white insides removed
1 eggplant
olive oil, for cooking
1 clove garlic, finely chopped
1 fresh chilli, finely chopped *or* 1 teaspoon dried chilli (optional)
2 × 400 g cans crushed, peeled tomatoes
5 basil leaves
salt and pepper

Cut the potatoes in wedges and the capsicums and eggplant into thick rectangular pieces (there's no need to salt the eggplant for this dish). Heat plenty of olive oil in a frying pan and sauté the potatoes, eggplant and capsicum for a few minutes until lightly browned. In a large saucepan, heat some oil and sauté the garlic with the chilli, if using. Add the canned tomatoes and basil, cook for a couple of minutes on low heat, then add the vegetables to this pan. Cook until all the vegetables are soft, adding salt and pepper to taste.

Serves 4 as a side dish

Pranzo – welcome lunch

We're standing on the paver-wide footpath of Via Ferrara waiting for Gracie to open the door to the house my parents have rented for the summer. Someone at the airport had collected them and, like Gracie, had probably whisked them through the town centre on a brief tour before lunch. Our rented house is directly across from Gracie's house on Via Ferrara, so in two short paces I can be across this narrow stone street and at her front door.

'Lunch is at Zia Maria's on Via Marina. Your parents should be there already,' Gracie says.

'Is it far?' Ross asks Gracie.

'It's around the corner! You've got time to drop your bags and go, the pasta's almost ready!'

Gracie quickly turns the double lock on the white front door and pushes it open. It's a two-bedroom, stone house with thick white walls, high ceilings and tiled floors. Inside, it's mercifully cool. Ross and I put our bags down in the front room under a window that looks directly out into the street. Space is tight on this side of town and the windows merge into the traffic.

'I'm starving, I haven't eaten anything since Brisbane,' I say, and my stomach rumbles a little.

'Ahh, Brisbane,' Gracie says, 'hey, what did you bring me?' She's got a hand on her hip and she's pushed her Guccis back so that they hold the waves of curly black hair off her face. I step up close into her personal space and give her a hug.

'I've missed you,' I smile.

But it's more than missing someone. When Gracie left Australia she left a space behind her that no-one else was able to fill. When you grow up with some-one I think you always expect them to be there and then, when they go away, you're left thinking they'll just reappear; walk around a corner or back into a room. They were part of that place and without them, it doesn't make sense anymore. That's what Cameron Street and Norfolk Road felt like after Gracie was gone. But she's found herself another set of streets to call home now. Via Ferrara and Via Marina. We just can't get away from living our lives at the juncture of two simple streets.

'Do you know what I was thinking the other day?' I ask, disengaging myself from our hug but keeping my arm around her shoulders. 'You remember the day we had to pick up the pig feet?'

Gracie rolls her eyes. 'That was sooooo embarrassing!'

'I've brought you a packet of Tim Tams and a packet of Caramello Koalas.'

'Oohhhh,' she squeals and claps her hands together, 'give me the Tim Tams first. I've been waiting seven years for one of those!'

I open my hand luggage and pull out a long packet of biscuits. Gracie snatches them out of my hands and tears them open with her nails. She puts her nose close and takes a long whiff.

'Ah, smells like Australia,' she says.

'Did you say something about pasta?' Ross asks from the other side of the room.

I turn and look at him slowly, curious that he should remember a conversa-tion featuring food.

Back out on the stone street we close the front door behind us and I take a moment to look left and right. So this is where the Italo-Australian fascination with concrete and stone comes from, I realise. They surround themselves with it because it reminds them of home.

'So,' Gracie points directly across the road, 'that's where Mum and I live. That's where Zio Angelo and Zia Lina live,' she points to the house on the corner, 'and just around the corner is Zia Maria's house. If you go down Via Marina towards the *centro* you get to Zia Concetta's house. And in between there are a few hundred cousins. But I just limit myself to the closer relatives 'cos we're pretty much related to the whole town.'

'Everyone's so close,' Ross says.

'Yeah, well, this is where everyone comes from. They've been living here their whole lives. Usually in the house their parents lived before,' Gracie says and shoots a glance at No. 7.

We walk past two houses and turn right into Via Marina. Then we walk past three more houses to Zia Maria's house. She is my father's youngest sister and, like all the Di'Bartolos, except me, she has a stunning pair of liquid blue eyes and a sharp, angular physique. Her front door opens and a furry, brown bullet shoots out and takes off down the street.

'Whiskey! Whiskey!' Zia Maria calls out as the small brown dog disappears down a side street.

Zia Maria turns to me and cries, 'Look at you!'

She takes both my cheeks between her cool fingers and squeezes hard. Like a lot of my father's family, Zia Maria did a short stint in Australia and returned home after a couple of years. The last time I saw her I was four years old, but I remember her clearly because she was forever pinching and biting me with fondness. 'Look at those legs!' she'd cry and sink her teeth in, 'you could make *mortadella* out of them!'

'And this is Ross?' she asks, looking him over with admiring eyes. 'He's the image of my father when he was young. Exactly.' Zia Maria grasps his face in her hands and kisses him on both cheeks. I can see my brother wince with the pain of affection.

Before we know it we're shooed into the house and Zia Maria ducks her head out once more in the hopes that Whiskey will come running back.

'Whiskey's the town playboy,' Gracie fills me in. 'He's fathered most of the dogs around here.'

'Ahhh,' Zia Maria shakes a disappointed head, 'I don't know what to do with that dog. Through here,' she says and guides us to the rear of the house where she opens the door to her backyard.

My parents are sitting at a long table arranged on a tiled terrace that runs off into an enormous and very green backyard. Fruit trees and tomato plants line the garden on all sides, and there's even an Australian-style barbecue. Zia Maria catches me looking it over. 'Australia,' she smiles and nods, knowing what I'm thinking.

'Lunch!' Zio Biaggio, Zia Maria's husband, claps his hands together when we're all arrayed around the table. Zia Maria runs back into the house only to emerge moments later with an enormous bowl of pasta in red tomato sauce.

'Made from fresh tomatoes,' she tells us as she puts the bowl in the centre of the table, 'straight from my garden.'

I turn my head in the direction she's pointing and I see the little red gems glowing in the midday sun. They remind me of Great Uncle Charlie's tomatoes: meticulously cared for, evenly spaced, perfectly pegged and untouchable along the back of his garden. In my mind I can see him turning them over in his palm, their little bodies fresh and hot. Ross pulls up a chair next to me.

'I'm starving,' he whispers into my ear.

I turn to him, startled. 'You're hungry?' I ask.

'Starvin' Marvin'.' His green eyes look huge in his taut face.

'Ok, well, we're eating, take it easy,' I pat his knee in reassurance.

Zia Maria comes to Ross' side wielding a giant ladle. She dips it into the pasta and deposits steaming red penne into his bowl, filling it to the top. I see my brother's nose twitch, something I've never seen it do before.

Zia Maria reaches past Ross and picks up a wedge of hard cheese.

'Baked ricotta,' she says, and puts it to the side of a grater she's holding over his plate. A cloud of cheese settles over his bowl and he brings a hand to his stomach. His nose twitches again.

The food smells disturbingly good – the fresh tomatoes crisp and sharp, made heavy by the smell of the ricotta, but it's the scent of the fresh green basil that gets your nose twitching. I watch as Ross slowly takes a fork of pasta and puts it to his lips. He chews once and draws a deep sigh from his gut and into his full mouth. I watch as his shoulders slump in satisfaction and he grins.

'It's fantastic,' he mumbles at me from the side of his mouth.

He's never said that about anything edible before.

I look along the table. My parents. My aunts and uncle. My brother and my cousin Gracie. All eating Sicilian tomatoes grown in the Sicilian soil under the Sicilian sun.

I start to feel the satisfaction of connection.

Sarsa Day
Sarsa semplice using fresh tomatoes

I remember as a child thinking that Nonna was the head witch of some bizarre backyard cult. Every once in a while she'd build a fire on the concrete out the back of her West End home and place a cauldron-sized pot on top. She'd stand over it and stir its red simmering contents with an enormously long wooden spoon.

With Nonna dressed in her usual dark garb, standing over a cauldron with her hair pulled back in a black scarf, how could I not think that I was bearing witness to some dastardly satanic ritual? In reality it was nothing more sinister than 'Sarsa Day' (Sauce Day). Bubbling away in the pot were hundreds of red tomatoes destined to be boiled down to a thick liquid and bottled for future use. I don't remember a lot about Sarsa Day except this slightly uncomfortable feeling that Nonna might be a witch, but I do remember how all the neighbours, Greek and Australian alike, would perk up at the crackle of the fire and the smell of melting tomatoes. They'd saunter over and casually lean on the chicken-wire fence while Nonna, talking in a mixture of Greek, Sicilian and English, would explain the painstaking process of bottling tomatoes.

My mother would soon revolutionise this age-old custom of making fresh tomato sauce by discovering canned tomatoes and the bottles of Italian passata that were then starting to make their way to Australia. Watched suspiciously by Nonna and Great Aunt Rosa, my mother successfully made pasta sauce with tinned tomatoes and single-handedly changed the course of cooking in our family forever. Not long after that day in the late 1970s, the cauldron was tipped upside down and stored in a corner of Nonna's backyard, where it still sits today and still manages to give me the shivers every time I see it.

But there is still something crisp and sweet about making pasta sauce with fresh, ripe tomatoes.

8 large ripe, red tomatoes
olive oil, for cooking

1 clove garlic, finely chopped
½ white or brown onion, finely diced
salt and pepper
4–5 fresh basil leaves

Pierce the base of each tomato with an 'X' (this makes them easier to peel), then immerse them in a large pot of unsalted boiling water for a couple of minutes. Remove and allow them to cool for a minute or two, before peeling off the skins with your fingers.

Heat some olive oil in a large pan, add the garlic and onion and sauté until the onion is translucent. In a bowl, squash the tomatoes with a large spoon to break them up, season to taste, then add to the hot oil and cook on low heat for about 15–20 minutes, stirring frequently. A couple of minutes before the end of the cooking time, throw in the fresh basil leaves and stir through.

Serves 4

A TOWN ASLEEP

We all sigh at the end of lunch.

It's been a long trip and it has taken a full stomach and some warm sun on my face to realise how far I've come and how long I've been awake.

Zia Maria comes over and pats my brother's hair. 'He looks tired, the little thing, maybe you should head home for a nap.'

Ross' eyes are drooping and he's rubbing his stomach with his hand.

'You ok?' I ask.

'Yeah, just feeling . . .' he stops and searches for the word, 'full?'

I smile at him. 'I've never heard you say that before.'

'You go ahead,' my mother says, 'we'll stay.' She looks around her. 'It's been so long.'

'Ah, before you go,' says Zio Biaggio, 'let me give you something.'

He takes off down the long garden and disappears behind some trees. When he emerges he's clutching four round fruits in his hands.

'Here,' he says to me, and I hold out my hands to receive the gift, 'take these back to your house, they're lemons from my yard. I bet you don't have lemons like that in Australia! These are the real thing,' he winks.

Out of the corner of my eye I catch my father smirk. Now it seems, the lemon wars have gone international. I can just see, upon our return, my father, his brother and Great Uncle Charlie indignantly bustling into Australia Post to ship samples of their lemons back to Sicily.

'Thanks Zio,' I say, and look back at my father who has silently crossed his arms in thought.

'Let me have a look at those,' my father says, and I pass one of the fruits over.

My father rolls it in his palm and brings it delicately up to his nose for a little sniff, then hands it back to me and leans back into his chair, all without comment.

Perhaps the Sicilian lemon cannot be bettered.

Gracie, Ross and I find ourselves standing on Via Marina outside Zia Maria and Zio Biaggio's house. I've got the lemons in my hands and that familiar fruit scent in my nose. It's quiet and still: there's no traffic and all the doors and windows along the street have been pulled shut.

'Look left,' Gracie says, and turns me gently by the shoulders. From where I'm standing the stone houses on Via Marina sit side by side and curve in a gentle concave. 'Now look up,' she says.

At roof level the peak of Mt Etna is framed between the houses on either side of the street. I'm lost for words at the sight of it, so close and so perfectly placed in the sky.

I can't imagine waking up to this every morning or seeing this every day on your way to something as mundane as work or to the shops. There's an old lady on the other side of the street walking along the footpath, but she doesn't even bother to glance up at the view.

'Do you ever feel her?' I ask Gracie over my shoulder, unable to tear my eyes away from the mountain.

'Sometimes,' Gracie says, 'you feel a bit of rumbling and shaking but you get used to it after a while.'

Ross and I turn to our left and then to our right: we both seem to be thinking the same thought and our eyes meet. To the left up Via Marina is Etna, to the right down Via Marina is the sea. It's a vision of beauty counterbalanced by potential disaster, and in one bad day the entire town could be washed out to sea. Slowly I begin to understand why Sicilians live life in such a headstrong and chaotic way.

'What now?' I ask, changing the topic and moving my thoughts away from natural disasters.

'Well, we can go for a walk or something, but it's siesta time so there's not much to see or do right now.'

'Hmmm, siesta,' moans Ross at my side and rubs his stomach again. He looks physically incapable of withstanding this new level of digestion.

'When will everything be open again?'

'Not until 4 p.m.,' Gracie replies.

'4 p.m.? But that's two hours away!'

Gracie just nods her head and starts walking towards the corner of Via Marina, where it meets Via Ferrara.

'That's Sicily,' she says.

'So what do people do here in the afternoon?'

'They sleep. Then they get up and go back to work at about 4 p.m. Those that have jobs anyway. Then they come home, have dinner and go out.'

We make the turn into Via Ferrara. Looking at this street again it seems more like a laneway, and I can imagine that raised voices on one side would float all the way over to the other.

'I'm ready for a nap,' I suddenly realise.

After almost thirty hours of no sleep, not even the adrenaline rush of being in Sicily is enough to keep my eyes from involuntarily closing. Besides, my stomach is full of pasta and fresh tomatoes, and the Sicilian sun is warm on my face. Sleep feels like the next comfortable step in the progression of the day.

The old lady I had seen earlier has disappeared into a pink plastered stone house. By now, I'm sure she's slipped off her shoes and fallen lightly asleep.

'Later on tonight,' Gracie says and wraps one arm around me and one around Ross as we draw up to the front door of our rented house, 'we'll go to Giardini for a gelato. And to check out the boys,' she giggles at me.

The sheets on my bed are white and crisp.

Ross has fallen asleep on the single bed on the other side of the room, with one hand on his stomach and a pleasurable look on his face. My parents are still at Zia Maria's; my father, unable to withstand it any longer, is by now no doubt listing the various merits and vigorously defending the particular features of the Australian lemon. Apart from this raging debate one street over, the quiet is absolute; there's not a single murmur or sound on the street. There's not even the beep of a wayward car horn.

I suppose that's what it sounds like when an entire town lies down and falls asleep.

The Sicilian lemon
Polpette a limone

Like the tomato, the lemon resonates with something deep inside me. It's the symbol of this beautiful island: a gift and a curse. Many a man has died and many a battle has been fought on Sicilian soil, all for the power to control the lemon groves.

There is more to the lemon than just the fruit. In true Sicilian style, even the leaves have a purpose and a place.

a few handfuls of large, waxy green leaves from the lemon tree
1 quantity meatball mix (see page 66)

Wash the leaves lightly under cold water and pat them dry. Take a handful of meat and spread over a lemon leaf, then place another lemon leaf on top and pat down. Repeat with the remaining meatball mix, then cook on a hot barbecue, turning once, until the meat is cooked through. Serve the meat wrapped in the lemon leaves, and remove the leaves just before eating. The result is a hot roasted meatball with a hint of lemon and a smell that will make your mouth water.

Serves 4–6

A *STRACCIATELLA* STROLL AT GIARDINI NAXOS

By the time Gracie knocks on our front door I'm almost ready. The dry Sicilian heat is doing wonders for my newly-straightened hair. It sits perfectly, with no threat of waviness. My skin has dried a little so there's not much shine to be covered up with make-up, and the pasta at lunch has filled me up enough to make me want to skip dinner. Our bathroom window looks out onto the house next door. As I'm patting down my hair I hear a familiar sound coming from outside. I look out and can't help but smile. Over the fence are two fat hens, clucking to each other in conversation.

The front door crashes open with the sound of laughter and high intensity chatter. Gracie's voice floats down the hall but it's drowned out by younger voices yelling 'Ciao!' The nerve endings in my stomach are like wild electricity wires. I feel refreshed and excited again about being here and I want to get out; I want to see Sicily.

The voices grow louder until they fill the house and it sounds as if a hundred people have suddenly drawn up outside the bathroom door. I poke my head out to find six young, lean, bronzed bodies circling my brother.

'Ciao,' I say.

They turn as one and rush towards me.

'Ciao!' they yell and grabble to kiss and hug me all at once.

'These are some of our cousins,' Gracie says. 'They thought they'd take Ross out tonight while we go to Giardini.'

Their eyes are bright on my face, and their young heads with sleek, dark locks turn from me to Ross.

'OK,' Ross says, '*andiamo*?' he flexes his new Italian skills.

'Si!' they cry with the joy of hearing their Australian cousin stumble on the rounded vowels. In seconds they swarm back to Ross, encircle him and escort him out the door. Their voices are loud with dozens of questions. 'What's Australia like?' 'How long did it take to get here?' 'Didn't you get bored on the plane?' 'Do you like it here?' 'What's Australia like?' They close the front door behind them but that only muffles the racket they make out on the street.

'Where are we going?' I ask Gracie.

'Giardini Naxos,' she tosses her mane of dark hair, 'we'll get a gelato for dinner and take a stroll.' I like the way she says the word stroll, like it's taken for medicinal purposes here.

Giardini Naxos is strung along the East Sicilian seaside in a glittering display of lights and cafes. It sits in the curve of the coast beneath the famous town of Taormina, which is high above it on the mountainside.

'We'll do a drive-by first,' Gracie says, 'so you can soak up a bit of the atmosphere.'

'There are about a billion German tourists here,' Gracie hums, trying to avoid a group of them that have meandered out onto the street and in front of her car. But I'm too entranced by the lights and cafe after cafe filled to bursting to take notice of people hurling themselves in front of the car.

Up through the windscreen I can see Taormina suspended high in the sky. It's all lit up with amber lights and juts out into the night like the prow of a ship. Above Taormina, the lights of an even higher and more remote town are visible.

'What's that place up there?' I ask Gracie, pressing my finger to the windscreen.

Gracie takes her eyes off the road and leans forward. 'Castelmola,' she says, 'it got its name from the castle up there.' The castle is a ring of lights in the night sky with the circle of the town lights behind it. It's so high up in the air, it seems like an unreachable, almost ethereal town, and I start to wonder if people actually live there. And if they do, how they get down.

Below in Giardini Naxos, across the road from the cafes people stroll along the seaside in pairs or groups. Young men and boys sit and stand along the low stone wall that runs long the coast and stops the sea from crashing into the town.

Suddenly Gracie brakes hard and I lurch forward, hands against the dashboard. A pair of dark Sicilian eyes are caught in her headlights and they shoot her a brooding glance.

'God, he's gorgeous!' she breathes, gripping the steering wheel with both hands and putting her face as close to the windscreen as she can reach. 'I should have hit him,' she slumps back into her seat.

'Gracie!'

'At least then I would have had a chance to meet him!'

With a hungry gaze she follows the pedestrian she almost killed and reaches to tuck a dark curl behind her ear. I look out of the window into the deep darkness that's masking the sea beating against the shoreline.

I want to get out.

I want to be in the thick of the action.

I want to see and be seen.

And on this hot summer night, I want to be part of Sicily.

'So, have you thought about what flavour gelato you want?' Gracie asks. She's spotted a parking space and whips her compact Toyota into position for a reverse park. The wheels are locked hard and she starts to back in. Immediately, the traffic behind her starts to bank up, and one rogue driver revs and dives out onto the wrong side of the road to get around us. Gracie locks the wheel hard the other way, her arms pumping furiously. Swiping a dark curl off her face she straightens the car up, rips up the handbrake and pulls the keys out of the ignition.

'Where the hell did you learn to park like that?' I ask. Only a centimetre-wide sliver separates her bumpers from the cars at either end.

'You learn how to park pretty quick in Sicily,' she sighs and shoves open her car door. A boy clad in tight blue jeans zips around her on his Vespa and beeps his horn. There don't seem to be any give-way rules here; drivers just have to be prepared for anything – pedestrians leaping from the footpath onto the street, Vespas diving in and out of traffic, and people like Gracie who swing open their car doors without looking.

Out of the car I find myself standing on the seaside of Giardini Naxos. Against my back I can feel the waves hitting the Sicilian shore. On the footpath

I wait for a break in the traffic so I can cross to the other side.

'What are you doing?' Gracie, standing on the fringes of the street, turns and looks at me as the traffic curves around her.

'I'm waiting to cross.'

She waves an impatient hand at me. 'If you wait you'll never get over. No-one ever hands you an opportunity in Sicily, not even to cross the road. Come on,' she waves me down from the footpath where she's standing, oblivious to all danger.

'There's a bit of a technique to crossing a road in Sicily,' she says, tucking her arm into mine. 'You have to pick the driver you're going to step in front of. Always go for a male driver – they're more likely to stop for you. Give him a side glance but don't stare him right in the face because then he'll think you've seen him and will give him right of way, rather than the other way around.' Gracie draws in a deep breath. 'Then just concentrate on the other side; don't look, just go.'

In this one small moment, Gracie manages to take me back in time. We're not in Giardini anymore, we're in our school uniforms standing on the side of Melbourne Street, waiting to take that first step onto that first zebra stripe.

'This is my favourite gelato shop,' Gracie pulls me in by the elbow. It's a tiny space almost entirely taken up by a glass-fronted display cabinet. A cash register is wedged tight into a back corner, and people are lined up cheek by jowl inside and spilling out onto the street. It's hard to see how they know who's next in line to order, but people are getting served and the line is moving quickly. It's Sicilian organisation – seemingly chaotic and yet working just fine in its own way.

'Pick your flavour,' Gracie says, and pushes me into a space in front of the cabinet.

'That's easier said than done,' I reply. There are hundreds of tubs sitting in the window, all individually labelled and all looking just as good as the one sitting either side of it.

Any scrap of impulse-control I may have will flee at the sight of ice cream. As Nonna says, 'Love and hate are two horns on the same bull', and so it is for me and the devilish dairy. In Nonna's deep freeze I was always sure to find a tub of chocolate-chip ice cream. For some reason it was always on special at Jack the

Slasher's, probably because the ice cream was a little powdery and the chocolate chips a little dusty, but it was cheap and it came in a 4-litre tub. That's all
that mattered. Besides, Gracie and I would smother it in Ice Magic so it didn't
really matter what it tasted like. And when no-one was looking, we'd squirt Ice
Magic straight from the bottle into our mouths.

'What are you thinking about?'

'I'm thinking about Ice Magic. Is that choc-chip?' I point at the gelato
window.

'It's called *stracciatella* here. You're not seriously thinking of getting choc-
chip, are you?' She looks at me and opens her dark eyes wide with horror.

I just nod in reply.

'Ohhhh, you're sooooo boring!' she cries. 'Try the *zuppa inglese*, try the *bacio*,
try the Nutella or the *nocciola* with cream. But not the choc-chip!'

'I can't help it Gracie, that's what I want!'

Gracie cocks a hand on her hip, looks at me sternly and says in a grave voice
'You want your first ever Sicilian gelato on your first night in Sicily to be
choc-chip?'

I search her eyes. The people in the shop are looking at us: we're even louder
than Sicilians.

'You'll never have this moment back again, you know, so think about it
carefully.'

She's serious. Food is serious business to the Sicilian.

I nod.

'I'm going the choc-chip,' I say slowly, standing my ground.

The *gelatier* on the other side of the counter picks up a cone and with a flat
spoon whips the gelato into a milky frenzy. Working the gelato into a roughly-
shaped ball, he deposits it expertly on the cone and hands it over the counter to
me with a broad smile. I wait until we step out onto the Giardini concourse
before I take the first lick of my first Sicilian gelato on my first night in Sicily.
I eat happily, greedily, joyously, but in the back of my mind lurks the memory of
how ice cream caused the greatest downfall of my early years.

My mother went shopping one Saturday morning, calmly leaving me, aged two,
in the care of Nonna and Auntie Gina.

'I want to come!' I declared, as best as a two-year-old can. I'm sure there was a bit of foot stomping and curly-hair tossing involved.

'You have to stay. Auntie Anna and I are going together.'

'Gracie?' I mumbled, thinking they were taking my cousin but not me.

'She's staying home just like you.'

This calmed me momentarily and Auntie Gina scooped me up in her sixteen-year-old arms and bounced me on her hip, while my mother walked out of Nonna's back door and into the driveway. I heard my Auntie Anna's voice coming up the drive, 'Ciao Rosetta,' she said to my mother, and then, to my horror, a smaller voice just behind called 'Ciao Zia.'

My cousin Gracie. Not at home at all, but going shopping while I was staying put.

By all accounts I took the revelation calmly. I even waved the shopping trio goodbye with a small smile, for I was planning something far more sly than bawling my eyes out right there and then.

Auntie Gina, the poor, unsuspecting victim of this story, took me into Nonna's lounge room where we spent a couple of minutes pretending the lounge was a trampoline. Then, *al'improvviso* as Auntie Gina later recalled, I dropped to my knees clutching my right arm and wailing. My cries were a siren call to Nonna, who ran in already screaming, 'Gina, what have you done?' accusing first, assessing the scene later.

'I didn't do anything,' Auntie Gina replied, but I'm sure her bottom lip would have quivered as Nonna stormed in, waving the warm wooden spoon she'd just been using at the stove.

'Why's she crying, what happened?'

'I don't know!'

They both looked at me. I was screaming the house down and clutching my unmoving right arm. My face was screwed up in agony; tears flowing, cheeks viciously red.

'What are we going to do?' Auntie Gina asked, looking from me to the wooden spoon. My Uncle Joe, spurred into action by the racket I was creating, came running upstairs.

'What's going on, Gina, what did you do to her?' he screamed.

'I didn't do anything!' she screamed back.

Uncle Joe reached out for my right arm, which was still clutched in my left hand. As soon as he got close my screams rose a couple of notches.

'She's hurt her arm,' he concluded.

'Gina, you broke her arm!' yelled Nonna, waving the wooden spoon in the air above her head.

'What's going on over here?' Great Aunt Rosa was at the back door. 'We can hear her all the way down the street.'

'Gina bloody broke her arm!' Uncle Joe called out over his shoulder as Great Aunt Rosa came into the lounge room.

'I bloody didn't!' Auntie Gina yelled back.

'It's her right arm I think,' concluded Great Aunt Rosa and started to reach out for it. As soon as she got within an inch of it my screams rose again and she hastily withdrew.

For some reason, perhaps because she was called back by the sound of my wailing, my mother returned early from her shopping trip. What she found was me still clutching my right arm, Auntie Gina beside me on the couch contemplating all the ways she was going to feel the burn of Nonna's wooden spoon, and Nonna, Great Aunt Rosa and Uncle Joe alternately staring at me and trying to get to my injured arm. Every time they got close, the screaming got louder.

'I'm taking her to Dr Lee,' my mother declared after a couple of minutes of taking in the scene. Dr Lee was our family doctor down on Boundary Street.

And so I was transported to the doctor, screaming and warily protecting my injured limb. When we got to the Boundary Street clinic, they sat me down howling in Dr Lee's office. Feeling none of my family's terror and concern, he took one objective look at me and narrowed his eyes. In one shrewd moment he'd summed up the situation, and he delivered his diagnosis.

'This is what you do,' he said calmly to my mother, standing as he took her gently by the elbow, turning her away from me. 'Take her out for an ice cream.'

The howling continued and the unmoving right arm was locked in position all the way to the ice cream shop in the West End Markets, where my mother calmly ordered a vanilla ice cream. As she was not without a hint of slyness herself, she held the cone out just far enough that I'd have to reach for it.

Without thinking my right arm shot directly out from my side.

Like I said, devilish dairy.

Thus my broken arm was cured, and my master plan for ultimate attention and sympathy scuttled. All for a vanilla cone.

'It's good isn't it?' Gracie says as she takes a long swipe at her *nocciola* with cream on top.

'It's the best choc-chip I've ever tasted.'

In the hot night the gelato melts quickly and turns to liquid around the edges. I lick to keep it from dripping down the side of my cone. We're licking in silence, walking in slow, half paces away from the shop. People walking slightly faster swing around us and let us stroll at our own pace. My tongue hits something heavy imbedded deep in the vanilla gelato. I stop and hold up my cone for a closer look. It's a giant shard of chocolate. I put the cone to my lips and suck the chocolate into my mouth with the runny vanilla. Our short stroll soon brings us to a row of restaurants with busy tables crowding the footpath ahead.

'Now what?'

'Now,' Gracie slips her free arm through mine, 'we cross the road and we stroll.'

Something sweet and a little different
Mustarda, the original grape jelly

Beneath Great Uncle Charlie's house, before he converted it into a downstairs flat, one corner was dominated by a round, timber grape crusher. Once a year, he and Nonno would buy cases of ripened black grapes, tip them into the grape crusher and turn the juice into their home-brewed wine. Nonno's hobby was to collect tall brown XXXX beer bottles which he'd use to store the wine and stack in case upon case beneath the house. Before all the grape juice became wine, though, Nonna would rescue some and make us all a special Sicilian dessert. Musta is Sicilian for the frothy grape juice left after the grapes have been crushed. From that, Nonna would make mustarda, *the original grape jelly, and the perfect accompaniment to vanilla ice cream.*

The traditional method of making mustarda *involves taking some burnt timber ash, wrapping it in cloth and putting it in the juice while it boils, but you can skip this step.*

500 g very ripe black or white seedless grapes
6 cloves
pinch of cinnamon, plus extra to sprinkle
3 tablespoons cornflour

Crush the grapes in a blender and then pass the juice through a fine sieve to remove the skins. Transfer the juice to a saucepan and bring to a boil. Add the cloves and a pinch of cinnamon and simmer on low heat. Dissolve the cornflour in a little warm water and gradually add to the juice, stirring until it has reached a custard consistency.

Pour into individual dishes and sprinkle with cinnamon while it's still warm. You can eat it hot or cold.

Serves 2

THE THINGS YOU MISS

We walk towards the groups of young men and boys leaning, sitting or standing along the sea wall. The young girls and women seem more mobile – they walk up and down and flick their hair at the admiring glances. As we pass, dark eyes follow.

'So what's the game plan for these two months?' Gracie asks me, ignoring a low whistle in her direction.

The air is fresh here, right off the sea. The lights of Taormina are to our backs and those of Giardini Naxos are to our right. To our left is nothing but men and the sea.

'What do you mean?'

'What's the plan? Romantically, I mean.'

I flick a glance at her out of the corner of my eye. 'I don't have any plans. I just want to lay back, see a bit of Sicily, spend some time with you and eat some good food.'

'Booorrring,' she sighs, and shoots me a frustrated look.

I've finally gotten through the top of the gelato and my teeth are breaking the biscuity cone.

'Really. I don't have any plans.'

'Aha,' she glances at me again.

'Yes, really. Why?' For some reason, my cousin Angelo's warning to be careful of the boys swims across my mind.

'Oh nothing,' Gracie sighs.

'What do you mean, nothing?' I stop on the footpath and look at her over the top of my cone. We've been like this ever since we were children. One taunting the other, until finally one takes a stand and demands an answer. The group of men we stop in front of rake over us from head to toe, and I taunt them by tossing them an annoyed glance. It sparks their attention.

'What are you talking about?' I ask again.

'*Americana?*' one of the men calls out, but we ignore him.

'Look around you,' Gracie says, and waves a gelato-free hand over the group of men. Everywhere is deep-olive skin and small groups of people languidly strolling past, covertly shooting glances at each other from beneath long, dark lashes. The heat of summer is in the air and the sound of the sea breaking on the rocks provides a soothing background noise.

'This place is magic in the summer,' whispers Gracie. 'You won't be able to help yourself. Everyone falls in love here in the summer. You'll see,' she says and loops her arm back into mine. We leave our admirers behind and they move on quickly to the next set of women that stray across their path.

'It's beautiful here,' I sigh.

'It is,' Gracie replies quietly, 'but there are a lot of things about it that are hard too.'

'Hard? Like what?'

'Lots of things,' she sighs and drops her eyes.

I reach over and give her arm a squeeze. We've strolled away from the busy stretch of tourists and the people out to be seen. A quieter stretch of path curves out in front of us and it changes the mood of our conversation.

'It's hard living in a small town when you're used to living in a city. It's hard being surrounded by so many people you're related to who all want to know your business. And it's hard feeling on the outside of things.'

She startles me. 'You feel like an outsider here?' This was the culture we were raised in. This is the island of Gracie's birth.

She just nods in reply and then says, 'It's confusing growing up somewhere, then leaving it and starting your life somewhere else.'

'Do you miss home?'

I try to catch myself before it comes out of my mouth, but the word 'home' is left hanging between us, and I'm not sure what Gracie's definition of home is anymore. She doesn't answer straightaway.

'Yes. Every day,' she replies quietly, and then sighs heavily. 'I still dream about going shopping in Myer.'

'You're joking?'

'No,' she tosses her curly hair. 'I actually dream about Myer. There aren't any big department stores here.'

'I didn't think you could miss something like a department store.'

'It's not just the department store, it's what it represents.'

I raise an eyebrow in query. 'What exactly does a department store represent?'

'Freedom to wander, to do what you please, to go from one department to another without being bothered, to be where people don't know you.'

It seems that in her mind Gracie is confusing a department store with Australia. Blending one with the other.

'Aha,' I reply.

'Plus, I miss West End. I miss going to the shops, and I miss the bread from the Vietnamese bakery on Vulture Street. I miss getting Chinese takeaway from the restaurant on Melbourne Street.'

'Gracie!' I stop and stand facing her. High up in my line of vision is glittering Taormina. From where I'm standing I can lean over and see the sea thrashing itself against the rocks of the Sicilian coast, and the moon is shining brighter than all the cafe lights of Giardini Naxos behind us. 'Look at this place! And you're missing Chinese takeaway?' I want to slap her.

'It's what I miss, OK?' she cries without explanation. 'I can't explain it.'

I look into her eyes. I suppose you can't know what you're going to miss until you leave it behind. In her eyes I can see her retracing the lines of Cameron Street, and Norfolk Road down to the point where it meets Boundary Street and broadens out into the centre of West End. In her eyes I can see how much she misses the simple place where we grew up and that she so quickly left behind. In her eyes I see the same look that sparks in Nonna's when she makes the same journey in reverse. It's the glaze of every immigrant.

'It's not the same place anymore Gracie, West End,' I say. 'It's different now. I don't even know if I like it that much anymore.'

'Changed how?' she asks softly, and we start walking again.

'I don't know how to explain it. It's become cool,' I use the word with disdain.

'It used to be so easygoing. It was just us, you know, the Sicilians, the Greeks, the Vietnamese. Now it's, well, trendy or something. All the shops are now cafes.'

'All the shops are gone?'

'They've renovated Jack's now and it doesn't make any sense to me anymore.'

Every time I go down there to do Nonna's shopping, I expect to find the inside of the West End Markets, the way it was before they redeveloped it. If I don't stop to think about it, I still head up the shopping centre driveway like I used to every afternoon after school, only to find my way blocked. It seems that the memories of my childhood are stronger than reality.

'The roundabout is gone now,' I say, referring to the giant traffic obstacle that used to take up the space where Boundary and Melbourne streets meet. 'It's traffic lights now.' But then we can remember back to when there was no roundabout at all.

'Now there's a cafe there named after the roundabout,' I laugh.

Our steps have become slow and short and we look to our feet in order to let our minds wander back to the past. Gracie smiles slowly; she's seeing it all in her head.

'Remember the gun shop?' I ask, and lift my face to hers with a smile.

'Of course,' she says, because that's where we were sent whenever Nonna or Gracie's mum needed a set of keys cut.

'It's gone too. Replaced by a cafe named after the gun shop,' I laugh again but Gracie says nothing.

'Gracie,' I touch her shoulder and bring our walk to a halt. 'You can always go back, you know.'

'Yeah, I suppose,' she sighs, but doesn't sound too convinced.

'You don't have to live in one place your whole life.'

'I know, but after seven years this is starting to feel like home now. It was so hard at the beginning, I worked so hard to make it work and now it's starting to pay off. I'd feel like I was throwing it all away if I went back now.'

'But if you're not happy . . .' I start to say.

'My family's here, this is where I'm happy.' She smiles with that particular brand of Sicilian pride I know so well.

Miniature pears, Whiskey's nonna and *L'Australiano*

'Zia,' Gracie says to my mother, 'I've had calls from your Zia Adele, Zia Enna, Zio Salvatore and Zio Mario. Then I got calls from Zia Concetta, Zia Lina, Zia Maria and Zia Rosa. They all want you to go over for dinner or lunch, whichever suits you, but as soon as possible because they all want to see you. Now.'

We're sitting round the kitchen table of our rented house on Via Ferrara.

'I don't know where your father's gone,' my mother says. 'He's been getting up at six every morning and disappearing.'

'He's probably gone to the bar to catch up with his friends before they go to work,' Gracie says. I imagine my father walking back into the neighbourhood bar like a man returning from war. His childhood friends, now aged and worn, walking up to him in wonder and saying, 'Pippo, is that you?'

'Where's Ross?' Gracie asks.

'He's still in bed,' I say.

We both look at the kitchen clock and see it's already nine am.

'I think it's the jet lag,' my mother suggests.

'We've been here a week already,' I say.

'Or it could be the food.'

'The what?'

'Your cousins have been coming to collect him almost every night. Last night they went out for gelato, the night before pizza, and the night before that it was crêpes.'

'What?'

'I know,' my mother shakes her head, 'it's like he's making up for all the meals he hasn't eaten. Now he's sleeping it off; he's got a food hangover.'

'Anyway Zia,' Gracie brings us back to the topic she started on, and I take a sip of my coffee. 'What am I going to tell all your aunts and uncles?'

Without a phone in our rented house or a mobile, Gracie has become our receptionist in Sicily. Her mobile number was being passed from hand to hand as the point of contact if you want to come and meet the Australians in town. Walking into Fiumefreddo has become like walking into a giant family reunion.

'We're going to have to make a list I suppose,' my mother says.

Gracie rummages around in her bag. 'Who do you want to start with?' she pulls out a piece of paper and a pen.

'You're gonna write it down?' I ask.

'When you see how many people you're related to in this town, you'll realise you're going to need a schedule.'

My mother sighs. 'Before we start with relatives we're going to have to start with the police.'

'Huh?' Gracie and I turn to her.

'Our citizenship papers. Your father and I have to go to the immigration section of the police station in Catania to collect and sign them. So we can become Italian again.'

'No use going now,' Gracie says and looks at the clock. 'It's nine a.m. already, they'll be closed at midday, and there'll already be a line out the door. You'll need to go bright and early if you want anything done.'

My mother's stunned by the news that a nine a.m. start is too late for a twelve p.m. finish.

'We'll go to Catania tomorrow morning,' Gracie says. 'I suggest you knock over a few relatives today and get them out of the way. Which one do you want to see first?'

Gracie waits with pen poised over paper.

'That's easy,' my mother says slowly and looks at me. 'I want to see my Zio Salvatore first,' she says, speaking about Nonno's brother.

Gracie pops the lid on her pen and puts the blank piece of paper back in her bag.

'No problem, we can go see him right now.'

'Shouldn't we call him first?"' I ask, but Gracie's already on her feet.

'No need,' she smiles. 'We're not going to his house. You're not going to find him at home during the day.'

'Where are we going to find him then?' my mother asks.

'You'll see,' Gracie says and smiles.

On our way out the front door we look in on Ross who is still fast asleep. His skin and hair are dark against the white sheets, and one of his hands is resting lightly on his stomach.

We open the front door and look down. Sitting on the top step is a box covered in a tea towel. My mother bends down and pulls the cloth away.

'Look at that,' I sigh over her shoulder.

In the box are miniature pears tiny enough to fit into a fist, their pale green skins lightly dotted, and each fruit perfectly blushed with a spot of pink. Next to them are round cherry tomatoes still on the vine, wedged tight beside a pile of long, deep-purple eggplants.

'That happens,' Gracie says and slides on her Guccis. 'People know you're in town and where you're staying. They probably don't want to disturb you so soon after you've arrived, so they'll just leave things at your door.'

Like a week's supply of fresh vegetables. Sicilians always give the most practical of gifts.

'But who?' my mother asks, bending down to pick up the box. As is her way, she gives the vegetables a slight sniff and runs her broad hand over the eggplants.

'Could be anyone, cousins most probably, you've got enough of them around here.'

My mother takes the box inside and Gracie and I step out into the street.

Whiskey is further up the road scratching on someone's door. He's got a tired set about his shoulders, but there's a mischievous quality to him that tells you he's been up to no good.

'Zia Maria mustn't be home,' Gracie says. 'God knows what he's been up to. Almost every newborn puppy in this town looks like him. He's got Zia Maria at her wit's end.'

'Whose door is he scratching on?'

Whiskey turns, looks at us, barks a hello and then goes back to scratching.

'When Zia Maria's not home he goes to her mother-in-law's place and waits there until he can go home.'

'Smart dog,' I smile. It seems that even Sicilian dogs go to their nonna's house when their parents aren't home.

'I don't know what we're going to do with all those pears,' my mother says as she joins us on the street and we set off for our walk.

The area known as Castello, the part of town where both my parents' families come from, sits behind the main church and piazza of the *centro*. Once you come up the side of the church and onto *il centro* you're faced with the string of bars and boutiques that give that side of town its name, Botteghelle.

'Where are we going?' asks my mother, as we come up through the back of the church and cross the piazza, the stone pavers ringing beneath our shoes. At a bar on the fringe of the piazza, groups of middle-aged men stop and watch us walk by.

'No-one's scared to look you in the face here, are they?' I say.

The men are loitering around the piazza, standing in groups, talking and gesturing wildly in mid-conversation. Out on the street, car horns are blasting in the air, and someone raises a hand in greeting to Gracie who waves back with a cheery, 'Ciao!'

Gracie steps onto the street and stops the slow-moving traffic with a raised hand, and we cross the street behind her.

'Do you see him yet?' she asks, as we head towards a group of tables lined up on the footpath beneath the awning of a bar.

'Not yet,' my mother says.

'You won't miss him,' Gracie says to my mother. 'No way you could ever miss him. He looks just like your father.'

In my mind I see Nonno's smile and a wedge of red melon. What I wouldn't give to see his face again.

A group of old men are sitting, chatting and sipping coffee in the mid-morning sun, outside a bar further down. They all have their dark hair slicked back like they probably did when they were twenty years old. Even in this heat, they are wearing an array of smart shirts and long, perfectly pressed trousers.

They look like they live in those seats, at those tables, under that awning. I can tell just by looking at them that they each have their preordained places – each one of them arriving at the same time every day and sitting in the same place, drinking the same drink and discussing the same sorts of things, day in and day out. They'll probably keep doing it day in and day out until slowly, one by one, they stop turning up.

'Oh my God,' I say and stop dead on the footpath.

My mother and Gracie are a pace ahead and they turn to look at me.

'You okay?' my mother asks.

I know he is Nonno's brother the instant my eyes skim over his face – the same face I had seen fleetingly the first day in Gracie's car but couldn't get a good enough look at. I had felt a flash of recognition then, but now I was stunned beyond words.

Nonno's image, long gone, comes out of the halls of my memory and hits me between the eyes in full living colour. Tears from the well inside of me come up to lodge in my throat and I start to choke on them. This man's face, his hair, the way he sits, the way he smokes and even his hands, belong to my nonno. I want to storm up to him and demand them back.

My mother turns to look in the direction I'm staring, and a few seconds after my initial shock I see her hazel eyes grow wide. A small gasp comes out of her and her tears begin.

'He looks like him, doesn't he?' Gracie says softly as she watches us. 'I always think I'm talking to your nonno when I see him.'

It's more like watching the dead come to life.

Being the first to compose herself, my mother takes a bold step forward. 'I want to see if he recognises me,' she says, and walks up to this man who seems more like a ghost to me than a real person.

'Do you know who I am?' my mother asks him as she steps into the middle of this group of octogenarians.

What were my grandfather's eyes blink and take in the vision of my mother's face. I see his skin drain of colour as if he too is seeing an apparition.

'Rosa?' he breathes between his teeth, and tries to stagger to his feet and reach out for his cane at the same time. Even his walking cane is the same style my nonno used.

Zio Salvatore, my nonno's brother, reaches out and takes my mother's hand, hers a smaller version but in the same style as his. His actions are cautious as if he's not sure she's real.

'Yes,' she replies, 'it's me Zio.'

'Rosa,' he says again slowly, before his face cracks into an enormous smile and he pats my mother's hand again.

'Come in,' Zio Salvatore says and then turns to us, 'come in all of you, let me buy you breakfast.' His grip on my mother's hand grows stronger and he drags her into the bar, with us following close behind.

'Are they from Australia?' one of the old men calls after us.

'Yes!' Zio Salvatore calls back to his friends, 'they're from Australia, the greatest nation on earth!'

The group of old men burst into peals of laughter and slap their thighs as if Australia and my great uncle are some long-standing joke.

'Hey l'Australiano,' they call after him, 'maybe you should go back!'

They start laughing again, but Zio Salvatore just waves a hand at them over his shoulder and pulls us deeper into the bar.

Australia over *GRANITA*

Unlike Nonno, Zio Salvatore's eyes are not a stunning sky-blue. Instead they are a warm and mischievous chocolate-brown, but they twinkle all the same in his heavily lined, worn face. His hair is thick and swept back in that same movie starrish way of my nonno's, and I can't keep my eyes off him.

'You look just like Nonno,' I say, as we head towards the back of the bar.

'He was very good looking, my brother,' Zio Salvatore says, and chuckles in a way that makes his shoulders move up and down.

'What would you like for breakfast?' he asks with a wave at the display case nearby. Zio Salvatore reaches out and takes my hand in his so that's he's holding my mother's hand on one side and mine on the other. I turn and feel my eyes grow wide in my head. The pastries in the display case are like perfect jewels behind the glass. *Cornetti*, filled with either marmalade, custard or Nutella, sit in icing-sugared rows. The *cannoli* are in straight, even rows and are filled to bursting with custards and creams. The *baba* are swimming in clouds of liqueur, the *cassate* are encased in their heavy shrouds of icing, and the biscuits are heaped cheerily on top of each other, pressing urgently against the glass. The smell in the air is that heady mix of vanilla and almonds that takes me straight back to Great Aunt Rosa cracking open her suitcase.

'Let's have a *granita!*' cries Gracie.

'Good choice!' exclaims my great uncle, and releases my hand to squeeze Gracie's arm. His brown eyes are bright and he is charmingly flirtatious for an eighty-year-old who can barely walk. Gracie squeals in reply – obviously my great uncle's charm is still effective, even at his age.

We walk in silence to a table and wait for a waitress. The back room of the bar is full of people wearing bright summer clothes, bathing suits and sarongs, and almost all of them are eating something icy out of glasses, occasionally dipping in pieces of bread. Their dark eyes swivel to us and look us up and down. It's obvious that we're not from here, and their curiosity is heavy in the air. After a few seconds of inspection they turn away, satisfied with their perusal, and go back to their breakfast.

'What flavour do you want? I suggest coffee with cream on top,' Gracie asks and answers at the same time.

'I'll have the original. Lemon,' I reply.

'Ohhh, you're so boring!' Gracie huffs.

'I'll have lemon,' I say to the tiny, dark waitress who is taking our order, 'and a brioche.'

'So how is your mother?' Zio Salvatore asks my mother.

'She's good,' she replies.

'What a woman she was,' he says and makes a fist, 'a strong woman. My brother couldn't stop talking about her when he first saw her. "That's a woman," he said, "that's a woman."'

'She still is a strong woman,' smiles my mother.

'No-one could get the better of Anna,' he shakes his head. 'And how are your brothers and sisters?'

'They're good,' says my mother.

Great Uncle Salvatore leans forward, reaches over and squeezes my mother's hand tightly, his voice dropping to an earnest level. 'And how is Australia?' he asks, as if he's talking about a person. His eyes are impatient for the response.

'It's beautiful,' breathes my mother with a smile.

'Ahhh,' he falls back into his chair and spreads his arms wide. 'I tell those fools outside every day what a beautiful place it is. What a good place it is. And all they do is laugh at me.'

Great Uncle Salvatore makes one hand into a fist and brings it down into the palm of his other hand. 'They don't know how everything in Australia works. Here there is only chaos. But Australia, Australia works. Do you know,' he turns to me and Gracie, 'I worked in Mareeba for ten years. Ten years!'

he holds up all ten thick fingers for emphasis. 'And do you know, I am an Australian citizen,' he pokes himself proudly in the chest, 'the best thing that ever happened to me. And the Australian government,' he waves a thick finger in the air to make a point, 'is the best government in the world.'

I grin to myself. I came to Sicily thinking I was going to another world. Instead, I find eucalyptus trees and Australian citizens in the unlikeliest of places.

'Ten years!' Zio Salvatore holds up his hands again. 'I wanted to take my wife back with me to Australia after I got married, but she refused to leave this town and her parents. Ten years,' he shakes his head slowly as the *granite* arrive along with a basketful of brioche.

'Met my wife at the deli,' he said, 'was on my lunch break and wanted some cheese with my olives. So I walk in and there she is. Fell in love because of a piece of cheese. Could have eaten dry bread instead that day and been in Australia now. Strange how life is.'

We all look into our glasses, amazed how a piece of cheese can change the course of your life. My glass is frosty and the lemon *granita* is opaque with little pieces of lemon rind mixed in like pieces of sunburst, yellow in my frozen glass. I dip my teaspoon in and take a mouthful. The lemon *granita* sparkles in my mouth, gleams across my teeth and snaps my tongue back to life. It's divinely bittersweet for what only amounts to lemon, sugar and ice.

'Dip in the brioche,' Gracie says, watching my face change. She's swirling the heavy cream through her coffee *granita*. I pick up my brioche and feel its warmth on my fingertips. Breaking it apart in my hands, I dip a piece of the sweet bun into my glass. The lemon *granita* melts against the heat of the bun and soaks into the sweet dough. It hits my tongue as a warm icy mass and melts all the way down the back of my throat.

Gracie was right – you do fall in love in Sicily during the summer. The problem is there are too many things to fall in love with. Right now, it is breakfast. We eat our *granite* and brioche slowly in the upbeat company of Zio Salvatore, who wants to talk more about Australia than anything else.

'Best country in the world,' he sighs, 'there everything is organised, everything works. The trains, the buses, the government, all run on time. I dare you to try and find out what time the buses run in this town. I don't think the bus drivers even know. There used to be a timetable stuck to a pole on the main road, but someone crashed their car into the pole and no-one ever replaced it.'

He sighs again. 'Australia,' he hums the word slowly.

Our *granite* and brioche are finished and my mother tells her uncle that it's time we got home. By now my brother should be awake and my father will be back from his early morning coffee.

'Ok,' he says, and we get up and move towards the door. 'I just have to speak to this old lady,' chuckles Zio Salvatore. He even laughs like Nonno: their chuckles start mid-chest and their shoulders move slightly up and down with each gasp.

'*Si vecchia!*' says the elderly woman sitting behind the cash register, 'who are you calling old, old man?' she says, pushing eighty herself.

Zio shoots her a wink and a grin as he pays. He receives the reply of an arched eyebrow with grace and another cheeky smile.

Back out on the street we're greeted again with the vibrant sounds of car engines, car horns, Vespas, church bells and the random shouts of 'Ciao!' from one side of the street to the other.

'How's Australia?' One of the old men looks up and asks my great uncle.

'Better than here!' he replies. 'Old fools,' he mutters under his breath and waves another dismissive hand at them.

'Come here,' he says, taking my mother by the elbow. 'See that house,' he points directly across the street from the bar, 'that's my house. You come over whenever you like. If you don't find me at home just look across the street and I'll be here. Except Wednesdays,' he shakes his finger and points at the ground. 'This bar's closed on Wednesdays, so we move up to the one over there,' he points two doors down the street.

I kiss my great uncle, Nonno's brother, on each cheek in goodbye. As we move away down the street I look back and see him settle into his seat amongst his friends under the awning. The word 'Australia' floats out from their chatter and down the road after us. This is the life my grandfather would have had if he had stayed here. That would be him getting up every morning, getting dressed and walking across the street to join his brother and their friends to sip coffee and watch the girls walk by. Like what he did every day at his Valley cafe before he got too tired and too defeated to make the trip anymore.

My mother's ghost and the perils
of being single

'While we're here, we might as well
drop past your Zia Enna's house,' Gracie says.

'Does she live far?' my mother asks.

'No-one lives far from anyone here,' Gracie replies, 'she's just around the
corner.'

'Will she be home? Maybe we should call her first.'

'Your Zia Enna is always home,' Gracie says.

The footpath narrows to barely a paver wide – this is all the space the town
could spare for pedestrians on this road – and we walk single file up an incline.
Gracie makes a left-hand turn at the top and we find ourselves on the street parallel to the main road we were on before. Across from us is a petrol station, and a
large raven-haired girl is pumping gas into a beat-up, rust coloured Fiat that looks
strangely like Uncle Joe's. One of its headlights even bears the same shotgun
scar, although in this part of the world it is more likely to be the real thing. We
pass a tiny tobacconist where there is barely room for the shop assistant let alone
any customers, before arriving at a green security-gated door. Above the buzzer,
written in large capitals, is the maiden name of my great aunt, Nonno's sister. As
is the way with Italian women, they prefer to keep their father's names as opposed
to taking their husband's. I wonder if Zia Enna looks like Nonno too.

My mother presses a finger to the intercom button and we wait.

'*Si?*' a childlike voice replies.

'Zia, it's Rosetta, I'm . . .' but my mother doesn't have time to finish, nor does
she need to remind Zia Enna who she is.

'Rosetta!'

A series of buzzes snap open the locks and we push the door open to reveal a steep staircase of two dozen tiled steps. We all look up and a small, round woman comes into our line of sight. She smiles and claps her hands together, then reaches up and pushes her glasses back up her nose. They take up her entire face and her eyes blink quickly behind them. I notice that her eyes are a brilliant blue.

We climb the stairs and I leave my heart somewhere on the tenth step – no wonder I haven't seen any weight problems here. At the top of the stairs, Zia Enna takes my mother by the shoulders, cups her face in her hands and brings each of her cheeks to her mouth, just like Nonna does to me. This small old lady giggles like a young girl in the same chuckling motion of her brothers. Her hair, which she brushes back into a bob, has the same thick sweep as her brothers', and her widow's peak is identical to my mother's. I look to my great aunt's old mouth and see my mother's lips. Her small, rotund physique and miniature legs remind me of Uncle Joe. My mother and Uncle Joe look more like Zia Enna's children than Nonna's. It is a startling connection of features. I have the sensation that if I step out onto the street I will see people passing by with my features, my limbs and my body, with someone else's soul inside.

'Come here, I have to show you something,' Zia Enna pulls us into her dining room. 'Look at that,' she says to my mother, and points to a large framed photo on the wall. 'I found this photo of your grandmother.'

For the second time that morning I stop dead. It isn't my great grandmother, Nonno's mother, staring at me from a photograph from sixty years ago. It's my mother.

I understand now why Zio Salvatore's face had drained of colour earlier.

While we were seeing the ghost of Nonno in him, he was seeing the ghost of his mother in mine.

'And this is my husband,' Zia Enna points to a framed photo sitting on a sideboard. She kisses her fingertips and brushes them across his face. Around her neck she's wearing a cameo with the same photo set in it.

'He's been dead so long now,' her features drop and I fear she'll start to weep. Her fingertips reach up and caress the cameo around her neck.

'Come, come,' she says, snapping back to life, and waves us on into the kitchen. Her enormous glasses keep slipping down her nose and she keeps pushing them up with a light finger and a quick chuckle.

'How's your mother?' Zia Enna asks my mother.

'She's good Zia.'

'She was always good your mother, strong as a lion. And your brothers and sister?'

'They're good too, Zia.'

'How's you're brother Joe? You know he's got a special place in my heart, when he was little I wanted to adopt him,' she smiles.

I smile back because Uncle Joe would have fitted in perfectly as her son. It could have been his Fiat filling up across the road.

'I asked your mother but she said no. And here I am, with no children,' she sighs. 'Would you like a drink?'

We shake our heads.

'Cup of coffee?'

We shake our heads.

'Ice cream? Wait, I'll get some ice cream.'

'Zia, really,' my mother protests. I can see her mentally trying to figure out how many calories she's already eaten this morning.

'Ssshhh, you're having ice cream!' Zia Enna's girlish voice issues the command, then softens. 'I can't really have any because I'm diabetic, but once in a while . . .' she trails off with a dismissive wave of her hand and dives into her freezer. She comes back with her hands full of assorted ice cream cones, and we each choose one under her glowing smile and bright eyes.

'Do you like it here?' Zia Enna asks us.

My mother stays silent. I know that since the airport, Sicily's lack of organisation has begun to grate on her nerves.

'It's beautiful Zia,' I reply, and she rewards me with a brilliant smile.

Like a young girl Zia Enna is taking delicate swipes of her ice cream. She's sitting perched on a chair with one hand resting on her stomach and her eyes dancing around the room. Everything about her demeanour suggests a perfect delight with life. Nonno's family certainly has happy genes.

'The air here is like nowhere else,' Zia Enna breathes, 'the mountain, the sea, there's nowhere else like it. Tell me,' Zia Enna leans forward and we all stop eating to concentrate on what she's going to say next, 'do you like *pasta al forno?*'

I catch my breath at the mention of it. It's one of those dishes that takes a lifetime to master, and I've never met a Sicilian woman under the age of fifty who has yet perfected the art of *pasta al forno*. It is, quite simply, a feat of culinary engineering.

Zia Enna pushes her giant glasses back up her face and, having finished her ice cream, she rests both her hands on her comfortable stomach. Her eyes have that mysterious twinkle I saw in her brother's and in Nonno's before that, and her face is a perfect study of cheeriness and satisfaction. I look around her kitchen and feel a warm familiarity; it feels a lot like Nonna's kitchen, and I can tell it's been put to good use over the years.

'I make the best *pasta al forno* in town,' Zia Enna breathes, and I believe her.

'You have a son don't you?' Zia Enna asks my mother.

'Yes, his name is Ross.'

'Ohhh,' Zia Enna giggles, 'you must bring him,' she turns to me, 'you must take care of your brother. I never got to see my brother Carmelo again.' Her face crumbles at the thought of the brother who went to Australia and only returned once more to see her, in 1974. She loved him as much as I did.

'Are you single?' Zia Enna suddenly asks me, her face instantly happy again.

'Yes Zia,' I nod.

I can feel Gracie turn and smile at me.

'Ohhh,' Zia Enna giggles again and claps her hands together, 'with the sun and the air here, you won't be for long!' She pushes her glasses up her face again and her eyes are brilliant with the prospect of romance. Zia Enna, it seems, lives in another world of her own making, a romantic and simple world. She has, like her brothers, a beautiful and tender soul, and I decide in that moment that when I grow up to be a little old lady, I want to be just like her.

We finish off our ice creams and a round of coffee which Zia Enna insists we drink. For all her girlish charms, her will is strong. It's not yet lunchtime and already I've eaten a *granita*, a brioche, an ice cream and drunk two rounds of coffee.

With a flick of a switch from the top of the staircase Zia Enna releases all the locks on her front door. She bids us goodbye and we promise to return next week with all the family for what we know will be the best *pasta al forno* of our lives. The green front door swings inwards and we're met by a tall old lady standing on the doorstep, her finger poised over the buzzer at Zia Enna's door. Her dark hair is perfectly lacquered, her thin eyebrows are tweezered into distinct lines and her black clothes are accentuated by heavy gold jewellery.

'I was just about to ring,' she says, and looks us up and down, dark eyes sharp and curious. 'Are you Enna's niece from Australia?' she asks my mother.

'Yes,' my mother says.

'Ahhh,' the tall old lady cries, as she grasps my mother by the arms and gives her a resounding kiss to each side of her face. 'I knew your mother when she was a girl, we'd go out to the countryside to pick *verdura* together. Ah, your mother, what a woman!'

There's something about this old woman that seems a little dramatic, a little over-performed. My mother's at a loss for words.

'Rosaria, is that you?' calls down Zia Enna, bunching her face up in a deep squint.

'Yes Enna, it's me, I'm just introducing myself to the Australians.'

I hear Zia Enna chuckling from the top of the stairs.

'You must come for dinner at my place, your mother was like a sister to me. My sister is in Brisbane you know, she sees your mother all the time. She tells me they meet for coffee. Isn't that lovely?'

'You're Carmelina's sister!' I pipe up, and find a sparkling pair of eyes on me. I get a dark-eyed inspection that starts at the top of my head and ends up all the way to the tips of my polished toenails. I think it best not to tell her that the coffee they meet up for is incidental to their primary purpose of blackjack.

'You must come, I make the best *pasta al forno* in town,' Signora Rosaria says and reaches up subconsciously to pat her dark, wavy hair.

'Uhum,' coughs Zia Enna whose sense of hearing is far more acute than her sense of sight, 'I've already invited them over here for *pasta al forno*,' she says slowly, 'you might have to cook something else.'

The two old ladies lock eyes and for a couple of seconds wage a war of meaningful glances over our heads. It seems Zia Enna isn't as ingenuous as she would have you believe, because it's Signora Rosaria who backs down quickly with a cough. 'Of course,' she waves a hand through the air, 'your Zia Enna makes a fantastic *pasta al forno*, I'll make something else, just as good,' she slips the dig in, 'but you must come over.'

'We'd love to,' sighs my mother, who has been accepting invitations left and right all morning.

'How old is your daughter?' Signora Rosaria suddenly asks my mother as if I'm not there.

'She's twenty-eight, turns twenty-nine this year.'

'Is she engaged, married?' Old, dark eyes flicker to my wedding-ring finger.

'She's single Rosaria,' calls down Zia Enna, and the two old women smile broadly to each other over our heads. Signora Rosaria's long grin finds my face and she beams at me. I feel strangely like I'm being sized up for something.

'Grazia,' Signora Rosaria sweeps her gaze quickly to Gracie who, caught off-guard, takes a small step back. 'I will call you to arrange. I have your number – I hear they don't have a phone at their house.'

How does everyone know where we are staying and how we can and can't be contacted? I get the feeling our arrival was discussed long before we landed, and all these little old ladies had obtained the necessary contact numbers in preparation.

Gracie just nods, 'OK *cummari*,' she says, and we make our quick escape into the street.

'You might want to get dinner at Signora Rosaria's out of the way first,' Gracie suggests as we make our back down to the *centro*.

'She's that much fun hey?' I ask.

'She's one of those really Sicilian Sicilians, if you know what I mean. You think it was an accident she just happened to be at your Auntie Enna's door when we were there?'

'I know what you mean,' my mother replies. So do I. They're as hard as stone, these old Sicilian women, and in a glance they'll shear you to the bone. Conversations with them are dances in which everything you say is weighed and measured, cross-referenced in their minds against your previous statements, and scanned for untruths. Suspicion lies heavy on everything – the Sicilian assumption being that you're always lying until proven otherwise.

'I suppose we should stop and get something for lunch. I have a feeling your brother is going to be hungry when he wakes up.'

Fiumefreddo has one supermarket, which in Australian terms is roughly the same size as a large suburban convenience store. All the trolleys are chained to each other and you have to pay a euro to use one. I assume you get the euro back when you return the trolley. Out the front on the street there are a total of four parking spaces, and a skinny guy in nylon shorts and a bumbag strapped to his waist is directing people in and out of them. A woman emerges from the supermarket and gets in her car to leave. The man in nylon shorts comes over and taps her window with an air of authority. I see her face contort at the sight of him. He taps again and she winds down her window to unleash her fury.

'This is a public street! I don't have to pay for parking here!'

'Hey, I looked after your car while you were shopping,' he replies.

'I didn't ask you to look after my car, who the hell do you think you are! Get out of my way!'

He backs off and mumbles under his breath, 'You gotta earn a buck some-how lady.'

Inside, at the deli counter, my mother contemplates a purchase of small-goods. Most people ask for fifty grams of this or a hundred grams of that, but my mother's purchases are more like 250 grams of this and half a kilo of that. The deli attendant is stacking our pile of purchases on the counter top and wait-ing on my mother to decide which cheeses she'll take home, when Gracie's mobile starts to ring.

'Pronto,' she cries into it and whips her head around so that her dark hair bounces down her back. The deli attendant momentarily loses concentration, and my mother has to repeat her cheese request twice before he can pull himself together. Gracie shoots him a twinkling smile and then goes on with her conversation.

'*Si cummari, certo.*'

She hangs up and the deli attendant reaches up to readjust his paper hat.

'Told you, you should get her out of the way first. That was Signora Rosaria and she wants you over as soon as possible. She's thinking tomorrow night.'

My mother and I just look at each other.

'Actually, I'm not sure you have much of a choice, she didn't really ask. She kind of just said that she was booking you for tomorrow night.'

Gracie slumps her shoulders a little, then straightens up when she finds the deli attendant's eyes flicker down to her hips.

'Put her in the schedule then,' my mother says and reaches up for her pile of mortadella, prosciutto, salami, pastrami and cheese.

We make the turn into Via Ferrara with all our shopping bags and find a tribe of old ladies camped on Gracie's doorstep. Auntie Anna, Gracie's mum, is holding court in the street.

'Here we go,' Gracie breathes quietly.

'Ahhh,' calls Auntie Anna, 'you're finally home! Come! Come!' she shooes my mother and I into the centre of the circle. 'This is Zia Lina, Zia Concetta and Zia Rosa.' Half a dozen Sicilian eyes look us over. Before long, more old women step out of their front doors and into the street, and our small group soon swells to a throng of tightly-curled, lacquered, dark-haired heads with roaming eyes set in worn, curious faces. One of them leans in close to my mother and asks, 'Is your daughter single?'

'You should stop drawing attention to yourself,' Gracie says to me, and I throw her a look, 'you'll be lucky if you get back on the plane to Australia,' she giggles.

'Here,' my mother throws me the shopping bags, 'go feed your brother,' and she allows me a timely escape before someone marries me off right there in the street.

I find Ross sitting at the kitchen table in front of a tiny cup of espresso, cradling his head in his hands.

'You okay?' I put the bags on the table and the scent of salami drifts out of one of them.

'Is that food?' he wipes a hand across his stomach. 'My stomach hurts.'

I nod.

'I'm so hungry.'

Ross reaches out in the direction of the salami smell and starts tearing the bag apart. Out of nowhere a knife appears in his hand and he's slicing a bread roll open, and tossing slices of salami in his mouth and into the bread roll at the same time.

'Ross, what's gotten into you?' He stops suddenly and looks at me. 'I don't know,' he slumps in his seat. 'There's something about the food here, or the air, I don't know. I'm just hungry all the time.'

I look at my so-far skinny brother. Somehow, between snacks and breakfasts and constant invitations to lunch and dinner, I don't think any of us are going to remain our former selves for very long.

Sicilian culinary engineering
Pasta al forno

Pasta al forno *is, quite simply, the sort of cooking men get married over. It is the pinnacle of Sicilian cooking. It's a triumph of ingredients and technique that I am unlikely to master until I become a very old lady.*

Everyone has their special trick to making the perfect pasta al forno. *For some, it's the pasta, others the cheese, some say it's the layering, but I'm sure you'll find your trick and swear your grandchildren to secrecy as well. Nonna has sworn me to secrecy over hers and I can never repeat it to another living soul.*

To a Sicilian like Nonna, viva l'omertà.

2 large eggplants
salt
1 quantity meatball mix (see page 66)
3 quantities *sarsa semplice* (see page 11), simmered for 1½ hours
olive oil, for cooking
1 kg dried penne
1½ cups grated *pecorino pepato* cheese
1 cup grated parmesan cheese
½ dozen hardboiled eggs, sliced

Cut the tops off the eggplants. Standing the eggplants upright, and without slicing all the way through to the bottom, cut into slices about ½ cm thick. Sprinkle salt over each slice, front and back, and squeeze gently together. Salting them this way draws out their bitterness. Leave the eggplants to one side for about an hour.

Form the meatball mix into thick, round patties. Brown the patties on each side in olive oil but don't cook them all the way through, then set them aside.

Warm the *salsa semplice* in a saucepan then slide the browned patties into the sauce and cook for 1 hour.

Preheat the oven to 200°C. Slice the eggplants all the way through, then rinse thoroughly and pat dry with kitchen paper. Heat 1 cm of olive oil in a frying pan, and fry the eggplant slices in batches until golden brown, then drain on kitchen paper. Meanwhile, cook the pasta in salted water, then drain.

Remove the meat patties from the sauce, cut into thin slices and set aside. Spoon about ⅓ of the sauce into a clean bowl and reserve (a small amount of this will be added between each layer to keep them moist). Stir ½ cup grated *pecorino pepato* and all of the cooked pasta through the remaining sauce.

Grease the base and sides of a large, deep baking dish with olive oil, then add a few spoonfuls of the reserved sauce. Add half the pasta and cheese mix and press down firmly. Add a few more spoonfuls of sauce, then scatter over about ⅓ cup parmesan and ⅓ cup *pecorino pepato*. Add the eggplant slices in one layer (overlap them if necessary), followed by another few spoonfuls of sauce, then the sliced meat patties in one layer (again, overlap them if necessary). Add the sliced hardboiled eggs in one layer, then a further few spoonfuls of sauce, followed by ⅓ cup parmesan and ⅓ cup *pecorino pepato*. Add the remaining pasta and cheese mix and press down firmly again, then finish with the remaining sauce and the rest of the cheese.

Bake for 20 minutes, then remove from the oven and cover the dish with foil or a lid, and bake for a further 20 minutes. Remove the foil or lid and bake for a final 5 minutes uncovered.

Remove the dish from the oven and allow to stand for 15 minutes. Slice into square serving pieces with a very sharp knife or an electric knife.

Serves 8–10

CATANIA'S *QUESTURA*

'According to the Italian consulate in Brisbane, all we have to do is go to the *questura* in Catania, give them our name and sign some papers.'

My father has skipped his early morning coffee in order for us to get a head-start to Catania, and my mother has dragged Ross out of bed early. He's sitting in front of me groaning.

'Get it together!' my mother snaps at him, 'you can't come all the way to Sicily and spend the entire time in one town eating. You have to see Catania.'

'Zia, you sure it's going to be that easy getting your citizenship back?' Gracie asks. She's offered to drive us to Catania and assist my parents in dealing with Sicilian authority.

'Well, that's what the consulate told me,' my mother replies, shrugging her shoulders.

My father slaps a palm on his thigh. 'You know, I still don't understand why it should be so difficult getting my citizenship back! I was born in this country, I was raised here and I worked here! I am an Italian!'

'You know, Papà,' I sigh, 'when you become a citizen again they may ask you to complete your military service.'

He blanches at the thought, then quickly regains himself. 'I'm too old,' he says, waving at me, 'and besides, it's not compulsory anymore.'

'Oh well, at least I don't have any of those worries,' I smile. 'Getting my Italian citizenship was a piece of cake.'

'See!' my father cries again, 'see what I'm saying! Here's my daughter, born in

Australia, raised in Australia, and yet she's an Italian. All because she was born before I was naturalised. Then I get naturalised, and she's an Italian and I'm not!'

'What about me?'

We all turn and look at Ross.

'According to the Italian consulate in Brisbane,' my mother quotes again, 'you'll have to live here for three years before you can become a citizen.'

'Three years!' Ross yells and then stops. I watch his face drop and then come back up again. 'I suppose that wouldn't be so bad.' Something tells me he's thinking about three years of eating salami, gelato, pizza and crêpes.

'Do you see what I'm saying?' my father goes on. 'We'll be Italian citizens,' he points to my mother and himself, 'my daughter's an Italian citizen, but my son can't be. Does that seem right to you?'

Gracie just shrugs, 'Zio, that's Italy for you. But I wouldn't count yourselves Italian citizens until you actually get your passports. I have a feeling it's not going to be as easy as you think.'

From the sky, it seems that everything in Catania is made from stone. At ground level, this impression is not altered – everything is made from stone, and the place is completely manic. It feels like a million cars are squeezing themselves through the impossibly narrow spider web of streets, bottlenecking in the middle of the city and popping out the other side. Everyone is in a rush, everyone is loud, and there's a thrilling sense of tension in the air. There is no cacophony of car horns here – just one continuous blast.

'Oh my God,' my mother breathes slowly. I can see her sitting in the front seat of Gracie's car, hitting the air brakes and hanging onto the overhead handle like her life depends on it. Ross, my father and I are squeezed into the back seat. Gracie weaves in and out of traffic, dodging cars and cutting people off. Bumpers appear left and right and make their own spaces in the traffic. It's like dodgem cars, without the safety of rubber padding.

'Zia, will you relax!' Gracie yells and slams on the brakes as a car jerks into her path and cuts her off.

'Relax?' my mother yells back, as a driver next to her leans his whole body into his horn. 'How can you relax? How can people drive like this?' my mother waves her free hand in all directions.

Up ahead a two-lane street has been converted to three lanes by a driver who's just decided to do his own thing.

'Zia, I know it looks like madness, but it works. Trust me, everyone gets to where they're going, and we'll get to where we're going to. It's not organised like Australia but there is a system and it works,' Gracie looks ahead, 'in its own way.'

She slams the brakes on again and we all pitch forward, then back.

'I hope so,' sighs my mother behind tight lips, and I see the muscles in her leg contract as she presses down on the invisible brake beneath her feet.

'This looks familiar,' I say, turning my face to the window.

'We've been around the block a couple of times,' Gracie informs me, 'if you see a space, or anything that looks like a space, or just anywhere I can put my car, yell out.'

'What about there?' Ross points to a tiny space between a bin and a corner.

'Looks good enough to me,' says Gracie, 'let's just hope it's there when we go around again.'

Cars look like they're piled on top of each other rather than actually parked, and after a number of attempts Gracie finally manages to cram her car into the only available space left.

I get out of the car, looking left and right. 'Which way do we go?' I'm completely disorientated even after three turns around the same block. This place is a maze of streets with every centimetre taken up with the incessant buzzing of people, cars, Vespas and noise. It's hot and dusty and wonderfully alive.

'My God!' my mother puts her hands to the side of her head, 'how do people live here?'

I take a deep breath and draw the noise into me, 'It's fantastic.'

'This way,' Gracie says, and we follow her up an incline and out onto a main road. Catania's *questura* is a nondescript, grey building in a street of office blocks and dirty, rundown shops.

'This isn't exactly the nice side of town,' Gracie sighs.

'I gathered that much,' I say. I see the entrance to the *questura* and from where I am it looks like a little slice of West End. On the footpath outside the door is an African man. He towers over everyone around him and his skin has a perfectly smooth darkness which makes me sigh in delight. Not far ahead of him is an Indian woman with her long, dark hair piled on top of her head, and in front of her is a Chinese family.

I turn and look at my parents. 'I suppose they're immigrants just like you,' I smile.

My father looks from the *questura* back to me. Until I had pointed it out to him, I don't think he had considered himself an immigrant to Italy.

'I'm not an immigrant,' he says to me.

'Well,' I goad him even more, 'technically you're not Italian, and neither are they.'

We get to the end of the *questura* line and take our places.

'Yes, but in here,' my father points to his chest, 'I am Italian.'

'Are you in line for citizenship queries?' Gracie asks the African man in English. She's got her head tipped back and her hand to her eyes shading the sun. He looks down at her with creased eyebrows.

'You don't speak English? Do you speak Italian?' Gracie asks him in Italian and he nods quickly.

'Are you in line for citizenship queries?' she tries again in Italian.

'Yes,' he says, 'I've been here for half an hour now.'

I take a quick step back and squint up at this tall man from a far continent. He's answered Gracie perfectly, but not in Italian. In Sicilian.

I look at him closely. 'Where do you think he learnt to speak Sicilian?' I lean into Gracie and ask her quietly in English.

'He's probably been working odd jobs, the sort Sicilians don't want to do, and he's just picked it up. It's only the oldies and poorer people who still speak dialect here. Everyone's making an effort to speak proper Italian now.'

'Why?'

'Because it's just the way it is. No-one our age would be caught dead speaking Sicilian anymore, it's just not done,' she sniffs, 'it's a little uncouth.'

Something in my heart breaks.

My beautiful tongue is shunned here, looked down upon. That lovely rubbing together of syllables is dying, only kept alive in its perfect form by the immigrants that left long ago. But it's not dead yet, because here, standing in this line, are the unlikely custodians of the Sicilian tongue. I look up quickly at my African friend and smile. He smiles back with a gorgeous flash of white teeth.

The line moves forward in increments, half a body at a time, until finally we are at the door. The *questura* is a small, rectangular room with bored-looking policemen sitting behind security grilles directly opposite the door. People sit along the walls waiting. Africans, Indians, Afghans and Chinese. There's something warm and hopeful about this congregation of people, about this tightly-packed immigration room. Hope, destiny and possibility brush shoulders here, draw up close to each lonely immigrant and drape an arm around them. It's a room brimming with humanity.

'I feel sorry for them,' my father sighs, looking around him. 'They've come for a better life.'

'Yeah, but why would they want to come here?' my mother asks sharply. It seems Sicily is starting to wear a little thin on her.

I don't know what it is about this room. Each of these people seem a little raw and vulnerable to me, and I want to go up to them and touch their hands. 'It will be alright,' I want to say, 'you'll be fine.'

Time ticks on, hours pass and bodies shuffle and realign. The temperature goes up and it makes us all itch, as the security grille gets closer and the policemen look more and more bored. The touching warmth of this room is wearing off after almost two hours of waiting. Finally, we hit the counter and Gracie explains the pitiful plight of my wilting parents. Born here, immigrants to Australia; rightful citizens of both their countries, returning now to become citizens of Italy again because of the new law. The policeman looks a little less bored with us, thankful I think to be able to converse in his own language.

'Wait a moment,' he says and gets up.

Time passes as the policeman shifts around the office, moving from desk to desk, rifling through a filing cabinet, lifting up a stack of papers somewhere else and putting them down.

'No papers, Signora,' he comes back and shakes his head at my mother.

'What do you mean, no papers?' my mother grips the steel mesh separating her from the policeman.

'No papers yet, Signora. Maybe Australia didn't send them,' he throws his hands out, palms up, as if he has nothing to do with anything.

'Oh, Australia sent them!' my mother's gritting her teeth and I worry that she's going to rip the steel mesh right out of the wall.

'Signora, you'll have to come back when we have the papers,' the policeman shrugs.

'And when will that be?'

He sighs again. 'That will be when we get them,' he replies, *'pazienza* Signora, *pazienza.'* Patience.

Defeated, we slump away from the counter towards the door. I look back at the immigrants lining the room, the same faces that were there two hours before. Looking at them now I realise that it's not vulnerability on their faces, but sheer exhaustion. A side-effect of dealing with Sicilian bureaucracy.

'What now?' my father asks unfazed.

We all look at our watches.

'Looks like lunch to me,' smiles Ross.

A PAIR OF SICILIAN EYES

I can smell something frying from the staircase. Signora Rosaria lives on the second storey of an apartment block in the centre of town. She opens her apartment door and greets us with a broad smile, open arms and a special twist on the cheek for me. The first thing I see the instant I walk in is a black and white photograph of her husband on a sideboard.

She follows my eyes with hers.

'Been dead fifteen years now,' she sighs, and brushes a kiss on her fingertips which she deposits on the photo. It seems that outliving your husband by at least two decades is a normal part of life for every Sicilian woman. These old birds only get tougher and hardier with age.

'Come, come,' she says, shooing us into the kitchen. So far in Sicily I had been shooed, pinched, poked, squeezed and inspected from head to toe. I love that people aren't afraid to be expressive here.

Signora Rosaria's kitchen is the source of the frying smell I had detected in the hallway.

'Oh, smells good,' sighs Ross, and I look at him out of the corner of my eye.

'Do you like artichokes?' Signora Rosaria asks.

They're sitting, murky-green, in a large baking tray. Broad leaves are flowered open and stuffed deep with breadcrumbs and cheese. Signora Rosaria was busy frying the tops of the artichokes to seal in the stuffing when we arrived.

'Do you have these in Australia?' she asks.

My mother laughs. 'We have everything in Australia, Signora.'

'Ahh,' the old lady nods, 'of course you do. I hope you don't mind but I haven't made anything too filling.'

'Not at all,' my parents reply together.

'You know,' Signora Rosaria says, leaning in close, '*pasta al forno* is nice of course, but in this heat I don't think it's the best thing to eat.' She smiles, contented that she got that in, and starts to make her way back to the stove.

A buzzing sounds from the hallway.

'Excuse me,' says Signora Rosaria apologetically and pats her hair softly into place, 'that's the front door. I hope you don't mind but I asked my grandson to come for dinner as well.' She shoots me a smile as she bustles past me into the hallway to get the door. We're left in the kitchen with the fantastic smell of hot olive oil and the fried tops of artichokes.

'This,' says Signora Rosaria as she reappears in the kitchen and we all turn to face her, 'is my grandson, Gianni.'

All I see is an enormous pair of chocolate-brown eyes and the flash of perfect white teeth.

'Hello,' he says and extends a hand.

I reach out and slip my hand in his and feel his strong fingers squeeze. He leans into me and brushes his cheek lightly against each of mine. When he steps out of my personal space I notice his dark brown hair and the deep olive tan of his skin.

He's still smiling at me, probably because I'm suddenly stuck to the spot and unable to look away. I'm fascinated by the way the lines around his eyes crinkle up with his smile, and the way I can see happiness dance deep in the darkness of his eyes.

Reality taps me on the shoulder and I'm suddenly uncomfortable and not sure where to stand or where to look. Not at him, I say to myself, but beneath my lowered lashes my eyes follow him around the kitchen table. He brushes a kiss on each of his grandmother's cheeks and squeezes her shoulder with his broad hand.

'What are you cooking Nonna?' he asks.

The old lady swoons, the way old ladies do when they see their handsome, grown-up sons and grandsons.

'Ahhh,' she sighs, and waves an admonishing but affectionate finger at him, 'your favourite of course. *Carciofi.*'

That grin never leaves his face. It lights up his eyes and his skin and I can feel my stomach start to churn.

'I raised this one,' his grandmother says proudly and pats Gianni on the arm. I wonder if he feels the same about his nonna's house as I do about mine. If this place feels more like home to him than the place where he sleeps every night.

'So how long have you been in Sicily?' he asks us.

'Only a week and a half,' my mother replies.

'It's not like Australia is it?' he grins again.

'Nothing like it.'

His dark eyes drop to the floor and his features gather into something a bit more serious. 'What's it like, Australia?' he asks as he reaches out, pulls out a chair from the kitchen table and seats himself directly across from me.

'Beautiful,' says my mother, 'so very beautiful.'

'I hear everything is very organised in Australia.'

What is it with these Sicilians' fascination with organisation?

'They even have artichokes there!' adds Signora Rosaria.

My father just nods confirmation and smiles in reply.

'That's the problem with Sicily,' Gianni says. 'It's every man for himself here. No-one has any sense of service or organisation. Everything gets done whenever someone feels like doing it.'

I'm reminded of buying a gelato at Giardini and the ordered chaos we found there. We still achieved the goal of getting an ice cream cone though.

'But it's so beautiful here,' I say.

Gianni flashes his perfect teeth in my direction and my stomach churns a little more.

'It is beautiful, and if you can ignore the people, it's even more beautiful.'

I prickle a little at his reply. I had found nothing wrong with the Sicilian people. I love that they look at you frankly in the face, especially if they don't know you. I love their friendly abruptness and their sense of dramatic expression.

'People are people,' I say. 'I think they're essentially the same everywhere you go.'

Gianni shakes his head slightly. 'Not the Sicilians. Sicilians are always out for themselves. You can never trust a Sicilian.'

'I think that's the same for a lot of people,' I reply harshly, and talk us directly into an impasse. His dark eyes float quickly across my face and I feel like I'm holding my breath. Signora Rosaria drops one of the artichokes upside down into the hot oil and breaks the silence.

An artichoke is sitting in a white bowl in front of me. With a fork I pick the fried breadcrumbs and cheese off the top. I pull one of the outer leaves off, turn it upside-down and drag the fleshy side along my bottom teeth. We eat in comfortable and warm silence, the empty bowl at the centre of the table slowly filling up with defleshed leaves. Signora Rosaria has opened the double doors that lead from the kitchen onto her balcony. From down below come the sounds of the town moving about its noisy business, another family across the way sits down to dinner, and the air blowing in is cool. It feels a lot like Nonna's kitchen in here, just like it did in Zia Enna's. It's the sort of place where you can nestle down in front of a plate of hot food and let all the stresses of the modern world fall away from you. It's a place where you take all your troubles and deposit them on the table for your nonna to sort through. If Signora Rosaria is anything like my nonna, she'll sort out life's issues with some well-worn one liners, like 'the one who goes slow goes far', 'never let flies land on your nose', or, my favourite, 'better the egg today than the chicken tomorrow'. 'I hear Australia is a very dangerous place,' Gianni says, and drops a leaf into the bowl.

'Ah, that's what everyone says about Australia!' my father joins in.

'Snakes, spiders, crocodiles, that's all we see on TV about Australia. And kangaroos.'

'There are two kangaroos for every person in Australia,' I say, remembering that statistic from somewhere. Gianni looks at me over the top of an artichoke leaf, confused. I realise that my Italian/Sicilian mix has made it sound as if every Australian citizen is given two kangaroos, like a gift from the Australian government.

'Every person has two kangaroos?' he asks and blinks.

'No,' I smile, 'what I mean is that for every person there are two kangaroos. There are twice as many kangaroos as people.' Finally I talk myself out of the grammatical fog I've created.

'And is it true that there are kangaroos that are bigger than a man and they kill people?'

I nod, although I'm not really sure.

'Do you see them often?'

I want to laugh, not at him, but at the vision of a giant kangaroo in Nonna's concrete backyard.

'No, they live in the desert,' I say, not entirely sure if that's true either.

Gianni just nods and accepts my authority on the matter.

I look over at Signora Rosaria and remember the story Nonna told me of the day she left Sicily. I can still hear the screams about another world. If only Signora Rosaria knew that in that other world they were living lives much the same as the ones they do here. I look up to find a pair of dark eyes wandering across my face. They stay a while, meet mine and hold for mere moments, before they drop down to his artichoke. For some reason Nonna's face and her look of foreboding drifts through my mind.

Green globes
Carciofi pieni

When they're in full bloom and fresh, Nonna buys cases of artichokes and stuffs them with all things Sicilian – parsley, garlic and pecorino pepato. When they're cooked, they're heavy and fleshy and their hearts melt on your tongue. You marvel at their delicate but powerful taste and finally understand why their centre is protected by so many leaves.

Nonna, Uncle Joe and I will sit in our usual places at Nonna's kitchen table, an artichoke in front of each of us and a large bowl between us. We take the leaves one at a time in our fingers, turn them upside-down and pull them across our bottom teeth, collecting the green flesh on our tongues.

2 fresh artichokes
1 cup breadcrumbs
¾ cup finely chopped flat-leaf parsley
3 cloves garlic, finely chopped
½ cup grated *pecorino pepato* cheese
salt and pepper
olive oil, for cooking
1 egg, beaten
potatoes (optional)

Cut the stalks off the artichokes, and remove the outer layer of leaves. Trim the top leaves by about ½ cm, then cut an 'X' in the top with a sharp knife. Run the artichokes under cold water to rinse clean, and then hit their base on the countertop to spread their leaves open a little. In a large bowl combine the breadcrumbs, ½ cup parsley, half the chopped garlic, grated cheese, and a pinch of salt and pepper. Take each artichoke and stuff this breadcrumb mixture between the leaves.

Heat some olive oil in a frying pan, drizzle a teaspoonful of the beaten egg over the top of each artichoke, then lightly fry them, top-side down. You only need to fry them long enough to seal the mixture (about 2–3 minutes), then set them aside.

In a large heavy-based saucepan, deep enough to sit the artichokes upright in, sauté remaining garlic and parsley in olive oil for a minute or two. Pack the artichokes tightly together in the pan, sealed-side up. If you have gaps between the artichokes, squeeze some potatoes in between to fill the gaps and keep the artichokes upright. Then add water to the pan, making sure it does not cover the artichokes – it should come up to about 1 cm below their tops so that the stuffing does not come out while they're cooking. Cook uncovered on medium heat for approximately 30 minutes. When you can easily pull off one of the inner leaves, they're ready.

Serves 2

The next morning Gracie is on our front step dressed in a low-cut swimming costume and blood-red sarong. In one hand she's gripping a blue and white striped beach umbrella, and in the other she's swinging her car keys.

'Time for the beach!' she smiles. Behind her, Whiskey strolls past down Via Ferrara in the direction of Via Marina and the sea.

The long road that runs along the length of the beach, Marina di Cottone, is like all things Sicilian: complete chaos. Yet everything is moving. People are parking, people are leaving and people are getting to the beach. There's no system but there seems to be some unseen, unspoken code of conduct that everyone knows and adheres to, and it keeps everything on track.

Cars are squeezed into every available and unavailable space. Vespas shoot in and out between cruising and stationary cars, with half-naked, bronzed bodies on the back of them. Families trailing floaties, beach chairs, umbrellas and numerous children stroll in and out of the traffic and across the road without so much as a glance at oncoming vehicles. A dark, skinny man on a dirt bike roars up and down the row of parked cars, collecting small payments of protection money at one or two euros apiece.

'You have to pay for parking on a public street?' I ask Gracie as she turns into the car park instead.

'If you want to find your car when you get back, you do. These guys are smarter than the guy at the supermarket – they take your money first, protect your car second,' she replies.

Gracie manoeuvres her car between two towering walls, and a wide expanse bordered by ancient stone walls opens up in front of us.

'I prefer to just park in the car park,' she says.

'What is this place? Or was this place?' I ask as a short, portly man points us frantically towards his colleague who directs us into a tiny parking space. They're squeezing the cars as close together as possible.

'It used to be the stable to the country house back there,' Gracie waves a hand over her right shoulder, 'but now the house is a ruin and they use the stable as a car park.' She locks the steering wheel hard and parks her car as close as she can to the one next to her. It's nice to know that no-one seems too concerned about getting their car scratched or dented here: they all seem to be notched with a healthy amount of scrapes and bruises.

Gracie bends over and pulls her giant beach umbrella out of the back of her car, momentarily distracting the car parking attendant.

'Ciao *bella*,' he breathes at her as we walk past, but Gracie just ignores him. With her stunning tan glistening and a riot of black curls trailing down her back, she's collecting every male glance from the car park to the water's edge.

We hit the beach and beneath my feet are pebbles: grey and black, some white striped, some sparkling a bright blue or orange in the hot sun.

'There's no sand!' I cry, looking down at my feet.

Strung along the water's edge for what appears to be kilometres in both directions is family after family of Sicilian beachgoers. They're sitting beneath giant umbrellas or laid out on beach chairs, and everyone's in bikinis or very small swimmers, sporting deep olive tans. Incredibly tall African men stroll through the crowds, draped with sarongs and beach towels for sale in a rainbow of colours. Beyond, the Ionian Sea traps the Sicilian sun and reflects it back in a clear wash of blue.

Gracie shoehorns us into a space as close as possible to the water's edge as we can get. Further up the beach comes the cry of a Sicilian man.

'*Luppini!*' he yells, 'I've got *luppini!*'

'Did I hear that right?' I ask Gracie and she just nods as if it's nothing unusual. I follow the Sicilian man with my eyes and see someone call him over and hand him a euro. He reaches into his esky and hands over a bag of chilled *luppini*. Legumes by the sea. I shake my head.

'Welcome to Marina di Cottone,' Gracie says and drives the beach umbrella between the pebbles.

Our towels flutter down to the stones and we throw ourselves under the open umbrella for some shade from the hot sun.

'You're a bit quiet this morning,' Gracie says as she rearranges the top of her swimming costume to give the most flattering view.

I shift a particularly big rock out from under my towel and try to make the ground beneath me as smooth as possible. The rock I pull out is flat and grey with a broad white stripe.

'Show me that,' says Gracie and holds out her hand. I drop the rock into her palm. She turns it over and examines it quickly.

'Keep that one. The ones with the stripes that go all the way around are said to be good luck,' she hands it back to me, and I close my fingers around it tight.

'So what's the matter with you?' she asks.

'It's nothing,' I say, and look out to sea, rolling the rock in my palm.

'What's the matter?' she persists.

'Fhhhh,' I blow out some hot air, 'dinner last night . . .' I start.

'Aha,' she lifts herself up on an elbow and looks at me. I can't see her eyes behind her dark sunglasses but her generous lips are curved into a small smile.

'Well, there was someone there.'

'Yes?'

'Nothing.'

Her mouth turns down in doubt.

'Oh, it's nothing,' I try waving her away but she won't be deterred. What was I thinking anyway? The butterflies in my stomach and all the hairs on my body standing on end surely couldn't mean anything?

'Gianni,' she says, and flops back on her back.

My eyes slide to her quickly.

'I know,' she reaches over and pats me on the arm, 'trust me, I know. He's gorgeous, he's the most eligible bachelor in Fiumefreddo.'

I don't say anything.

'You have to think about it though. I mean, if there's something there what are you going to do? Summer fling? Sicily isn't for you,' she shakes her head, 'if you're thinking more than a summer fling that is.'

'I'm not thinking of marrying him if that's what you're saying. I only met him last night.'

'*Luppini! Luppini!*' the man with the legumes gets closer. When we're all together at Nonna's for lunch or dinner she'll buy bags of these *luppini* and serve them in small bowls before dinner. We nibble on them while we wait for the pasta to be served. You put them in your mouth, slip their casings off between your teeth and crunch their salty bodies.

When am I going to see something different in Sicily, something I hadn't already seen at Nonna's house or in West End? Sicily is not for me, Gracie says. Right now, Sicily was proving to be nothing more than what I had been taught and what I had already lived my whole life.

The sun is baking my white legs, Africans are strolling past flashing white smiles, I'm running my palms over the smooth, hot rocks and the water is lapping the shore close by. I barely have time to say, 'This place is magic,' before Gracie's mobile rings.

'*Pronto!* Ciao!' she blasts into her phone, then sits bolt upright. 'Yes, of course, what a great idea. Not a problem. I will let her know. OK, ciao!'

Gracie lies back down and avoids my gaze.

'Who was that?' I ask.

'No-one in particular,' she says, rolling onto her side to face me.

'You seemed pretty excited,' I mumble, and toss another *luppino* into my mouth.

'Oh nothing,' she sighs and moves some rocks around, 'it was just Gianni.'

The *luppino* shoots down my throat and lodges itself in an excruciatingly painful position.

'What?'

'He wanted to know what we're doing on Saturday night. He wants to organise dinner with us and a group of his friends.'

Gracie turns onto her back but watches me out of the corner of her eye. I smile slowly.

'Really?'

'Ahuh,' she sighs, 'you gonna ask me where?' Gracie smiles up into the stripes of the beach umbrella.

'Where?' I cough up my *luppino*.

'Castelmola,' she sighs.

I remember my first sight of Castelmola the night we were at Giardini Naxos, and the way it seemed strangely suspended in the night air. It seems like the perfect location for so many things.

'Saturday is so far away,' I sigh and cough again.

A lesson in legumes
Chickpea soup

The legume figures heavily in Sicilian cuisine, probably because Sicilians were traditionally peasants. Ordinarily I love winter, but as a child I would dread it for one reason. A slight drop in temperature and my mother would start dragging out the entire legume family – lentils, chickpeas and beans of all shapes and sizes. 'This was how we paid off our first house so quickly – all we ate was lentils,' she says. It was also an opportunity for my father to recount the tales of poverty and misery that were his Sicilian childhood. Every winter's evening I'd skulk to the dinner table and push my spoon through the murky depths of my lentil soup, and my father would say, 'I hated them as a child too, but as you get older you will appreciate them.' I don't really want to admit it, but he's right. As an adult your tongue starts to appreciate the warmth of the freckle-sized brown lentil and the smoothness of the bean. But more than those, I now look forward to the lentil's curvier and nuttier cousin, the chickpea.

2 cups dried chickpeas
1 potato, diced
1 carrot, diced
1 white or brown onion, diced
salt and pepper
1 cup dried shell pasta
drizzle olive oil

Soak the chickpeas in tepid water overnight. Drain and transfer to a large saucepan, adding enough cold water to cover by about 10 cm. Add the diced potato, carrot and onion. Cook on medium heat until the chickpeas are soft, and then add salt to taste. Add the pasta and cook until al dente. Serve hot with black pepper and a drizzle of olive oil. This also tastes great cold the next day.
Serves 4 as a side dish

CASTELMOLA

The days in between pass in a slow, hypnotic rhythm. We get up late and eat a *granita* at the bar for breakfast. We drive to the beach where we bake for half a day and then come home for lunch, which is usually a *panino* with cheese and salami, some olives and a couple of glasses of red wine. We finish off with some fruit and maybe a scoop of gelato. Then we take to our beds for an afternoon nap on cool, white sheets between cool, white walls. In the late afternoon we get up, get dressed and go to whichever aunt, uncle or cousin has offered to feed us for the evening.

Zia Enna's *pasta al forno* proves to be up to the hype. I look at my brother as we walk up as a family to Zia Enna's.

'Have you put on weight?' I ask.

'No!' his hands shoot automatically to his stomach and he rubs it.

'I think you have!' I stop on the footpath and look at him.

'Have not!' he rubs his stomach harder.

The smell at Zia Enna's door is of baked pasta and fried eggplant. It seeps out of the front door and creates a cloud of scent on the footpath.

'Have so,' I whisper as my mother presses the buzzer.

The locks snap open, the door swings in and we are engulfed by the warm smells of baking that draw us up the stairs and into Zia Enna's kitchen by our noses. We find her tucked into a checked apron, pushing back her giant glasses and giggling softly to herself.

'Zia, it smells great!' says my brother, as he rushes to her and gives her a kiss on each cheek. She gushes like a schoolgirl and picks his face up in her hands.

'He's so good looking,' she sighs, 'he will get an extra big piece!'

Ross just smiles and I look to his tummy, which has started to fill out nicely.

Zia Enna bends down and opens the oven door. From inside she draws out a baking dish of *pasta al forno*. The sauce has turned a deep red and the cheese on top has melted and turned into a hot crusty lid. With a long, sharp knife she starts slicing through the pasta, cutting large square portions. She slips a spatula under one corner and lifts out the most perfect piece of *pasta al forno* I have ever seen. The layers of penne sit perfectly moulded to layers of fried eggplant, meatballs and hardboiled eggs. Melted cheese binds it all together.

'Go sit in the dining room,' she shooes us all away with a smile.

Drool appears at the corner of Ross' mouth and I know that Sicily has changed him forever.

'Ross gets the biggest piece,' says Zia Enna as she appears in the dining room carrying a plate. She lays a hunk of pasta down in front of my brother.

'He's a growing boy,' she giggles.

'He's growing alright,' I cough, and Ross shoots me an evil glare in reply.

'So what do you think of Sicily?' Zia Enna asks Ross when we've all been served dinner.

'It's beautiful, Zia,' he smiles around a mouthful of pasta.

'Ah!' Zia Enna claps her hands together, 'it is beautiful, isn't it? The air, the mountain, the sea – you can breathe here.' Her eyes lock onto my brother's. 'You should find yourself a nice Sicilian girl and stay here.'

Ross smiles again.

'And I'll make you *pasta al forno* every week.'

He looks like he's seriously considering it.

The same week we have dinner at Zio Salvatore's house and he spends the whole night speaking about Australia, regaling us with stories of the Australian sun, the Australian soil and the band of Sicilians who worked the earth in Mareeba. He chides his wife for not wanting to move there and mumbles again about the price that he paid for a piece of cheese. Zio Salvatore's wife smiles at him indulgently, 'It was the best piece of cheese you ever ate,' she says, and he winks at her.

We have coffee at my father's aunts' houses, where I'm completely sidelined because they're too busy admiring my brother and how much he looks like their long-dead brother, my father's father. They cup his face in their papery hands and ooh and aah at his green eyes. When he's not being admired by great aunts, he's collected by the same gaggle of cousins who take him to nightclubs by the sea and places where they can eat crêpes at midnight.

So the days pass in this easy, hot, food-fuelled rhythm, until finally, Saturday night arrives.

Castelmola is reached only by braving a number of tight hairpin curves, with nothing but a sheer drop below. Gianni spins his car expertly around the tight corners, only occasionally veering slightly to one side and swiping a few trees. My fingers are locked in a white-knuckle grip on the armrest.

'What's the matter?' he asks, turning to me and taking his attention completely off the road. The fingers on his right hand are pressed together to a point and he opens and closes them in a strange gesture, like a flower opening and closing.

'What does that mean?' I ask, my eyes wide. The road suddenly narrows and the headlights of an oncoming car flare up in front of us.

'That means fear,' he says, opening and closing his fingers again.

'I'm not frightened,' I lie.

Gianni flicks his lights on and off at the oncoming car, telling the other driver he can go first. 'Yes you are,' he smiles, and starts driving again without taking his eyes off my face.

We reach Taormina, half way to Castelmola, and he shifts the car down to a lower gear as the road gets tighter, steeper and curvier. I have been holding my breath all the way up to Taormina, but Castelmola is even higher, even more difficult to get to.

Between Taormina and Castelmola I barely draw any oxygen. We wind our way up, slowly turning up to the very top, up to my ethereal town. Without warning, the assaulting mountain road spreads open and turns into a car park, flat and wide. I release the breath I had been holding and try to draw one in at the same time.

'You alright?' Gianni asks. His eyes are soft and warm and all I can do is nod.

'I don't always drive like that, you know. Usually I hit more trees.'

I swallow and he starts to laugh.

Gianni swings his door open and we both get out of the car and step into the night air, me on shaking legs. Gracie slides out of the back seat.

'That was impressive,' she gives Gianni a once-over from beneath fluttering lashes and I can't tell if she's talking about his driving or him.

'Grace,' he smiles at her, 'behave yourself.'

'Ahh,' she sighs, 'I wish I could, I really wish I could.'

'Follow me,' he smiles and takes the lead.

We walk a long, curving tarmac road up into a square and past the ancient castle that gives the town its name. Gianni is slightly ahead of us and I'm trying hard not to let my eyes linger too long. Instead I turn my eyes to the town that had captured my imagination from the ground. There is a fairytale quality to this place. Once upon a time it would have been a remote, towering outpost, the residents comfortable in their isolation. Below us, the tourist mecca of Taormina is brightly lit and overcrowded. Up here the lights are soft and muted, swept stone alleys are lined with hundreds of steps, and there's a soothing quiet in which you could happily lose yourself. Gianni winds on ahead, turning left and right down streets the width of staircases and studded with sand-coloured steps. Gracie loops her arm in mine and we continue to climb.

I exhale slowly and know that, even though I have hardly seen the rest of the island, I have just found my favourite Sicilian town.

Dinner is on a stone terrace, and like most of Castelmola we have to climb a steep incline of steps to get there.

'Pizza,' Gracie says, 'I'm definitely having pizza.'

I tip my head back so that I can see the stars in the sky. This far up the mountain they look like you can reach out and touch them. The terrace is awash with soft amber lights and our company is an assortment of Gianni's friends and their girlfriends, all of them glowing and tanned. To one side I have Gracie and directly across from me is Gianni, his eyes turning a shade of light chocolate in the soft light, which sets his tan perfectly against the light blue of his shirt.

'Margherita,' I say to the waitress.

'Booorrring,' hums Gracie at my side.

The air is cool and it makes me shiver a little. Pizza and beer seem like the perfect meal tonight.

Pizza at home
Margherita

I like the simplicity of Sicilian food – the fresh, unprocessed flavours which, when combined, are elevated above the individual components. To me, the Margherita is the perfect pizza, and it's the one my father makes when we have pizza at home every Friday night. He sets to work on the dough early, and when he lays it to rest beneath a red-checked tea towel, we have to take care not to disturb it.

'Is it ready yet?' my mother will ask.

'Leave it be,' my father will sigh and hush my mother with a slow hand. 'I'll know when it's ready,' he'll say, as if the dough itself will tell him.

The Margherita is a combination of tomato sauce, melted cheese and the piercing taste of basil. I let my nose play over the smell when it arrives. Then I attack the thin dough with a knife and fork, starting in the middle and working my way out.

45 g fresh yeast
1 tablespoon salt
375 ml warm water
750 g plain or Italian 00 flour
1 × 400 g can crushed, peeled tomatoes, drained
½ cup finely sliced spring onion
salt and pepper
dried oregano, to taste
olive oil, for cooking
2 cups grated mozzarella cheese
½ cup fresh basil leaves

Put the yeast and salt into a large mixing bowl and pour the warm water over the top. Stir until the yeast dissolves. Gradually sift in the flour, stirring the

mixture as you go, then mix the dough with your hands until it is elastic and no longer sticky. Add more flour if necessary to make a smooth, bread-like dough. Cover the dough in the bowl with a tea towel and set aside in a warm place until the dough rises to roughly double its original size.

Whilst the dough is rising, you can prepare your topping. In a bowl, mix together the tomatoes and spring onion and add salt, pepper and dried oregano to taste.

Preheat the oven to 250°C. When the dough is ready, work it into 4 large pizza shapes, about 30 cm in diameter – remember that the traditional Sicilian pizza is made thin. Drizzle some olive oil on a baking tray (you may need more than one), lay the pizzas on the tray and top with the sauce, grated cheese and fresh basil leaves. Add another drizzle of olive oil over the top and bake for 20–25 minutes, or until the cheese has melted and the base is crisp.

Makes 4 large, thin-crust pizzas

Cuzzola is what Sicilian children really hang out for on pizza night. My father puts aside a piece of dough while the pizzas are in the oven and we watch him with quick eyes as he reaches for the frying pan.

'A cuzzola!' he'll cry out in Sicilian five minutes later, and adults and children alike will come running. Decades after Nonna was a girl, the cuzzola *still brings a smile to her face.*

Take a piece of dough and stretch it into a shape that will fit your frying pan. Heat plenty of olive oil in the frying pan and fry the pizza dough well on both sides. Put it on a flat dish and dust one side with a good helping of white sugar. Eat while hot.

A SEA OF YELLOW

'Have you gotten tired of our little town yet?' Gianni asks me across the table. To my side Gracie is embroiled in a conversation with one of Gianni's friends, and the rest of our dinner companions are talking amongst themselves.

'It's a good town if you want to relax,' I smile.

He gives me a throaty laugh in reply.

'I don't mind it,' he says, 'sometimes it's boring, but I like that everyone knows everyone else. I like that I can go to the bar on my own and know that there'll be someone there to talk to.'

It seems like a nice thing to know everyone else.

Gianni's dark eyes won't leave my face. 'What are you doing tomorrow?'

'I don't have any particular plans.'

'Have you been to the beach?'

'Every day,' I smile.

Chocolate-brown eyes look me over from my forehead down. 'I can tell,' he breathes. 'You know, if it weren't for your accent no-one would ever know that you weren't from here. You have the looks of a classic *Siciliana*.'

'I was born somewhere else Gianni, but this is where I'm from.'

'Come with me tomorrow.'

'Where?'

'To the beach, *Siciliana*.'

Gianni takes me gently by the arm and helps me down the stairs on our way out of the restaurant. The pizza has filled my stomach and the beer has turned my knees to jelly. Gianni's aftershave winds itself around my head; I'm so close I can smell it coming right off his skin.

'You like it up here, don't you?' Gianni asks as we take the final step down.

'Yes,' I say, 'how did you know?'

'I can tell by your eyes,' he stops and looks down at me. He's tall for a Sicilian and I have to tip my head up to him. 'Come on, let me show you the best view in all of Castelmola.' Gianni links his arm through mine and turns to lead us out to the fringes of the town.

Tucked into a back corner of Castelmola is a white stone church. The main entrance is a tall, narrow archway that looks away from the town and out to sea. There are only a few metres between the church door and the side of the mountain, which slides straight down beneath us, broken up only by a few houses built into the side along the way. At night the view is mostly darkness, punctured by sparkling lights that show you where the land ends and the sea begins. Gianni is at my side and his friends are strung out along the rock wall that stops you from falling over the edge.

'This is my favourite place in all of Sicily,' Gianni sighs next to me. 'Up here you can forget all the things that are wrong with this place and just concentrate on how beautiful it is.'

In the night his features soften and it makes me want to reach out and touch his face. Instead he brushes mine with a soft finger.

'You know, *Siciliana*, I quite liked it when you were pale as well, when I saw you at my nonna's house. Tomorrow, nine a.m.,' he says quietly.

The couples silently watch the view, occasionally leaning into a kiss. Gracie is keeping a slight distance from Gianni and me. We stand side by side looking out into the night, with not much else to say because there's something about this place that inspires quiet. You could stand here for hours and do little else but watch the night pass you by. After a while someone mentions our great enemy, time, and all of a sudden we're floating back down the mountainside.

'What are the drivers like in Australia?' Gianni asks, while I brace myself for the white-knuckled terror of the descent.

'They stick to the rules,' says Gracie from the back seat.

Gianni spins us around a curve.

'Well, they don't drive like they do here,' I add.

Gianni accelerates out of the corner then brakes hard, and angrily flares his headlights at an oncoming car that's approaching the bend on the wrong side of the road.

'Ooooooohhhhh!' Gianni cries as if he's on a fun park ride. He hits the accelerator again and turns to me laughing.

'Lighten up!' he says, and reaches over to pat me on the knee, 'I've only had a few accidents!'

We get to the bottom of the mountain in one piece and come to a stop sign, which Gianni completely ignores and shoots straight through. I see headlights and a fast-moving object coming across the intersection and I reach for the armrest with clenched fingers. A horn blares and the oncoming car picks up speed and dives around us.

'See what I'm saying!' Gianni waves a hand at the windscreen and beeps his horn in reply. 'No-one cares about the rules here!'

'I think you're the one who ran the stop sign,' I deliver softly, looking out the passenger window for anything else oncoming. Gianni turns his head towards me and when I look at him I can see the smirk on his handsome face.

'Stop signs are more of a suggestion in Sicily than an actual direction,' he says out of the side of his mouth, then waves a hand and accelerates. 'They're optional,' he shrugs.

'Maybe they should write 'stop' in Italian instead of English so everyone knows what it means,' I suggest.

He takes his eyes off the road and looks at me with the same smirk.

'You know, you're very funny, *Siciliana*. I bet you even wear your seatbelt when you're in the back seat.'

I sigh with relief at the sight of Fiumefreddo. How sensible my ancestors were to have chosen a town sitting so quietly on flat ground just off the coast. All is quiet and the street lights are glowing. Gianni stops the car in the middle of Via Ferrara, taking up the whole width of the street. Gracie slides out of the back seat on one side and I open the passenger door on the other.

'*Sogni d'oro, ci vediamo domani,*' Gianni says. Golden dreams, I'll see you tomorrow.

Somehow I don't think it will be a night that inspires much sleep. I climb into my single bed and try to sort through what is happening in my stomach.

The problem is that it's not just Gianni that is causing me this pleasurable discomfort. It's the taste of that simple and perfect pizza, the view from Castelmola, and the sound of my feet on the stone steps as I climbed high into the mountain. My head and my stomach are swimming, and I know it is going to be a long and restless wait until nine am.

But then I am awake. Suddenly. Inexplicably.

Someone is yelling outside my window. I rub my eyes. My ears feel blocked because I can't really be hearing what I'm hearing.

'Eggplants! Capsicums! Pears! Apples! I've got pears as big as apples! Apples as big as eggplants!'

The orator drags out every syllable as if in an opera. The Sicilian is rough and ancient. It's the language of the peasants from fifty years before. It's my nonna's language, and it's booming from the street.

'What the hell is that?' Ross groans.

'Someone selling fruit and veg. I think.'

'From the street?' Ross pulls the white sheet over his head. 'Food, it's all about food, there's food everywhere in this place. I can't take it anymore!'

I get up and pull open the blinds. Parked in the middle of the street directly outside our window is a three-wheeled truck loaded with boxes on the back. The driver is yelling his wares into a microphone that he has hooked up to a PA system, beamed out to the street via a megaphone mounted on the roof of his truck. Behind the truck a cluster of old women is starting to form, and I can see more heading down from Via Marina. Drawn, I think, by the prospect of apples as big as eggplants.

I smile to myself. I thought all of this was soon to be a fading memory. I want to take a picture of this perfect and simple Sicilian scene and take it back to Giovanni. 'Look,' I'll say to him, 'at least in Sicily the street vendor is alive and well.'

'Hey Ross,' I say, still poking my nose out through the blinds. 'Ross?' I call, but he's wound himself back into a white cotton sheet.

'Uuuuhhhh,' he grunts.

'Do you want to come to the beach this morning?'

'Uuuuhhhh,' he moans.

'I'll take that as a no,' I snap the blinds shut.

'What's wrong with Ross?' I ask my mother in the kitchen.

'He went out again last night with your cousins, and he's been eating a lot lately.'

'Must be something in the air,' I sigh. 'I'm going to the beach today, what are you doing?'

'As soon as your father gets back from his morning disappearing act with his friends, we have to head back to Catania to have our fingerprints taken.'

'Fingerprints?'

'Yes,' my mother talks slowly, 'fingerprints. In order to reclaim our citizenship. Although at the moment, I'm starting to think it might be easier to just be Australian. I don't think dual citizenship is worth it!' She gazes silently into her morning espresso. A takeaway container of *granita* is empty at her side. Her tone is enough to tell me that further questions are not a good idea, but I still arch an eyebrow in query. She draws a deep breath and huffs it out. 'While you've been at the beach, eating pizza, having fun,' she waves a flippant hand in my direction, 'and while your brother has been roaming the town with his cousins on the back of a Vespa, eating everything in sight, and while your father's been reconnecting with his youth at the local bar, I've been trying to reclaim our heritage!'

I bring my eyebrow down.

'Except,' she goes on, 'it seems that it's not as easy as the Italian consulate in Brisbane would have you believe. They don't tell you,' she shakes her head, 'that Sicilian officials are very good at losing paperwork, or that the *questura* in Catania is hidden along one of the busiest streets in Italy, or that when you do find it you'll have to stand in line for two hours only to find out that "we have no papers, Signora"', she takes a deep breath.

'Ma, I was there, remember?'

'You were there the first day,' she throws a finger in my direction. 'You haven't been there the other two times!'

I drop my head. My mother's voice is going up and down and the mixture of screeching and whispering is causing a knife of pain in my head. Her hand is like Nonna's often is, turned into a fist on the kitchen table.

'And then you're told, after your papers have finally been located under someone's coffee cup saucer, that you'll have to come back another day to sign them because they close in five minutes and are only open half a day anyway.'

'Ma!' I put up a limp hand in protest but she cannot be stopped.

'Finally, after we've made the hellish trip to Catania for the third time, the police call us to say that before we can be issued with an Italian passport we have to be fingerprinted in case we're terrorists. Me and your father, terrorists! And that you can't just be fingerprinted by just anyone, oh no,' she drops her chin and shakes her head, 'you have to go to the criminal police and be finger-printed by the forensic fingerprinting expert, and getting to see him is only pot luck because if there's a crime scene that needs dusting he'll be called out! Then,' her voice drops to a dangerously low level, 'if you have the good fortune of catching him in his office between crimes, usually about nine am because not much criminal activity happens here before breakfast,' she takes a breath, 'you have to wait until your fingerprints are sent to Rome and then to Interpol for cross-referencing. So basically, before a person who was born in Italy gets to become an Italian citizen again, they might as well just be dead and save them all the bureaucratic trouble!' She finishes with a gust of exhaled air and a mad look to her eye. I'm saved by a quick knock on the door.

'At least they have an effective immigration policy,' I smack a quick kiss to her cheek, 'only the tenacious get through. Gotta go, see you later, have a great day!' I grab my beach bag and run down the hall to the front door.

Gianni's standing on the front step in a blue T-shirt and dark blue shorts. His dark skin is glowing and his classicly-styled sunglasses frame his face perfectly.

'*Buongiorno Siciliana,*' he says and smiles a row of white teeth.

'Ciao,' I breathe, and as usual my voice gets stuck at the back of my throat. I pull the door shut behind me and we stroll the two short steps across Via Fer-rara to his waiting car.

'Before we go anywhere, we go to breakfast,' he says.

'Sounds good to me.'

Gianni has parked his car into a sliver of a space on Via Ferrara. He spins the wheel tightly to get out but doesn't quite make it, and I feel the tap of bumpers bouncing off each other.

'Did I hit it?'

'I think so.'

He reverses a bit more and taps the bumper to the back of him.

'Did I hit it?'

'I think so.'

The shocked look on my face registers and he grins. 'We have to get out somehow!' he throws a hand, palm up, in the air and shrugs a shoulder.

'Are you going to leave a note?'

'A what?'

'A note, to say you hit their car.'

'Is that what you do in Australia? You leave a note?'

'Aha.'

Gianni smiles, shakes his head and finally squeezes us out. 'A note,' he grins, 'I like your Australia, very civilised.'

We fly to the end of Via Ferrara and head towards the sea.

'Where are we going?'

'Riposto,' he turns and looks at me. 'It's by the marina and the bar has the best chocolate *granita* in all of Sicily!'

We drive through the town of Giarre to get to Riposto. It's a small seaside town with streets made out of solid squares of black lava rock that make your teeth chatter as you drive over them. Gianni comes to an intersection and waits for the traffic to present a space. While he has his head turned the other way I take a quick moment to look him up and down.

'See the stop sign here,' he points to the sign through the windscreen. 'Did you see me stop? You want me to turn the ignition off and then re-start the car?' he smirks.

'Very funny,' I reply.

I look to my left and see a building with long glass windows. Inside people are gesturing wildly and yelling at each other. All the men are dark and swarthy with cigarettes dangling from the sides of their mouths. Something slick coats the floor of the building and is running out of the doors in small streams.

'Fish market,' says Gianni and accelerates into the hint of a break in the traffic.

'Now, if I'm not mistaken, it's along this road somewhere,' Gianni breathes and looks left and right.

We pass the marina on our left.

'Marina was back there,' I point over my shoulder.

'Really?' he says. 'I'm sure the bar is up here somewhere,' he slows the car down slightly. To our right are houses and apartment blocks built up a hill, to our left is a low stone wall and the sea.

'Do you know where you're going?'

'Of course!' he shrugs, but doesn't look too certain and pulls the car over to the side. 'Maybe I'll just turn around,' he says, and puts us into a three-point turn. 'See,' he knocks a knuckle against his window. 'I told you it was along here somewhere,' he says as he heads back to the marina we had overshot.

At the bar Gianni finds us a table outside so that we can look at the boats docked in the marina while we have breakfast.

'Taste this,' he lifts a spoon of chocolate *granita* to my mouth and it melts all the way down to my stomach like a smooth river of cocoa.

'You have this for breakfast every day?'

'In summer, yes.'

I look to the sea, blue against the white hulls of the yachts. I look to the stone buildings on the other side of the street, and up to Mt Etna which, in this part of the island, dominates the sky. Just across the road people are buying fresh fish hauled from the sea, and I'm eating chocolate for breakfast under the watchful gaze of a pair of dark Sicilian eyes. It's not bad, this Sicilian summer life.

'So, which lido do you prefer?' Gianni asks, as he angles his car into the stable car park at Marina di Cottone.

'Lido? I've never been to a lido.'

Gianni takes his eyes off the burly man frantically waving him into a car space and turns to me.

'You went to the free beach!' he looks horrified.

I just nod my head because the Australian in me didn't realise you could pay for a stay on a public beach.

Gianni takes the lead and I follow his casual, meandering walk. He's a strange mix of manic energy and languid poise. A dark towel is slung over his shoulder and his steps fall in a slow rhythm on the wooden walkway that leads to his favourite lido. The walkway turns and all of a sudden, everything is yellow. Perfectly spaced yellow beach umbrellas flutter in the air, long yellow sunbeds stretch out beneath them, and to my right, yellow cabins act as change rooms. It's a bright sea of yellow set against the backdrop of the blue Ionian Sea and the white of passing boats.

'Do you like to swim, *Siciliana?*' he asks when we're stretched out on our *lettini*. His body is long and dark. I smile at him and lie back on my sunbed. Our heads, I notice, are only centimetres apart.

'I'm afraid of the water,' I confess.

'What?' he sits up. 'An Australian, afraid of water?'

'I know!' I sigh, 'I've never been swimming in the ocean.'

'Never?'

'Never.'

'But you can go swimming here,' he waves a hand at the sea and props himself up on an elbow. 'It's the sea, not the ocean; there are no waves, no sharks, no jellyfish. There's barely a current,' he looks out.

I follow his gaze and have to admit he's right. There's barely a ripple and what there is is being created more by the bathers than anything else. Still, I shake my head and smile.

'So, I'm not going to have the pleasure of taking you for a swim?' he flashes his white teeth and I feel my fear ebb a little.

'I'll wait for you here.'

Gianni sits up and cocks his head to one side, giving me a stern look from the corner of his eye. He stretches his long, strong limbs and gets up.

I watch him as he strolls slowly down the wooden path to the water's edge until he disappears from sight. For the twenty minutes he is in the water, I try in vain to read my book and occupy myself with my tan, but my eyes keep wandering off the page and out to sea. Finally I see him emerge and come back into my line of sight. Long, dark legs eat up the distance from the water's edge back to our *lettini* and he comes, dripping the Ionian Sea all the way back to me.

A sea of yellow 225

The *ARANCINI* OF LINGUAGLOSSA

The sun continues its slow rise into the sky and the heat gets drier. My book lies abandoned on the stones of this Sicilian beach. We start to talk and our proximity loosens our tongues and our thoughts. Beneath our umbrella and the shades on our sunbeds no-one can see the looks that pass between us.

Without the amber light of the night before, his eyes are almost black. He's dark and strong and everything one would imagine a Sicilian man to be. We talk about the past, our thoughts, our desires, and realise that everything we discuss strikes confirmation and agreement with the other. We swap stories of relationships past, of the illusion of love and the pain that two people can inflict on each other. When I stumble on a word or a turn of grammar he rushes in with words or phrases of what I might mean. He smiles and tells me he understands, even if I can't explain.

'You're different to the women here,' he says, and turns on his side so that he can face me while we talk. I notice his eyes stray from mine, float down the length of my sunbed, and back up.

'In what way?'

'You're natural, normal. I don't know what it is. You laugh a lot, you always have a smile on your face.'

'Don't the women here smile?' I ask.

He runs a hand through his dark hair. 'Not as much as you.'

The sun hits the centre of the sky far too quickly.

'You hungry?' he asks, and trails a hand from his chest to his stomach which

I follow with my eyes.

'A little.'

'Do you like *arancini?*'

I smile a slow smile in reply.

'We have to go up the mountain for them,' Gianni says, and watches as a little colour drains from my face.

Linguaglossa is a small town on the rise of Etna's volcanic slope. It is, like all Sicilian towns seem to be, made completely out of stone, with streets made from a building material found in abundance in this part of the world: lava.

'This place,' Gianni points out a bar on the corner of an upcoming intersection, 'makes the best *arancini* in all of Sicily.'

He hits the brakes, the intersection springing up on him while his head is turned. My nails dig into the dashboard in front of me.

'Scared?' he asks with a twinkling smile, and turns back to the road long enough to dart across the front of some oncoming traffic. In the closeness of the car I notice that he smells like warm sun and the sea.

'Do you see a space anywhere?' his eyes are darting left and right and everywhere other than in the direction the car is travelling. I shake my head. Parking spaces seem to be a very rare commodity on the bustling island of Sicily.

'There's one!' he points.

'I don't know if that's a park Gianni,' I look out the window. 'I think it's just a corner.'

'Yes,' he agrees, and nods vigorously while racing towards the imaginary spot he thought he saw, 'but we're going to turn it into a park. In Sicily,' he starts, and waves a finger as if lecturing, 'you have to take every opportunity and use it to your advantage!'

There's a squeal of tyres on lava rock as Gianni stops the car, puts it in first gear, revs the engine and climbs the footpath. The car tips onto its side, two wheels on the footpath and two wheels on the road, with the corner underneath. He rips up the handbrake.

'I bet they don't park like that in Australia, *Siciliana*,' he smiles, as he pats me on the knee and swings open his car door into the path of another car. A beep sounds and a Fiat swerves around him. 'Watch where you're going!' Gianni and the passing driver yell at each other in unison.

'You coming out for an *arancino?*' he asks, sticking his face back into the car.

My knees have turned soft and I can't seem to get my breathing under control. It's the sheer adrenaline rush only a Sicilian behind the wheel of a car driving up a mountain can give you. I realise, after being in the car with Gianni, that it's not Uncle Joe's fault that he drives the way he does. Even though he grew up in Australia, if it's in the genes there's nothing that can be done about it.

'Give me a minute,' I take a gulp of air.

The *arancino* is a small, deep-fried rice ball shaped like an orange or a pear. On the outside it's a deep golden brown and on the inside it's all fluffy rice with a melted centre of sauce and cheese. It's one of only a few things that can snap my scattered senses back into focus.

Gianni takes my elbow gently between his fingers as I come around the side of the car.

He leans into me and whispers, 'You're always safe with me, *Siciliana.*' He leads me through the traffic and into the corner bar, but all I can think about is the feel of his breath on my neck.

Everyone at the bar looks up as we enter.

'*Buongiorno,*' says Gianni.

'*Buongiorno,*' staff and customers chime in reply.

Gianni leads me, still by the elbow, and deposits me gently on a stool at a chest-high counter along one wall.

'I'll be back,' he says, letting his fingers stray up the back of my arm as he moves away.

In the facing mirror I see him ordering and I watch covertly, mesmerised by his strong features and his dark good looks, waiting for the flash of white teeth every time he smiles. I'm still wearing my swimming costume beneath my clothes and Gianni is still in the shorts which this morning doubled as swimmers. He looks comfortable and sure of himself, and he walks his languid walk back carrying two *arancini* wrapped in serviettes. Silently he passes one to me and leans into the counter beside me. Our faces are to the mirror as we eat our warm *arancini*. I look at myself and don't recognise the person I see. I'm eating a fried rice ball without the slightest idea of its calorific value and more surprising still, without any desire to find out. All I know is that in this moment, I am hungry and it tastes good. Our faces are toasty from the sun, our limbs varying shades of brown, and we are happy.

Gianni grins at me like a child, with a mouthful of rice. My teeth hit the centre of my *arancino* and I find the cheese perfectly melted and the sauce a smooth and thick consistency. The cook's thrown a couple of peas in as well. It's an amazing meal that fits perfectly in the palm of my hand.

I sigh deeply and crumple the paper serviette. I look up and find Gianni's dark eyes on me in the mirror's reflection.

'Good?'

I nod.

'Thirsty?'

I nod.

'Wait here,' he says, and brushes my arm again as he passes.

Again, I follow his reflection in the mirror and he catches me out with a quick glance. I drop my eyes to the crumpled serviette but can't help myself for long and look up once more. He's ordering something at the bar in that casual, charming way of his, and the barman nods his head and reaches for two tall glasses. They're pressed to a machine that fills them with cold tea. With an ice cream scoop in hand, the barman dives into a fridge and comes up depositing something icy into each glass. He drops a long teaspoon into each one and hands them to Gianni.

'What is it?' I ask when he returns.

'Just try it,' he says, and as I start to bring the glass to my mouth he reaches out slowly and brushes some hair from my face. I freeze beneath the touch of his fingers.

'Drink, drink,' he motions.

I take the teaspoon out instead and stir. The lemon *granita* floating in the tea starts to melt and break apart. The outside of my glass has turned frosty and as I lift it to my lips I feel the chill before it even hits my mouth. It's pure lemony sweetness.

Where before there was the warmth of the rice, now the coldness of the tea spreads quickly and settles sharply in my stomach. It makes me gasp with pleasure.

'Good?' Gianni grins.

So far, I want to say, it's been one of the most pleasurable days of my life.

I start to get a familiar feeling.

The satisfaction of good food and drink, a pleasant exhaustion from the heat of the day, the touch of good company and a beautiful view. As much as you can capture the feel of a place, this is what Sicily is beginning to feel like to me.

A PARK BENCH IN ACIREALE

'You're tired,' he says softly, as he takes his eyes off the road and looks over at me.

We've left Linguaglossa behind and made it down the mountainside unscathed. My eyes have closed without me even realising it and now I'm caught in a dream world. I'm being drawn under by the sweetness of sleep and his warm smell.

'I'll take you home.'

'No!' my eyes pop open. 'I'm not tired, really. It was just the *arancino* that made me sleepy.' The truth is that my bed is calling me. While the warmth of the *arancino* cools with the tea and *granita* in my stomach, my mind is on white sheets between white walls and the stillness of Fiumefreddo at naptime. Something is telling me to stay awake though because there is more of this day to come.

'You're sleeping.'

'No, really. I'm fine. I don't want to go home yet.'

I sit up, rub my eyes and catch him smiling at me.

We're hurtling along the highway and the sun is moving down towards late afternoon.

Sicily is buzzing past in greenery and bush after bush of *fichi d'India*. My favourite fruit is something of a delicacy in Australia because it's otherwise known as the pestilential prickly pear. In Sicily it grows unabated and thrives in the slivers of dirt by the roadsides. Hundreds of bushes of them even thrust themselves out of the sheer cliff face beneath the glamour town of Taormina.

A good prickly pear will snap between your teeth with the first bite, its flesh taut with juice. If you can get through their tough, razor sharp skins, the prickly pear will explode on your tongue like a million starbursts. Peeling them is a skill in itself and everyone has their own technique. When he can get his hands on them in Australia, my father favours washing them under cold water with a cloth to remove the prickles, before executing a technique involving a knife, a pair of tongs, a surgeon's incision and a fair amount of swearing. I prefer Great Uncle Charlie's no-nonsense approach. He places his plastic garden chair in a corner of his West End backyard, and sits quietly peeling the fruit in a pair of bright yellow washing-up gloves. In Australia we're usually delivered a box from someone who's growing a contraband bush, and they only seem to come in a dull orange colour. In Sicily, you will find them in shades of red, yellow, orange, green, and the sweetest darling of them all – the white. Like most of our fruit and veg, a box of them had mysteriously appeared on our front stoop in Via Ferrara, and I knew that in our fridge a bowl of them was sitting: peeled, cold and waiting to be devoured.

Another run of cacti blurs past my eyes as my eyelids start their downward slide again.

'*Ninna nanna*,' he chides in a Sicilian coo, 'you're really not sleeping?'

'Really,' I say, opening one eye.

'One more stop and then you're going home for a nap. Your choice, where do you want to go?'

Everything is new to me and I tell him as much. A few kilometres pass while he thinks, and gentle sleep starts to seduce me again. I lick my lips at the thought of a cold *ficho d'India*.

'Acireale. Have you been there?'

I shake my head and open my eyes.

'There's a beautiful *villa* there, do you want to see it?'

'I'd love to,' I smile, just before I finally succumb to sleep. The last thing I see is him grinning at me and shaking his head.

I awake to the sight of tall, iron gates.

'This is the park?' I ask, getting out of the car.

We make our way along the narrow footpath towards the entrance of the park. I'm walking on the edge of the footpath and the traffic is moving at lightning speed. A Vespa buzzes past and Gianni reaches out and holds me by the elbow as he draws me in close to him. I am out of danger but his fingers stay on my elbow long enough for his touch to burn into my skin.

The gates that guard the entrance to the park have been left open and we step through onto a wide, paved path. Even in their parks Sicilians can't help but lay stone. The path becomes a sweeping semi-circular terrace, and Gianni takes me by my burning elbow again and draws me up to the railing.

'Look at this,' he says.

Over the railing, the hill that the town of Acireale is built on falls away. Beneath it the sea closes in all around and out as far as the eye can see. Sicily's jagged hills and cracked volcanic landscape carve out the most startling vistas. Just when you least expect it, you turn and see a sight that takes your breath away.

'Beautiful,' he says, but he's not looking out to sea. His eyes are on me.

I freeze again without a response and break his gaze by turning my face to the view.

My heart beats quickly. His hand slides softly across the railing until his fingers brush against mine. Those dark eyes are still on me and I can feel my cheeks start a soft pink flush.

'Shall we go for a walk?'

'Good idea,' I say.

The park at Acireale is a structured maze of pathways and old-fashioned benches with trees spreading shade from overhead. A little drinking fountain is surrounded by children jostling for a spray of water.

'Let's sit here,' Gianni says, and takes a bench close to the fountain. His long, tanned legs stretch out in front of him.

We're closer than we have been all day, so close that I can hear him breathe. We sit in silence watching the children tussle over the fountain. One girl holds back the dark hair of another while she takes a drink. I can feel Gianni's eyes move to the side of my face and notice, all of a sudden, that his leg is pressed against mine. His skin is warm and his face is turned to study my profile. I'm too scared to turn to him, knowing that if I do our faces will touch. My cheek is burning and I don't know how long I can look away for.

I don't know if I want to keep looking away.

Slowly I turn and see the dark of his eyes. I turn away again and take a deep breath. His fingers move to the skin of my cheek and they brush away a long strand of hair that's caught itself against my lip. When I turn back his kiss finds mine and I lose myself in the Sicilian shade.

Jealousy and Nutella

Nothing wakes you up quicker than a kiss. All the languidness and heat of the day disappears in a jolt of euphoria. Gianni's hand strays to my face and my hair, his lips find my neck.

'Can I see you later on?' he whispers, 'for dinner?'

My mind races through the lunch and dinner schedule Gracie has drawn up for us.

'I think I'm already booked for dinner tonight.'

'And after dinner?'

'And after dinner I have no plans,' I disengage and smile at him.

'Then after dinner you're mine,' his arms fold me to him.

He shakes his head gently, his forehead is pressed softly to my temple.

'Do you have to go?' he asks.

'To dinner?'

'To Australia,' he sighs.

The light in the park starts to soften and we take this as our cue to head back to our town. By the time we get back to Fiumefreddo, the sun has started to set and Via Marina is jammed with cars coming home from a day at the beach. The street lights come on and men and boys start to gather in the small piazza off Via Ferrara. Gianni comes to a standstill in the traffic on Via Marina. I look to the piazza and find a group of my great uncles having a noisy conversation.

'Ciao Zio!' I call from the traffic.

They turn as one, 'Ciao Mischella!' they call back.

Gianni inches forward and indicates to turn into Via Ferrara. Whiskey ambles across the road with a young *cagnolina* at his side.

'That dog is a terror,' Gianni says, as Whiskey looks up into the headlights and throws us a bark. The young, female dog at his side nudges closer to Whiskey's side. 'He's not even that good looking,' Gianni says, and throws his hands up as we watch Whiskey and his date step onto the footpath on the other side.

'Charisma, I suppose,' I sigh. 'Ciao Whiskey!' I call out of the window. He turns quickly over his shoulder and with a twinkle in his beady eye barks back.

That night, after I've come back from another round of dinner and cheek-squeezing and prospects of upcoming marriage proposals, I open the door to Gianni's knock.

'Ciao *Siciliana*,' he says as I step out into Via Ferrara, now shrouded in warm summer night. The sight of him throws me. His dark skin glows in his white shirt and you can see his Arab ancestors flash in the striking features of his face.

'Ciao,' I sigh back as he leans in for a kiss.

I'm wrapped in the scent of his aftershave and entranced by his slow amble across the road to his waiting car.

'Tonight I promise you the best walk in all of Sicily!' he proclaims when we're sitting in his car.

'Gianni,' I smile and shake my head, 'you should be a tour guide.'

'Why?' he looks at me, confused.

'Everything you've shown me so far has been the best in Sicily, and we've hardly strayed far from Catania.'

I'm rewarded with a flash of brilliant, white teeth. 'The best is the best, we're just lucky it's all here!'

Via Ferrara is empty as Gianni veers out of his parking space. We come to the end of the road and he turns away from the sea and angles the car towards Etna's slopes. My fingers find their usual spot on the armrest.

'What did you have for dinner?'

'Octopus,' I reply.

'Ahhh,' he sighs softly and touches his stomach. 'Do you know how to make it?' he scans me quickly from the corner of his eye like he's sizing me up for some future duty.

'Not really, but I make a great tuna salad,' I grin.

'Tuna salad?'

I nod quickly and smile some more.

'I suppose I could get used to that,' he reaches out and brushes the back of my head with his hand.

'Where are we going?'

'I thought we'd go for a walk and some dessert.'

'I could do with a walk,' I say, feeling a little uncomfortable after dinner. I want nothing more than a glass of *amaro* and a lie down, but with Gianni at my side I can suffer the discomfort with ease.

Zafferana Etnea is where fairytales are made. It's so beautiful, so picture-perfect, it doesn't seem real. Although it's high up on Etna's side, it's buzzing with activity and has none of the remote solitude of Castelmola. It is a town almost in the direct line of the lava flow, yet it sits defiant on Etna's flank. The centre of town is a giant piazza bordered all the way around with thriving bars and antique globe streetlights. Almost all the piazza is taken up by tables and chairs, and people are eating and drinking in the open air, in the centre of town beneath the soft amber glow of the lights.

'Dessert first, and then we stroll,' Gianni takes my hand and pulls me into a bar. Like every Sicilian bar I have stepped into, the smell of vanilla, almonds and icing sugar overpowers you. Only the strong, bitter smell of espresso cuts through to give you some relief.

When we emerge Gianni is holding two small white paper bags in one hand. He takes my arm and slides it through his and we stroll leisurely down the length of the piazza. Occasionally heads look up and study us as we pass. Female eyes, I notice, land on him and stay awhile. At the end of the piazza we come to a long set of stairs.

'Come this way,' he steps down and I follow.

'Where do they go?'

'To the garden,' he says, and I look over the railing into the paved and planted gardens below. I put my hand in his and let him lead the way. We walk across more stone through the gardens towards the back where a long balcony looks out to complete darkness, but which Gianni tells me masks the sheer drop beneath Zafferana Etnea.

I wonder how they built these towns, so precariously perched right on the edge of cliff faces and clinging to the side of an active volcano. Maybe it's the danger of them that makes them so wistfully beautiful.

It's quiet and peaceful here. It's one of those surprising pockets of silence that pops up in the otherwise chaotic buzz of this island.

'Have you tried a *cornetto* with Nutella?' he hands me one of the paper bags.

'Not yet.'

'Be careful,' he says, 'it's still hot.'

I'm crippled from dinner but Gianni, the romance of Zafferana Etnea and the smell of warm pastry are intoxicating.

The *cornetto* is warm between my fingers and the Nutella has loosened with the heat of the pastry. I take a bite and a chocolate river sweeps into my mouth, coating it with sticky sweetness. The icing sugar on the top of the *cornetto* rises like a small white cloud and dusts my nose. I look over to Gianni and see that he has a fine coating of icing sugar on his nose as well.

'So,' we're leaning against the railing side by side and Gianni looks out into the darkness, 'will you be telling your boyfriend about our kiss today?' he chews thoughtfully.

I blink and look at the side of his face. His nose is long and straight and his forehead arches square and graceful to his hairline.

'I don't have a boyfriend.'

He raises an eyebrow.

'You going to keep it a secret then?'

I lower my *cornetto*.

'I don't have a boyfriend,' I repeat slowly.

'I'm sure he'll ask you when you get back if you met anyone.'

I turn my eyes wild on his face and put a hand to my hip. My hand squeezes into a fist and my *cornetto* emits a blob of Nutella in protest. Gianni feels the heat of my irritation and it makes his shoulders slump.

'Maybe I'm a little jealous,' he says, his dark eyes roaming the night ahead. 'I had a beautiful day and I don't want you to go.'

I smile at him slowly, very slowly.

'There's nothing to be jealous about,' I say.

It would be difficult to replace those dark, Sicilian eyes and this magical island, I want to say to him. Instead I go back to my *cornetto* and, like Whiskey's *cagnolina*, I shuffle into his side.

Red tentacles
    Octopus in sauce

'You never do anything in even numbers,' Nonna says, standing by her stove. 'Always odd. Even is bad luck.' She takes the lid off the tall pot on the stove and reaches in with a pair of tongs. Out of the hot water comes a head with long tentacles attached. Under her breath Nonna starts to count, 'One, two, three.' The octopus gets pulled out of the water and dunked back in three times. Once she's finished the dunking and the octopus is cooked, Nonna will chop up the thick tentacles and make a salad with parsley, chunks of garlic and olive oil. But my favourite octopus are the baby ones. Tiny balls of tentacles swimming in the red of a Sicilian sauce.

1 kg baby octopus, cut in half and cleaned
1 large white or brown onion, finely chopped
olive oil, for cooking
1 × 400 g can crushed, peeled tomatoes
salt and pepper

Boil the octopus in unsalted water for about 20 minutes, then remove the pan from the heat and leave the octopus to sit in the water for another 20 minutes.

Meanwhile sauté the onion in olive oil then add the tomatoes, seasoning to taste. Cook on low heat for approximately 20 minutes while your octopus are swimming in the warm water. Add the octopus to the sauce and cook on low heat for another 10 minutes.

Eat hot with a piece of Italian bread and a glass of red wine.

Serves 4

Finally, Etna

Bliss accelerates time, that's a fact.

It's so unfair to be so happy and so sad at the same time. Your heart beats in the moment but your eye is firmly on the ticking clock. Life in these two months is bursting at the seams – everywhere is colour, noise and heat, and every day my heart beats at the base of my throat with the excitement of it all.

Castelmola, Zafferana Etnea, Acireale, Aci Castello, Acitrezza (where my nonno saw his mermaid), Siracusa, Catania, Forza D'Agro, Stazzo e Milazzo. Towns on the mountain or by the sea with names like lines from a poem that draw you in. All of them skim past me like the bushes of *fichi d'India* by the roadside. I see them all by his side, his black eyes following me. During the days when Gianni is at work, I wake up late and take a *granita* for breakfast with Ross and Gracie. Then we drive to the beach where we do nothing but sit under an umbrella and move the beach rocks around beneath our fingers. We return at lunchtime to find someone has come past to pay us a visit but found no-one at home so left a box of miniature pears or eggplants at our door. One day we found Whiskey curled into a ball on the stone step, both his mother and his nonna having gone out for the day. At night, about nine pm, Gianni comes past to pick me up and we take a gelato and a stroll along the sea or up the volcano.

'You realise that tomorrow night is your last night in Sicily?' Gianni asks. We're lying in the sun at what has become our favourite yellow lido.

'I know,' I shut my eyes against the sun and the realisation that we have less than forty-eight hours left together.

'You don't have plans for tomorrow night do you?' he asks, propping himself up on his elbow and looking over at me. The sea is still clinging to the dark hairs on his arms and chest, and he's run a hand through the hair on his head to slick it back.

'No,' I squint over at him and can't help but look at him from head to toe, 'why?'

'I want to take you somewhere nice tomorrow.'

'Somewhere nice?' I smile, as if all the places we've visited together haven't been perfect. My second last day on the island ends as many of the others before it did. With a gelato on one side and Gianni on the other.

The next morning I'm standing by the side of Gianni's car on Via Ferrara when he tells me where we're going on my last day in Sicily.

'Really?'

The sun is beating down on my head.

His dark head nods in reply, 'Really. Don't you want to go?'

'I want to go,' I say but my fingers clench without me thinking. 'I really want to go.' Gianni looks at me and how I've started to wind up into a tense ball.

'I'll drive slowly, I promise.'

'You promise?'

'I swear,' he breathes.

I look up into the sky. Even before my arrival I was mesmerised by her. Now I can finally stop teasing her by visiting the towns on her slopes, and go right up to her. Finally, I am going up to Etna.

Gianni is true to his word. He drives slowly, properly, sticking to the correct side of the road, sticking to the speed limit and stopping at all the stop signs. She gets closer and closer, we get to the foot of her slopes and the car tips upwards and begins the climb up the volcano. The roads here are wide, probably to accommodate the tourist buses, and the roadside is surprisingly green and lush at the bottom of the slope.

'We're almost there,' he says and reaches over to pat my leg.

We pass an abandoned house made of stone, tucked deep behind some old trees. But this is the last of the greenery. As we head further up, everything changes and we find the road bordered on both sides by enormous black boulders – the dried-up, crusty remains of Etna's lava flows. Off to the side is a small stone building with black rocks piled up against one of its walls.

'That used to be a church,' Gianni says. 'The lava stopped right at its door.'

My ears start to block and I have to clear them with a cough.

When I look up the road has flattened into a wide plain that's rimmed with tourist buses and has one tiny cafe in the middle of nowhere.

'This is as far as we can go,' Gianni says. 'There used to be restaurants further up but the last lava flow took them out.'

When we get out of the car I have to shield my face with my hands. The sun is beating down on the side of the mountain and there's no shade up here. I can see the path of the last lava flow because it has left a long river of black rock that's darker than the other rocks around it. It starts further up the mountain and sweeps down, stopping near the side of the road.

'We're crazy to live in Sicily,' Gianni mumbles to himself and looks up to the lip of the volcano in the far distance.

'It's beautiful,' I sigh at the black Martian landscape. It's desolate and quiet. Even the tourists have softened their chatter for fear of waking her.

Gianni just shakes his head. 'Sometimes I think you're crazy too, *Siciliana*. Australia must be such a peaceful, happy place compared to here.'

'Well, we don't have a volcano,' I smile.

'Sicilian curse,' he breathes and looks down at me.

'Curse?'

'Yes,' he nods and looks at me slowly. 'You've fallen in love with Sicily. She's beautiful, you can't get enough of her, but in here,' he taps his chest over his heart, 'she's hard as stone.'

We take a stroll up to the edge of the dried lava and I have a photo taken next to my first close encounter with volcanic activity. I'm coated in a fine layer of lava dust and my mouth is dry.

'Time for an espresso,' Gianni slings an arm around my shoulders and we cross the road to the makeshift chalet which acts as Etna's only bar. It looks like something that belongs in the Swiss Alps, not deep in the Mediterranean. Inside we sip espresso on the side of the volcano. After our coffee we take to the beach chairs lined up outside the bar. We sit and lounge, our volcanic coffee throbbing through our veins. We lie back and look up to the blue Sicilian sky in silence.

Fish at Capo Mulini

'There's so much more to today,' Gianni says and looks at his watch. We've spent almost all day on Etna and I don't want to come down.

'You've got time to go home, have a nap and get ready.'

'For what?' I ask.

All I get is a smile in reply and a quick kiss.

I'm glad Gianni doesn't tell me where we are going in the evening because it comes as a sweet surprise to find out that while we spent the day on the volcano, we'd be spending the evening by the sea.

'Let me guess,' I say to Gianni as he angles his car into a tiny spot, 'the best seafood in all of Sicily.'

He stops and looks at me with mocking wide eyes, 'How did you know!'

'A good guess.'

Capo Mulini sits on the eastern Sicilian coast, and its most famous restaurant has tables that lead all the way to the water's edge. When we arrive the waiter smiles at Gianni and leads us out to our table. We find ourselves seated on the shore under the stars and, in an old-fashioned way which suits him well, Gianni orders for me.

'Eat,' Gianni says, spooning mussels stuffed with breadcrumbs onto my plate, 'you won't eat this in Australia.'

There are a lot of things, I realise, that I won't be doing in Australia.

'What are we going to do Gianni?' I ask suddenly, my fork looking for the sweet flesh in a mussel.

'About what *Siciliana?*' he says and takes in a deep breath. In his dark eyes I can see that he knows what I'm talking about.

'You know what.'

Gianni nods softly then tips his face back to look at the stars.

'*Destino,*' he says, 'do you believe in it?'

'Yes,' I reply.

'Then she will show us.'

'I think I've fallen in love with this place.'

Gianni looks down from the stars and into my eyes. 'Sicily is easy to fall in love with. But Sicily is not like Australia.'

'You've never been to Australia.'

'No, but I see the difference between this island and the mainland a few kilometres across the sea. So I can just imagine how different Australia is.'

'She's so beautiful,' I say and sound just like Nonna.

'On the outside. But sometimes it's a prison,' he says, sounding like her too.

I hate that everyone loves and hates this place in equal measure. So beloved and so reviled.

'That's what my nonna says.'

'It's true,' he sighs, 'you could never leave Australia for this,' he sweeps his hand out to sea and I follow it with my eyes. It sparkles under the moonlight and washes around the hull of a fishing boat purposefully run aground nearby. A table of six is sitting right next to the bow and all around us people are laughing and dining on morsels so fresh they are barely minutes out of the sea. This is my idealised, romantic version of Sicily where the simple pleasures of life reign supreme. In my own stubborn way I am going to hold onto it.

'And what's wrong with this? Don't you see how beautiful it is here?' I ask him.

'Yes, it's beautiful on the surface. But life here is hard. For you it would be like going from *le stelle alle stalle*.' From the stars to the stables. Australia to Sicily. Both beautiful and both calling me.

'Why do people hate this place so much? What is it about Sicily that's so awful, explain it to me. Is it the Mafia?'

Gianni huffs like I'm talking about something trivial, and he looks down to rearrange the napkin on his lap.

'The Mafia,' he waves a hand dismissively through the air, 'is everywhere, in every country. Mafia is in the simplest things. Paying the guy at the supermarket to watch your car, that's Mafia. It's not the Mafia that's the problem with Sicily, it's the Sicilians.'

I sigh hotly at this self-loathing.

'Ok, well, explain the Sicilians to me.'

His black eyes are strong on my face. 'Why can't you just believe that in Australia you live a good and prosperous life and here life is impossible?'

'Just explain it to me!' I clench my hand into a fist and place it on the table. Please don't let me give up on my dream of Sicily, I want to cry at him. I want to understand why people like my own grandmother and mother are repulsed by her. And why I, on the other hand, have fallen madly in fascination with her.

We've come to the end of our mussel entrée and the waiter appears almost instantly to take away our empty plates. Gianni reaches across the table and takes my hand in his, unclenching my fingers.

'In Sicily, the only people you can trust are your family. Your husband, your wife, your children and your parents. That's it. Everyone else is out to stab you in the back and ruin you, given half a chance.'

Across from me dark eyes are ablaze.

'Gianni,' I pat his hand, 'I think you'll find that that's the same the world over. There are very few people you can trust anywhere.'

'People live on jealousy here,' he goes on, 'there's very little work and not enough money, so as soon as you have something, others automatically want to take it away from you.' He shrugs his shoulders. 'Then again, there are also a lot of people who are too lazy to work for anything.'

I crease my eyebrows at his contradiction.

'I know it's beautiful,' he continues, 'but there's more to life than that.'

I just sigh. What more is there to life than beautiful places where you feel connected and happy and full?

'The only good thing about having to deal with Sicilians is that it makes you hard. If you can live in Sicily, you can live anywhere. If you can deal with Sicilians, you can deal with anyone,' he finishes just in time for the arrival of our *spaghetti alle vongole*. The pasta is glossy with olive oil and wound around little polished shells filled with delicate pale flesh, which lie hidden in the curves of the spaghetti. I'm already full from the mussels but as with everything in Sicily, there's always room for a little something more. The spaghetti twirls around my fork perfectly, the way it has since I was a child of three. It slides into my mouth and I taste the perfect blend of olive oil and the sea.

'Gianni,' I say, swooning under the moon and the influence of a little too much red wine, 'I know I haven't seen a lot of Sicily, but I've seen enough to know I want to see a lot more.'

I look out to sea. The moonlight is picking up the ripples of water like lines of silver in the night. Instantly I think of mermaids and Nonno Carmelo. If mermaids are real, this is where they'd be.

'If it's so awful here,' I say, narrowing my eyes at him over my spaghetti, 'why do you stay?'

His face softens. 'Because I know I'd miss her too much if I left her.'

Her. Sicily.

Something fishy
Pesce stoco

'What is that smell?'

'You smell it too?' Gracie asks, as we make our way home from school.

A trail has been left behind for us to follow all the way up Norfolk Road to the fork of Cameron Street. Gracie's nostrils flare, I hold mine pinched shut.

'You know what it is?' I say, realising there's only one thing that could leave this particular perfume.

Gracie looks deep into my eyes. 'Oh no,' she moans, and her whole body slumps.

'That's right,' I say, shaking my head and keeping my fingers to my nose, 'we're having stoco for dinner tonight. I bet your mum bought some too.' Nonna never shops alone. If there are artichokes or stoco or anything else on special or particularly fresh to be had she'll send word around to Great Aunt Rosa, Auntie Anna or my mother, and they'll all head to the shop to buy in bulk. If the smell of stoco is in the air we're guaranteed to find it for dinner in every Sicilian house in West End.

Gracie and I turn to look down Cameron Street. Up ahead are Great Aunt Rosa and my nonna, plastic bags clutched in their hands with the tails of the pesce stoco sticking out of them into the air. When she gets home Nonna will take the pesce stoco downstairs and place it in her wide concrete laundry tub. There it will sit, to soak and soften and stink out all of downstairs.

We don't see much of the pesce stoco anymore, but in Sicily there are signs for stoco everywhere. Nonna still makes this dish but now, instead of using dried fish that need hours of soaking, she substitutes frozen cod fillets.

1 white or brown onion, finely diced
1 teaspoon capers
olive oil, for cooking
½ × 400 g can crushed, peeled tomatoes

2 potatoes, cut in half
2 large fillets (about 250 g each) frozen cod, defrosted
handful green olives, pitted and cracked
handful fresh basil leaves
salt and pepper

Sauté the onion and the capers in olive oil in a large pot. Once the onion is translucent, add the tomatoes and ½ a litre of water and simmer for 5 minutes. Add the potatoes and simmer for a further 5 minutes. Then add the cod and the olives and cook over a low heat for 15–20 minutes, or until the fish is cooked through. Stir in the basil and some salt and pepper to taste, then serve.

Serves 2

Fish at Capo Mulini **253**

MESSINESE RICOTTA DREAMS

My arm is in his and we're strolling in
silence along the water's edge. A set of timber steps lead down to a deck that
looks out onto the water. In front of us is the sea, above us the moon is out, and
below the mermaids are swimming. The air is warm and the pair of dark eyes
beside me flash. His arm encircles my waist.

'I don't want you to go,' he says into my ear.

'It's magic here,' I say by way of reply.

'I know,' he breathes into my dark hair. 'Do you feel like dessert?'

'Dessert? I always feel like dessert!' I grin from ear to ear.

'For your last night in Sicily, we'll have something special. Something you
won't ever forget. Something typically Sicilian!' Gianni takes my hand and
pulls me away from the view, breaking the spell that had begun to wind itself
around me.

'Where are we going?' I ask as we pull away from the restaurant.

'Messina,' he breathes, and I feel strangely hypnotised by the Sicilian accent
on the double 's'. Nonna was born in the province of Messina before her family
moved to Fiumefreddo in the province of Catania. She has always been proud
to call herself a *Messinese* and in her own way she looks down on those from
neighbouring provinces.

From the city of Messina you can almost reach out and touch mainland Italy.
Maybe because of its proximity to the mainland, or because Messina has always
been a port city, you get the feeling that the *Messinese* consider themselves a little

more cosmopolitan than the rest of Sicily. For years the Italian government has been threatening to build a bridge from this charming city to mainland Italy. But I think Sicily is best left as an island. Best to leave her floating and free.

Messina was the last part of Sicily Nonna saw before she got on the boat, never to return, and I am in awe to be here now, so long after she left.

'My God, it feels like Australia!' my face is pressed almost flat to the passenger-side window. We're stuck in traffic but the streets are not narrow here, they're broad and lined with brightly-lit shops.

'Really?'

'The streets, the lights, everything seems so new here. I don't feel like I'm in Sicily at all.'

I cut my eyes to the traffic beside us. A young, dark-haired woman with almond-shaped eyes is staring past my shoulder. I realise that she's looking at Gianni. I turn back to him and find him staring straight at me and grinning like a cat.

'Don't let anyone ever tell you you're not Sicilian, *Siciliana*, even if you were born in Australia. *Occhi del'gatto!* You see everything!' he reaches out and ruffles my hair, puts the car in gear and moves us past his anonymous admirer.

'I was just wondering what she was looking at,' I say, feigning ignorance and shrugging my shoulders.

'*Si, si,*' he says, smiling and shaking his head.

Like everywhere we'd been for the past month, Gianni knows the ins and outs of this city. He winds down back alleys, past piazzas and cuts across choked intersections like a man who seems to know exactly where he's going and how to get there.

'Oh no,' he taps the brakes and brings us to a halt in a quiet street.

'What?'

'Wrong road,' he huffs, locks the wheel hard and puts us into a turn.

I just smile, 'You always seem so confident about where you're going.'

He shakes a finger. 'A man's at least got to appear like he knows what he's doing.' He looks left, right and left again with eyebrows creased. 'Over there, I think. No, wait,' he points in the opposite direction, 'over there. Even if he has no idea,' he smiles and sets us on the right road.

'You sure this is right?'

'Keep smiling and you won't get dessert.'

Finding a park seems to be a game of chance on this island, and nowhere more so than in Messina. Cars line the footpath three or four deep while people run into nearby shops, emerging moments later clutching packages of sweets or *cannoli* or *focaccia Messinese*. Gianni veers off a main road and down some quiet backstreets till he finds a parking space on a corner near a bollard.

'Wait here,' he says to me, 'I'll be right back.'

As he swings his door open two parking inspectors instantly appear at his side.

'*Buonasera*,' Gianni and the parking inspectors chime at each other.

'You can't park here,' one of the inspectors says.

'I'm just going to be two minutes,' Gianni says to them with a smile, and I see their faces harden. 'I'm just going in there,' he points to the bar, 'to buy a couple of *cannoli* and I'll be right out.'

As soon as they hear the word *cannoli*, something in their faces change and they break into smiles, waving him away and into the bar. Apparently *cannoli* are a compelling enough excuse for an illegal park in Sicily.

In the piazza across the road a group of teenagers are standing near a fountain and eating *focaccia*. They're concentrating on their food and one of them is gesturing to his slice as another comes over to examine it. On this island, even the teenagers are obsessed with their food. An evening's outing revolves, not around drinking, but eating. They go out for a gelato, a crêpe or a *cannolo*, and each person has their own favourite place for everything. I don't know where else people take food so seriously; where else it is an integral part of every moment's existence. Except maybe Nonna's house in Cameron Street, West End.

The driver's door opens and Gianni waves a thank you at the parking inspectors who are now standing across the street.

'*Buonasera*,' they all chime to each other again.

'Can you hold this?' Gianni asks and presents me with a package gift-wrapped in red and gold paper and tied with gold ribbon.

'What's this?'

'Dessert,' he says matter-of-factly.

I'm holding the little present carefully between my hands and contemplating the joy of living on an island that gift-wraps dessert. Gianni turns the keys in the ignition but doesn't go anywhere. He's looking out to the piazza.

'You want to go for a *passeggiata* over there and eat our *cannoli?*'

I look over and notice that the group of teenagers have finished eating and are sitting on a flight of steps that lead off the piazza and up to the doors of a stone building. The whole square is fringed in trees and except for the two parking inspectors there's no-one else around. Gianni opens his door.

'Do you mind if we go for a *passeggiata?*' he asks the parking inspectors. 'We won't be long, we just want to eat our *cannoli.*'

The male parking inspector looks to me and back to Gianni, and waves his hand as if it's no bother and we shouldn't have even troubled ourselves by asking.

'*Buonasera e buona passeggiata,*' he says and smiles at us as we leave our illegally parked car and commence our stroll.

The white stone rings beneath our feet. Gianni takes the sweet package out of my hands and slips off the ribbon. He spreads the wrapping paper open and reveals two golden pastry tubes filled with pearly white ricotta, sitting on a gold paper tray.

'*Ricotta cannoli,*' he says and smiles at me, 'you can't get any more Sicilian than this!'

He lifts one of the tubes off the gold tray and a thin cloud of icing sugar shifts.

'Take a bite,' he whispers, and puts the edge of the shell to my mouth. It breaks crisply under the pressure of my teeth and the ricotta slides onto my tongue. It's a blissful balance of sweet and mellow sour. It's the *cannolo* in its original, time-honoured state, and it's perfect. A slow hum comes from my stomach and out of my mouth.

'Good isn't it?' he smiles and I take the *cannolo* in my hand.

'Let me guess, the best *cannoli* in all of Sicily.'

'How did you know?' he grins.

I take a second and third bite as we stroll and I marvel at the perfect match of pastry and ricotta. Like all Sicilian food the mastery is in the simplicity of it all. Now I can't help but feel that I'm being wooed Sicilian-style, with dessert, and it's working. I've fallen in love with Sicily and all the beauty of this moment is being absorbed and locked into this single *cannolo*.

All things cheesy
Ricotta cheesecake

The cannolo *is too hard to make at home. It must be made by one of those magic-fingered Sicilian pastry chefs and eaten in the open Sicilian air. But if you want to taste a little sweet ricotta on your tongue, a cheesecake will bring some of the flavours of Sicily home.*

125 g plain chocolate biscuits
125 g amaretti biscuits
150 g butter
750 g fresh ricotta cheese
1 cup icing sugar
50 g grated dark chocolate
2 teaspoons vanilla extract
½ cup chopped red or green glacé cherries
½ cup mixed glacé peel
½ cup cream, whipped
extra glacé cherries and grated chocolate, to serve

Wrap the biscuits in a clean tea towel or put in a plastic bag and bang them with a rolling pin until coarsely ground. Melt the butter in a small saucepan. Pour the melted butter over the biscuits and mix well. Grease a 20–24 cm springform cake tin and press the biscuit mix into the base of the tin, then place in the fridge to firm up while you make the topping.

In a large bowl mix the ricotta, icing sugar, grated chocolate, vanilla, cherries and peel together. Pour this mixture over the biscuit base and leave in the fridge overnight. The next day remove the sides and base of the cake tin and dress the cheesecake with whipped cream and some more glacé cherries, then dust with grated chocolate.

GOING FORWARD AND GOING BACK –
LA SICILIA E L'AUSTRALIA

IS IT ANY WONDER
THAT CONFUSION REIGNS
WHEN YOU'RE TAKEN FROM
   ONE PLACE
AND PUT IN ANOTHER

ONE A PLACE OF ROCK
THE OTHER
A PLACE OF SAND

THEN BOTH
TURN OUT TO BE
DRAWN
BY THE SAME HAND?

Ciao *Sicilia*, Ciao Australia

'One more stop,' Gianni says, 'I want to show you one more place before you go.' We are back from Messina and driving slowly along the *centro* of Fiumefreddo. It is the early hours of the morning and everything is quiet – the stone buildings reflect like gloss in the streetlights. He takes a right-hand turn and drives all the way to the end of the street where two iron gates stand tall. Behind them there is only darkness.

'It's a fruit orchard,' Gianni says, 'but what I want to show you is up here,' he points up to the apartment block next to us.

On tiptoe we climb silently up four flights of stairs. Gianni fishes a key out of his pocket and opens a door out into the night. I'm standing on a rooftop terrace surrounded by the lights of the houses in the distance on the right and nothing but aching darkness to the front and to the left. Above me the stars are out in the summer night.

'Straight out there,' Gianni points ahead, 'is the sea. And over there,' he turns me slightly and points behind and to the left, 'is the volcano.'

'Where are we?'

'This is the rooftop terrace to my apartment downstairs. I haven't moved in yet but I like to come up here for the peace.'

Between the volcano and the sea, I breathe to myself.

'You can see the mountain from here in the daytime?' I ask.

'It takes up all the sky over there,' he waves an arm out into the night.

'It's so quiet,' I sigh.

'Up here, you're above all the noise and there is nothing around you but air.'

Gianni wraps me in his arms and draws me in. The spell that had been cast over me at Capo Mulini entwines itself around me again.

'I will miss you,' he breathes into the top of my head.

'I will miss you too,' I sigh against his chest. But at the same time I smile at the thought of Australia.

It seems I have begun tearing in two.

'*Sogni d'oro*,' Gianni says for the last time, as he delivers me back to my door. 'I'll see you tomorrow at six, we'll have our last breakfast and then I'll take you to the airport.'

'Ciao,' I reply and step into the little white house.

That night I dream of fish. In my dream I am at the Gold Coast in a high rise apartment and the blue of the ocean outside catches my eye. I go to the balcony and look down to find the ocean alive, brimming with fish.

'Gianni,' I call back into the apartment, 'look at this.'

Gianni comes to my side and looks out to the Pacific Ocean. There are so many fish that there's not enough water to contain them and they all start rising to the surface.

I don't want to wake up the next morning. I don't want the next morning to come at all, instead I'd be quite happy to be trapped forever in the waking dream of the night before.

I open my eyes and find myself presented with the morning I have been dreading for so long. The morning of my departure.

Ross is still asleep in the single bed near the door and I can hear my parents moving around in the kitchen. Like a dark, oppressive omen my suitcase stands almost bursting by the side of my bed. Stuffed inside is a box of *paste di mandorla* and I know that by now my clothes will already be infused with the smell of almonds and vanilla. My ears strain for the sound of the fruit and veg vendor, wanting to hear his cry of 'Eggplants, pears, capsicums!' one more time. But I hear nothing. A minute ticks past and I can feel my time in Sicily slowly draining away.

Already the days and weeks past feel like a sweet memory washed in amber glow. I see Gianni's dark eyes crinkle at the side with laughter. I can still taste the *cannolo* from the night before and Zia Enna's *pasta al forno* from weeks ago. My skin is branded by the Sicilian sun reflecting off the yellow of the lido, and burns with Gianni's salt kisses after he's come back from the sea. I can hear Gracie's flirtatious giggle and the cacophony of car horns blaring on our first day here. Already I am being stalked by the sentimentality of perfect memories and the blazing happiness of moments passed and gone forever.

In a matter of minutes I shower, dress and am waiting for Gianni to collect me. He's coming early so we can share one last breakfast together. My brother is being delivered to the airport later on by my parents and Gracie. My parents are grounded in Sicily for another week, or as long as it takes for the Sicilian officials to issue them with a passport. A favour here and a word in someone's ear there and they were cleared of all terrorist activities. Now they just have to wait for the powers that be to sign on the dotted line.

'So do you know when you'll be heading home?' I ask them.

My father just shrugs, I think he'd be happy to stay as long as it takes. My mother rolls her eyes, she just wants to escape the island of Sicily as soon as possible.

A soft knock falls on the door and I open it to a sad pair of brown eyes. Whiskey is standing on our front step staring up at me. He barks twice, sharply and then bends down to rub the tip of his nose against my sandalled foot. He looks up and barks one last time and then runs back to Via Marina. Behind him Gianni grins, 'I found him out here waiting – he's such a womaniser, that dog.'

'Are you sure you have to go?' Gianni asks as I slide my seatbelt on.

'I'm not that sure of anything anymore,' I reply, still fogged by sleep and sensing the sadness about to strike.

Every moment seems so fleeting. I taste and swallow every second left in his company, every second left in Sicily.

'*Mi hai stregato,*' he says, suddenly whipping his face towards me.

You have bewitched me.

I want to say the same thing about him and about Sicily. This magic island of stone around which the mermaids lazily swim.

'I would like to see Australia one day,' he says.

'You should come for a holiday.'

'I think I might. I've always wanted to see a kangaroo,' he smiles.

We are through the highway toll booth and heading towards Catania and the airport. I look over and find that his sunglasses have slid over his eyes. Gianni reaches across and with his arm he draws my head to his chest.

'Are you sure you have to go?' he asks again.

My face is muffled against the green of his polo shirt. I want more of him and more of this island, but I can't deny the little worm of pain inside me telling me I need to see Australia again, need to hear that distinctive Aussie twang, need to see a Southern sky.

My suitcase is checked in and we find our way to the airport bar. Gianni slides a cappuccino in my direction and hands me a warm *cornetto*.

'With vanilla custard,' he says, 'you haven't had one of these yet.'

Those dark brown eyes have lost a little sparkle and he looks away from me as he takes his first bite. The pastry flakes apart on top of the *cornetto* but holds together around the custard centre which has a lemony sharpness to it that surprises me. My cappuccino frothily washes it all away. We eat in silence, staring at the wall behind the counter.

'Will we call each other?' he asks.

'I think so,' I reply.

That's all we can seem to say as we dust our palms clean of pastry.

'Time to go,' I sigh, and then look up into the blackness of his eyes, 'it was a beautiful summer.'

He leans into me suddenly and kisses me gently on the forehead, his fingers digging into the flesh of my arms. I screw up my face and push down everything inside of me that is trying so hard to get out.

I see Gianni; he stands a head taller than anyone else. He raises his hand in farewell and his sunglasses slide down to cover his eyes again. Gracie is jumping up and down on the spot, waving frantically and craning for one last look, as Ross and I pass through the metal detectors. I blow them all a kiss and feel like someone has reached into my stomach and squeezed it tight.

I feel it again as the plane sweeps up into the air and leaves the coast of Sicily behind, the city of Catania shrinking away from me.

I feel the sudden need to take out a white handkerchief and wave it against the glass.

'Ciao *Sicilia, ci vediamo,*' I whisper, with my palm pressed to the glass as my little island disappears beneath the fuselage of the plane.

Ciao *isola bella*.

Ross and I step back in the time tunnel of travel. Hours stretch and seem to take forever and then suddenly speed up and disappear. Food trays come and go, movies begin and end. We're tossed about by the winds over the Bay of Bengal, and blink at the ordered efficiency of Singapore Airport. Until finally we arrive in a place where everyone is smiling at us and the friendliness is startling. Was Australia always this friendly or has it just changed in the two months I have been gone?

The smiling immigration lady takes my passport.

'Have a good trip?' she asks.

'Fabulous,' I reply, my mouth changing shape around the English words. I'm suddenly happy to be speaking and hearing English again, and the comfort of communicating with ease slides over me.

Ross and I go through to the baggage carousel and everyone's waiting calmly and orderly for their bags which are coming out quickly, one after the other. We only have to wait twenty minutes before our suitcases appear and we find our-selves in the Customs line.

A man in official uniform is walking briskly up and down the line with a small dog on a leash. The dog stops dead in front of a man carrying an enor-mous backpack.

'Can we look inside your pack, please?' the Customs official asks the back-packer, who happily obliges. The tourist starts pulling out thongs, a towel, a pair of shorts, but still the dog won't budge.

'Keep going, please,' the Customs officer says.

A pair of sneakers and pyjama bottoms end up on the growing pile on the floor. Finally the man reaches deep into his pack, his whole arm disappearing with the effort, and pulls out a single, blackened banana. The little dog goes pert all over and the Customs officer knows he's found what he's looking for.

'Please dispose of the fruit in one of the marked bins, Sir,' the officer says and bends down to give his dog a long pat.

It's so orderly and efficient and polite in this part of the world and it makes me smile, makes my chest swell with pride. This is one of the gateways to Australia, and everything that is Australia is squeezed between these airport walls.

Bright, efficient, friendly. Welcome to Australia.

The Customs dog starts tracing the line of travellers again and I see it come my way. It makes me suddenly remember that I'm packing half a kilo of Sicilian biscuits but the dog strides on and passes the smell of Sicily by. My suitcase is expertly handled onto the conveyor belt and the examiner pays close attention to the X-rayed vision of its contents. The machine is sparkling and state-of-the-art, and half a dozen more of them flank the facing wall. Someone presses a button and the belt spits my bag out the other side. It's picked up by another waiting official and politely handed to me with a friendly goodbye. How easy and smooth everything is, how perfectly coordinated. I smile with real happiness to be home.

But then I stop and blink, two paces from the exit. Thirty hours ago I wasn't sure I wanted to come home at all. So why was I so happy to be here now? Because you're home, a little voice says inside my head. I want to sink to the carpet and sit there for a while. How can I miss one place and be so happy in its complete opposite at the same time? I'm paralysed by confusion and I'm still standing on the inside of the exit door, not sure whether I should be going forward or going back.

I have no option. Finally, I move forward and out to Australia.

A lemony twist
   Sicilian vanilla custard

If Nonna knew what I'm about to reveal to you, she'd never speak to me again. I am saved by the fact that she cannot read English. I'd be banished to the hills of Sicily or the innermost desert of Australia. I'd be disinherited and disowned. All over a lemon peel and the secret to perfect vanilla custard.

1 lemon
¼ cup custard powder
¼ cup sugar
500 ml milk
cinnamon, for dusting

Using a sharp knife, cut off two strips of peel about 5 cm × 1 cm from the lemon. Dissolve the custard powder and sugar in a tiny bit of warm water in a saucepan. Add the milk and the lemon peel and stir over a low flame. Make sure you stir the milk continuously and, according to Nonna, always stir in the same direction, until the custard thickens (about 15–20 minutes). When it's the right consistency, remove the lemon peel and pour into individual serving bowls, dusting with cinnamon before serving.

   You could also buy some croissants, the French version of the Italian *cornetto*, and warm them in the oven. Leave them to cool a little then pipe in the vanilla custard for your own *cornetti* at home.

Serves 4

A NEW CAMERON STREET AND A BRIEF RETURN
TO NORMAL LIFE

'You should go see Nonna tomorrow.'

It's my mother on the phone from Sicily. My parents are still trapped there for at least another week until Sicilian officials can finally issue them with an Italian passport. The end of the most agonising wait of my mother's life.

'We've waited this long,' my father said, 'we might as well stay until we get it.'

On my return I had called the Italian Consulate in Brisbane to see if there was anything more that could be done to expedite the matter, to free my parents from their indeterminable wait.

'*Signorina*,' they had said to me with pity in their eyes, 'your parents are lucky to have gotten this far. Seventy percent of people get fed up and come home without their citizenship.'

How clever of Italy to have an immigration system with an inbuilt patriotism test.

'Is that Ma?' Ross says from across the kitchen. He has his nose in the fridge and is already missing Sicily. 'I could go a piece of Zia Enna's *pasta al forno*,' he sighs.

'OK,' I sigh in response to my mother's suggestion, 'I'll go see her tomorrow. I'm just not in the mood for any drama today.'

The next day I drive slowly to West End, dragging the journey out, going over in my head the questions I expect she'll pose and the answers I should give. She'll ask me if I liked it, if I could live there, she'll want to confirm that I'm never going back and that all of Sicily is starving and still war-torn.

Nonna had already been crying by the time I arrive. I can see it in her eyes and in the tautness of her face.

'You look tired,' I say.

'Bloody dealer,' she sighs.

Maybe what I mistook for tears was just tiredness.

'Do you want a cup of coffee?' she starts again and sits down slowly at the kitchen table.

'No, Nonna.'

'You've lost weight,' she eyes me up and down.

'Lost? I've been eating non-stop for two months!'

'You look skinnier – Sicily agreed with you then?'

Her question is loaded with meanings, her eyes flare open and her mouth pinches shut. I know she's saying one thing but meaning something entirely different. I also know that she knows about Gianni, but I'm not sure how much. Nonna may live in Australia but the telephone means that she knows all the up-to-date news from Fiumefreddo before its residents even know what's happening.

I have no choice now but to engage in her conversational dance. This is a particular art of Sicilians, who never say what they mean or what they think. They talk in circles and think four moves ahead. The Sicilian conversation is fraught with weaves and turns, traps and double takes, and is heavy with suspicion and speculation.

'It was beautiful.'

'Do you want a cup of coffee? I've got those biscuits you like.' Nonna ignores my opening parry.

'I don't want anything Nonna,' my voice is a little harsh, even to my ears.

Her eyes flare with tears. She's playing the drama card early and it surprises me – it usually comes at the end when brute force hasn't worked.

'So, did you like Sicily?' her voice trembles a little.

'Yes, it was beautiful, I just said that.'

Nonna shrugs.

'I told you it was beautiful,' her head whips suddenly towards me and the tears vanish, 'do you think you could live there?'

'I don't know,' I break her fierce gaze: not many people can stand toe to toe with her and hold those eyes for long. 'I suppose I wouldn't know unless I tried.'

My eyes turn back to Nonna's and I notice her eyes dart to my hands, checking for rings. She was blessed with a heavy dose of *furbizia*, my nonna, the gift of being nobody's fool.

'You must know after being there for two months that you couldn't possibly live there!' I'm startled by her tone. It's a mixture of anger and anxiety and her hand on the table has turned into a fist. She's mixing up her tactics now and it throws me off balance.

'Nonna, will you calm down!' I shout at her.

I am sure that she has been sitting at this table for hours, days, weeks even, contemplating my return and my thoughts and views on Sicily and how she'll counter them. She would have sat here terrified that we weren't coming back, that we'd all fall in love with the island and never return.

But I don't understand anything anymore. I miss Sicily. Deep inside of me I feel her, and the thought of her makes all the hairs on my body bristle. But I feel so comfortable here in West End, in Nonna's house, and so very proud of this efficient new country we call home. I'm anxious and frightened and completely torn in two. I can't bear to hear anyone degrade my Sicily or the beauty I found there. I can't bear to hear someone take away the perfect moments I spent within her shores.

'I have to go Nonna,' I say.

'Go? You just got here!'

She doesn't expect my new turn of tactics either.

'I know, but I have to go,' I turn and walk to the door.

'What's the matter with you?' she yells after me, but I don't reply.

I'm seeing red again and I'm not entirely sure why. I'm angry and confused and I fly out of the back door and down the concrete steps. I scowl at the chilli plants and the chickens clucking next door. I race down the concrete drive, the sound of it ringing beneath my shoes like stone. I'm out on the street now and Helen from across the road looks over and waves at me.

'Hello Michele,' she calls.

But I can't reply to her either.

All the dominoes in my head, and in my heart, start to fall, and finally I start to see what I could have only seen now. Could have only seen after I'd been to Sicily and back again. I turn on my heel and storm back up the drive. I fling open Nonna's back door. She's where I left her, sitting at the kitchen table with her fist clenched. Her jaw's working but there are no tears – she hasn't commanded them to fall just yet.

'What's the matter with me?' I yell, 'what's the matter with me?'

Her eyes are wide but she's not frightened of me, this woman's not frightened of anyone, she's just surprised. I never play the angry card with her because she does it so much better than me.

'Don't you understand?' I drop my face and flare my dark eyes back at her.

Nonna blinks again and says nothing.

'You raised me in Sicily!' I shake the finger I'm pointing at her. 'Everything. The language, the food, the *sarsa* days, the evil eye, the trips to the shops,' my finger turns accusing as I list off all the culprits, 'the chickens, Giovanni's truck, even this street with everyone living in each other's pockets, is Sicily. And you! So Sicilian, still living there in your head fifty years after you left it! How can you not understand me when you created me? How can you ask me to hate something you taught me to love?'

Nonna doesn't say a word. I'm not sure she understands everything I've just said and no doubt she will turn it into something else later. Besides, I'm not even sure I understand it myself, or where it's come from. All I know is that it's true and that I'm mad and confused. I was raised in Cameron Street, West End, but each and every one of its residents took a hand in turning it back into their respective homelands. Cameron Street lives trapped in time, and now modern life and modern times are closing in on it. I had found in Sicily what is being taken away from me here.

'Nonna's upset with you.'

It's my mother again, on the phone from Sicily.

'I know.'

'She says you flew off the handle. That you threw back in her face everything she's ever done for you.'

'I know.'

It's true. After I yelled at Nonna, I got in my car and drove to Wynnum. I needed to see water. I passed families in the playground and sitting at tables under the sun eating fish and chips. I envied what I thought was their simplicity. Australia is what they knew, all they knew. Australia was where they were born and where they grew up, and Australia is where they'll die. I sat on a bench by the water and tried to sift a way through my mess. I had a strange and dire affliction, an intense longing for a place.

'We're getting on the plane tomorrow,' says my mother and I can hear her smile, 'I can't wait to get out of this place.'

When she returns I know she will say how wonderful and bright and orderly and perfect everything is in Australia, and she will be speaking the truth, but at the same time she will try to kill my Sicily with every word.

I hang up the phone and sit by it for a heartbeat. It rings again – no doubt my mother has forgotten to tell me something, like how long it took to have her passport photo taken.

'Hello,' I pick up.

There's a second's delay like most international calls.

'*Pronto.*'

'Gianni?' I say.

'*Ciao, Siciliana,*' he drawls.

There is a moment of silence on my end.

'I miss you,' he breathes.

'I miss you too,' I say. 'What have you been doing?'

I hunger for the sights and sounds of Sicily, so for the moment I'll live them through him.

'We were working at Giardini today,' he says.

'Really!' I lean back into the chair, swooning. The lights of Giardini at night and the long walkway by the sea float through my mind. I wonder if he can tell that I'm swooning more over Sicily than I am over him.

'And then I went to Castelmola for a pizza.'

'No!'

Gianni just hums down the line.

'With who?' my voice thins and my eyes narrow.

'*Gelosa!*' he cries. 'With the boys.'

I am jealous. Jealous that he is walking the steps of Castelmola and that he gets to see my favourite mountain town while she only lives in my memories now.

For three months my life goes back to normal. I start a new job in the city, and every day I catch the bus there and back, and the service is punctual and efficient. Everywhere I go, people are friendly and polite and seem to be obeying the traffic rules. I am lulled again by the security of my bustling yet smooth-running and bright city. I am happy and I am sad. Comfortable and anxious. I don't want to leave but I don't want to stay. Until Christmas comes, and I finally find a way through my confusion and realise that I have to sort things out for myself once and for all.

A Chinese Christmas

'Where are we having Christmas? Nonna's, right?' I ask my mother as I clear away the dishes from dinner. We were all running late tonight so my mother threw together the Sicilian answer to fast food – pasta and ricotta. It takes as long to cook as it takes the pasta to boil.

'Well, where else would we have it? You know what your nonna's like.'

I know perfectly well what my nonna is like. Inflexible in her customs and rigid in her beliefs. Christmas Day is the central day of the Sicilian food calendar, and Nonna's preparation is intense and always starts months in advance. I look at the calendar hanging by the phone. We're already part-way through November and I haven't heard a peep out of Nonna about going to the shops, ordering the sausage meat, grating more cheese or making the macaroni.

'Shouldn't we be organising stuff by now?' I look to my mother. She's at the sink with her face turned away from me.

'What's wrong?' I ask.

'Oh, well, it's just we're having a different type of Christmas this year,' she's up to her elbows in washing-up water.

'What do you mean, a different type of Christmas?' my eyes narrow.

'Just different,' she says again without turning to look at me. 'Besides, you and Nonna still have your issues to work out.'

'We're still having it at Nonna's right? How different can it be?'

'Yes, we're still having it at Nonna's, but,' my mother finally throws the sponge into the washing-up water and turns to look at me, her face a mixture of triumph and pain, 'we're having a Chinese Christmas.'

'I'm sorry?'

'A Chinese Christmas. Your Uncle Sam's new girlfriend is Chinese and she's offered to cook us Christmas lunch. Besides,' she tries to justify herself again, 'your nonna has difficulty getting around.'

'And will his new girlfriend be learning how to make macaroni in sauce?' I throw one hand on my hip and with the other I start swinging a tea towel.

'I just told you we're having a Chinese Christmas. She's cooking Chinese!'

'Chinese?' my father asks from the lounge room.

'Chinese?' I ask again, swinging my tea towel in a big circle.

'Chinese!' my mother yells. 'Chinese!' She's waving her hands at us and little bubbles of washing-up water are flying around the kitchen. I look at my father. My father looks at me. Christmas is one of the only days of the year we get to eat macaroni. It takes an entire afternoon to make, and I love those little tubes of flour and water more than anything else.

'I'm calling Nonna!' I make a dash to the kitchen phone but my mother blocks my path.

'So you're going to cave in first and call her?' she smiles slyly. 'We're having a Chinese Christmas.'

'You can have a Chinese Christmas! I'm having macaroni even if I have to be the one to make peace!' I try to swing past my mother but she grabs my wrist with one of her strong hands that she inherited from Nonna and I can't break free. My mother is unequivocally anti-pasta and sometimes I wonder if she has a single Sicilian gene in her. While my father and I sit down with enormous grins in front of a bowl of white spaghetti on red sauce, my mother turns green. It made me think she had some sort of traumatic pasta incident when she was a child that turned her against the most traditional of Italian foods. 'Nonna made spaghetti with fresh tomatoes and their skins one day and force-fed me an entire bowl. From that day I've never been able to eat pasta,' my mother later confessed.

I struggle. I can see the phone. It's the only thing between me and macaroni.

'Ma-ca-ro-ni,' I gasp with each struggle.

'Chi-nese,' my mother gasps back.

We struggle for an entire minute until I see my father out of the corner of my eye calmly pick up the phone and dial.

'*Ciao sono Pippo. Si, non ce male, ti vuole parlare Michele,*' and serenely he hands the phone to me and I watch as my mother crinkles her eyebrows. Macaroni is a unifying force between my father and I, and we'll defend it to the end of our days.

'The one time we could have had something different and you've always got to go back to pasta!' huffs my mother and gives up the struggle. 'Haven't we had enough of things Sicilian this year!'

'Ciao Nonna!'

'Ciao,' her voice is a little strained. This is the first time I've spoken to her since I yelled at her, and I decide that the best tack is to pretend like it never happened. No-one knows how to sweep things under the carpet quite like Sicilians.

'Listen Nonna, do you want to make some macaroni for Christmas?'

'Pasta, always pasta,' my mother slams a cupboard door closed and plays the guilty card, 'you know your nonna can barely walk – now you want her to make macaroni!'

'Nonna, are you going to be able to make them? If you're not up to it, don't worry about it.' She's quiet for a few moments. I know she's contemplating whether to accept my olive branch. She's weighing and measuring.

'I'm not going to be making them standing up, am I?'

'She's not going to be making them standing up, is she?' I snap at my mother.

'Your mother will have to make the *sugo* though. I don't have the strength to make that anymore.'

'Nonna says you're making the sauce,' I inform my mother, and she turns a darker shade of red.

'I'm not making anything,' she says in a see-sawing, chiding voice that's thoroughly annoying. 'I'm Chinese this Christmas and I've conveniently forgotten how to make the sauce.'

'Well, last time I checked, I wasn't part-Chinese, so that means this year at Christmas you won't be my mother!' I guilt-trip her back.

'What is going on?' Nonna yells into the phone.

'Ask your daughter, she's become Chinese,' I say to Nonna.

'That's right!' my mother says and slams another cupboard door shut. 'I'm

Chinese, make your own sauce!'

My father rubs a hand over his face. 'All I want is a couple of macaroni at Christmas and now my wife is Chinese.'

'It's OK, Papà,' I reach out and pat him on the shoulder, 'we'll have our macaroni.'

Gourmet on the quick
Pasta and ricotta

This is the Sicilian version of a quick and easy meal. Even Sicilian fast food is made entirely out of fresh produce and tastes divine. This is what we eat when we're all running late or my mother wants a break from cooking.

500 g dried shell pasta
1 teaspoon salt
750 g fresh ricotta cheese

Boil the pasta in salted water until al dente, then drain, reserving some of the cooking water.

Meanwhile, in a bowl, mash 500 g of the ricotta with a fork, adding a little of the warm cooking water to loosen the consistency. Mix this through the drained pasta and serve immediately. The remaining ricotta should be served at the table. This dish must be eaten hot and can't be stored for the next day.

Serves 4

MAKING MACARONI

'Ciao,' Nonna says, in the same strained voice she used earlier, as she swings open the back security gate for me.

'Ciao,' I say and bend down to kiss her.

I only get one quick kiss on each cheek, none of the machine gun-style puckering that I'm used to. Obviously I'm still out of favour and will not be forgiven so easily.

'I bought the flour,' I hold up a plastic bag.

'Did you get it from the Greek shop at Woolloongabba?' she asks and turns into the kitchen.

'No, I just got it from Jack's,' I peek into my plastic bag, worried that there's something wrong with my flour.

'Ah,' she waves a hand, 'remember that when you make macaroni you have to get the special flour from the Greek shop at Woolloongabba.' I get a finger waved at me.

'Nonna, flour is flour.'

'Tsk,' she hisses, 'if you're going to do something you have to do it right.'

'What are we going to do if this flour is no good?'

I'm standing in the kitchen door clutching a plastic bag bursting with two kilos of the wrong flour.

'You're lucky I thought ahead and had your Uncle Joe pick it up yesterday.'

I slump in the doorway. 'You could have told me.'

'When was I going to tell you? It's not like you call me anymore.'

She takes the opening point. No-one does guilt quite like Nonna.

'More flour,' Nonna says. She's got her arms in an enormous mixing bowl. Flour is clinging to her wet, broad hands and the dough is slowly starting to emerge from the gluey substance it started out as. I slowly sift the flour from the bag into the bowl. Nonna cups her hands under the flour flow and rubs them together to dislocate all the wet globs clinging to her.

'I'm sorry for what I said that day, Nonna,' I say, so suddenly I even startle myself.

Nonna presses her lips together and says nothing, she just looks up at me with beady brown eyes.

'More flour.'

I keep sifting.

'Are you getting tired?' I ask. Each knead is straining the muscles in her arms and chest and pulling on the nerves in her neck.

'You do it for a little while,' she waves a dusty hand at me.

I roll my sleeves up a bit higher and straighten my apron. Nonna's eyes are on me and I know she's going to be critiquing my kneading technique.

I turn my left hand into a fist and push it deep into the centre of the dough. With my other hand I pick up a corner of the dough, bring it into the centre and place my fist through it. I move the ball of dough around in a clockwise direction.

'I raised you, you know,' she says, staring at the dough.

I look at Nonna and she's got tears in her eyes.

'You're like my youngest daughter.'

'Nonna.'

'Stop!' Her tears and guilt trip have ruined my rhythm and I've turned the dough the wrong way. 'If you go anti-clockwise you'll confuse the dough,' she says, as if it's a living thing. 'Always go the same way, whether it's dough or it's custard, you always go the same way.'

I wipe my hands slowly on my apron and Nonna takes over in a steady clockwise direction.

'I don't know what came over me.'

'Love.'

'What?'

'Love, that's what made you mad at me. You fell in love with that island.'

I drop my eyes to the floor.

'You can't trust love,' she goes on, 'it confuses everything. It's a beautiful place but it has a heart of stone.' She says again what Gianni had said to me before. They love and hate their home.

I look up past Nonna and into Georgina's house. Nonna's Greek neighbour waves at me through her window and I raise a floury hand back.

'You wanted to stay there, but you couldn't so you threw everything back in my face.'

Nonna stops me with her words because they are partly the truth.

'You're mad at me because you think that if we had stayed in Sicily things would have been less confusing.'

I wipe my hands on my apron again but don't respond. This is her conversation. I can't look at her but I know that her eyes are burning into my face.

'But you don't see everything you've gained here, or what your life would have been like if we had stayed.'

I feel her eyes move away from me and when I look at her she's staring down at the dough.

'I don't think you understand what we left and why we left,' she finishes.

Moments pass and nothing more is said. Nonna picks up the dough again and kneads it quietly. I sit and watch her work.

'You don't know what it's like Nonna,' I say quietly, 'being confused about who you are and where you come from.'

'What's so confusing,' she slaps the dough. 'You're a *Siciliana* and you were raised a *Siciliana*! In Australia!'

With broad palms she gently soothes the dough. 'Pass me that tea towel,' she points across the table.

I reach over and pass it to her. Nonna spreads the red checks wide and places them over the dough, tucking them around the sides.

'Now we let it rest for a couple of minutes.'

Nonna looks up. 'You have the best of both places,' she places the bowl with the dough to one side of the table. 'You know everything that is good and valuable about being Sicilian. You have Sicilian pride and family values and you know how to cook good food. But you have the wealth, the freedom and the organisation of Australia. What more do you want?'

'I know Nonna. But there is something that draws me there.'

'Love?'

'Maybe,' I say.

She shakes her head. 'Are you in love with him or the island?'

I look her dead in the eye. I don't have an answer for her.

'I cursed his whole family you know,' she wipes her face with her hand, 'his grandmother and all her children on the day we left.'

My eyes meet hers and she shakes her head. 'I suppose we'll have to find someone to lift it.'

'I had a dream about fish,' I say, and Nonna's eyes come up sharply to mine. 'I dreamt that Gianni and I were on the Gold Coast and I looked out of the balcony of our apartment and the whole ocean was full of fish.'

'Fish? Are you sure they were fish?' Her eyes search my face, anxious and sharp.

'Fish,' I nod, 'there were so many fish they were rising out of the water. What does it mean?'

Nonna wipes her face again and looks away from me.

'Good luck,' she says and meets my eyes again. 'Fish mean prosperity and good luck.'

I think about the rock I pulled off the beach at Fiumefreddo and which now sits on my bedside table – its solid white stripe a symbol of the same good luck.

A handful of white flour runs through my fingers. I'm sweeping my hand from one side of the table to the other. When I run out I dip my hand into the flour bag I'm holding at my side. I dust the entire width and almost the entire length of Nonna's kitchen table-top with flour, save for half a metre from the end. Nonna's washing and drying the macaroni pins and the dough has finished its siesta in the bowl.

When we're finished our tasks Nonna and I sit at the end of the table untouched by flour and put the dough in the bowl between us. She reaches in and pulls out a hunk of dough. Beneath her strong palms she rolls it out like a sausage, thinning it out at one end, then with a knife she cuts off little pieces, about two centimetres long and one centimetre wide. Nonna tosses a couple of pieces in my direction. I lay one in front of me and put my macaroni needle on top of it so that the sides of the dough rise up around the needle. I bring the dough together with the needle in the middle and start to roll the dough out along the length of the steel. With my palms moving back and forth across the needle, I stretch the dough out to a long tube of pasta. I see Nonna watching me as I work, she nods her little dark head and I slide the tube off the needle and toss it onto the floury table before me. And so we work, mostly in silence, until the feel of the dough beneath our fingers becomes more of a habit than a task. The chubby macaroni tubes are tossed, in no particular order, onto the flour-coated table.

'You'd better line them up before they dry out and stick to each other,' Nonna says.

I leave my needle, walk around the table and line up the pasta tubes in neat rows and columns on the flour.

'I know that Sicily has changed since I left it,' Nonna concedes quietly while my back is turned to her. I look around but she's not meeting my eye.

'I'm sure it has Nonna. It really is very beautiful.'

'It always was beautiful,' she nods. 'I still see the mountain and the sea in my head,' Nonna taps her temple.

'People aren't starving like they were when you left, you know.'

'I know,' she says, 'but they don't prosper either, they don't go forward, they just survive. They don't have choices and opportunity like people here do. Opportunity is what matters.' She stretches out a macaroni tube and tosses it in my direction. I don't know what to say to her.

It's true that here opportunity greets you at every turn. It's not the same in Sicily. People fled in search of opportunity. People still do. Instantly I am wracked with confusion.

'I'm not saying I don't love Australia, Nonna. I do, and Australia will always be home. But I've fallen in love with Sicily too.'

With the tubes all lined up I take my seat and continue my rolling.

'So why are you so mad?' she asks, keeping her eyes on her macaroni needle.

I don't say anything for a couple of heartbeats.

'Because I'm not sure which one I want. Which one I'm meant to have.'

Nonna whips her head up and her eyes burn into mine.

'*Babba!*' Fool, she hisses at me, and all I can do is blink in reply. 'Why would you want to give this up!' Australia, she means.

But I knew as soon as the words left my mouth that it was true, I was being a fool. Not because I was thinking of choosing one place over the other, but because I thought I had to make a choice at all. Opportunity switches a light on in my head.

'Why did you leave Sicily?' I ask Nonna.

'For a better life,' she says, looking at me warily. She senses I'm going to lead her into a conversational trap.

'For you?' I ask, closing my fingers around my macaroni needle.

'For my children, for you,' she says, 'so you'd have opportunity, freedom.'

'Choices,' I sigh, 'so that we could have choices.'

Nonna nods.

'Or the freedom not to have to make a choice at all.'

Nonna arches an eyebrow. The macaroni needle slides beneath my palms.

'I think you've just provided me with the answer *Nonnina*,' I smile.

Rolling them out
Macaroni

That's how Nonna and I make macaroni every year. We take an afternoon out of our schedules and we sit, side by side at her kitchen table, rolling out the pasta. We gossip, we laugh and she tells me stories of when she was a girl. Everything we discuss and we feel passes straight from our fingers and into the dough.

This is best made the day before you need it and stored in the fridge overnight.

250 g plain flour
250 g semolina
salt
2 long, straight metal pins (Nonna's are fashioned from old coathangers, but
   you can use thin metal skewers, as long as they are rounded and smooth)
plenty of extra plain flour

Put the flour, semolina and a pinch of salt in a mixing bowl. Gradually add water, a little at a time, kneading between additions, until the dough is elastic and no longer gluey. Let the dough rest for a couple of minutes and then break off a piece, roll into a sausage shape, and cut into smaller pieces about 2 cm long and 1 cm wide. Dust a tabletop with plain flour and sprinkle a little over the pins. Lay the pin lengthways over a piece of dough, join up the ends around the pin and roll it from the centre and out with both your palms flat on top of the pin. When the tube is about 5–6 cm long, slide it off the pin and sit it on the flour-dusted tabletop to dry. Continue until all the dough is used up. Store the macaroni in the fridge overnight, and then boil in salted water until al dente and eat with *sarsa semplice* (see page 11) or *sugo* (see page 305).

Serves 4–6

CHRISTMAS DAY

At Christmas, Nonna's house looks different. It's always warm and welcoming, but on this day it becomes central to everything we are as a family.

Uncle Sam's Jaguar is parked at my spot beneath the paper-barked tree and Auntie Gina's BMW is blocking the drive behind Uncle Joe's Fiat. My parents are parked further up and as I pull up I realise that we're all driving cars in shades of red. To ward off evil spirits. I park across the road in front of Helen and George's house.

'Morning,' they say to me from the balcony where they always sit. 'Merry Christmas.'

'Merry Christmas,' I reply.

I cross the road to find Nonna's next-door-neighbour hippies sitting on their front steps.

'Morning,' they say to me.

'Good morning, Merry Christmas.'

'Merry Christmas,' they reply.

Further down the street, cars have started to arrive at Great Uncle Charlie's house.

Angelo has pulled up in his old red Falcon, still going long after its heyday. Parked behind him are his brother's and sister's cars. From the street I can smell fried *polpette* and the heaviness of the pasta sauce. It's oppressively humid today, like it is every Christmas Day, but we're still going to sit down to a full hot lunch and enjoy every bite of it.

Voices float down the driveway. I turn the corner into Nonna's backyard and find Uncle Joe in shorts and a T-shirt stoking the coals of the barbecue. Uncle Sam's at his side pointing out what Uncle Joe should be doing and how he can improve on his barbecuing technique. If you look at photos of them when they were children, you will notice that they haven't changed that much from the day they got on the boat in Messina. Uncle Sam's stick-thin legs and knobbly knees are still there, although perpetually hidden, even in this heat, beneath a pair of long slacks. Uncle Joe has maintained his short, rotund and cheerful form, and mischief still flares in the warmth of his eyes. The two of them still use the side-sweeping hair parting Nonna Anna styled for them forty-six years before.

'Merry Christmas!' I call as I step towards them.

Their faces break into wide grins, and so does mine at the sight of them.

'Merry Christmas!' they call back.

Two houses down, Great Uncle Charlie strides out into his backyard and assumes his command post at his barbecue. He looks over and calls '*Buon Natale!*'

'*Buon Natale!*' we all call back, and Uncle Joe raises his tongs in greeting.

I leave my uncles arguing over the positioning of the coals and seeking Great Uncle Charlie's counsel on the matter, and walk up the broad concrete steps into Nonna's house. The security door creaks on its hinges and the sound of women arguing in short, sharp Sicilian cuts through the air.

'Rosetta!' yells Nonna, 'what are you doing?'

'I'm dressing the salads Ma, what does it look like!' my mother is frozen mid-pour with a tall, rectangular can of olive oil in her hands.

'It's too early!' Nonna yells back, 'they'll all go soggy!'

'Uhhh,' my mother groans and slams the olive oil can on the kitchen sink. Tin rings on steel.

'Merry Christmas!' I call as I enter Nonna's kitchen.

'Merry Christmas!' Auntie Gina gets up from the kitchen table and kisses me on each cheek. Auntie Gina is the youngest of Nonna's children and was born in Australia nine months after Nonna's arrival here. It seems my grandparents didn't waste much time getting to know each other again after three years apart.

'*Buon Natale*,' Nonna's forearm is around my neck and she draws my cheek to her mouth. The puckering starts and I know that somehow, while making the macaroni, we laid our differences to rest.

Sarah, Uncle Sam's Chinese girlfriend, is leaning against the windowsill that looks into Georgina's house. 'Merry Christmas,' she says, and we kiss each other on the cheek Sicilian style.

'Would you like a spring roll?' Sarah asks and motions towards the table where a platter of the golden tubes sit lined up.

'I'd love one,' I smile.

'Hello! *Buon Natale!*' comes an Aussie twang from the kitchen door.

'Auntie Fran!' I rush to smack a kiss to her cheek. This tall, blue-eyed blonde has been my Uncle Joe's girlfriend for thirty years. Sometime during the seventies, Uncle Joe clapped eyes on her long-legged, svelte blonde form and knew that he'd found his version of Australian nirvana. Drawn by Uncle Joe's twinkling brown eyes, stocky strength and permanent grin, Auntie Fran knew she'd found herself a little chunk of Sicilian manhood.

'Smells good Ma,' says Auntie Fran to Nonna, who smiles in reply.

'I don't know Fran, I'm too old now, I don't cook like I used to.'

'You wait Sarah,' Auntie Fran says to Uncle Sam's girlfriend. 'Thirty years ago I weighed fifty kilos – this is what good pasta does to you,' Auntie Fran pats her now voluptuous figure.

'After thirty years you've become one of us,' I smile at Auntie Fran and put my arm around her shoulders.

The air is warm and heavy with the smell of *sugo* and spring rolls. Every face is wearing a grin and outside the voices of my old West End float across the fences.

'God, it smells good,' my brother's form appears in the kitchen. He's developed a new habit of rubbing his stomach every time he's near food. Since we've returned from Sicily his appetite has become a force to be reckoned with. Gone is the skinny kid whose knees were once the widest part of his body. He's been replaced by a stocky and muscular Sicilian man.

'*Beddu*,' Nonna grins at Ross and calls him beautiful in Sicilian. I can tell she's happy to see the strong outline of his body. Nonna's main objective in life, to make everyone round and cheerful, is slowly being fulfilled.

'Are those olives Nonna?' Ross asks, picking the plastic wrap off a bowl on the table.

Nonna just nods and watches. Ross dips two thick fingers into a bowl and comes up with one of Nonna's perfect green olives.

'Have you got any bread Nonna?'

She inclines her head towards the end of the table where a corner of the tablecloth is covering a mound of bread.

'Are these from the Vietnamese bakery?' Ross asks.

Nonna just nods and smiles again.

He pulls the end off a bread roll with his strong fingers and takes a bite of his olive.

'Uhhh,' he sighs, 'there's nothing better than bread and olives.'

The table's been set, and there are bowls clustered together in the centre of the table with the start of our Sicilian Christmas lunch. Long, silver anchovies swim in olive oil. A bowl of Nonna's green olives sits next to another of dry, wrinkly black olives that stick to the top of your mouth and burn your tongue with their deadly dose of red chilli. A deep white bowl is turned red at its centre by roasted capsicums dressed in olive oil and speckled with chunks of white garlic. Beside them their fleshy cousins, the roasted eggplants, are cut roughly into bite-sized pieces and studded with diced garlic.

'*Mangia, mangia*,' Nonna says to Ross, as he dips a fork into the capsicum bowl and layers a slice on the end of his bread.

From the kitchen window my mother calls out, 'I'm putting the macaroni on!'

'OK, barbecue's almost ready,' Uncle Joe says, waving his tongs in the air.

'Mischella,' Nonna calls, 'go to the fridge and get the sausages for your uncle.'

I go to the fridge and pull out a long dish of Sicilian sausages, each one perfectly rotund and stuffed full of meat and pepper and fennel. Carefully I go down the stone steps and hand Uncle Joe the sausages.

Two doors down, Great Uncle Charlie has begun laying his sausages onto the hot barbecue while Great Aunt Rosa stands at his side. Behind them their grandchildren are laying waste to Great Uncle Charlie's tomato plants.

'Get out of there!' yells Great Uncle Charlie over his shoulder, and even from where I am I can see him turning purple.

''Melo, calm down,' soothes Great Aunt Rosa and chuckles. Calmly, she picks a ball out of a nearby tomato plant and tosses it back to her gang of grand-children. One of them has found the hose and turns it on full power, pointing it mercilessly at the parsley bush that loses half its green leaves in the watery blast.

'Oh my God!' Great Uncle Charlie puts his hands to his head and shakes it.

'Charlie, you OK?' calls Uncle Joe from two doors up, grinning ear to ear.

'I don't want to talk about it,' calls back Great Uncle Charlie, as he turns his back on the ruin of his backyard.

From both Great Uncle Charlie's and Nonna's backyard, clouds carrying the smell of roasting Sicilian sausages rise and float out over the rooftops of West End. Above our heads these little scent clouds mingle with the Vietnamese and Greek ones simultaneously rising into the air all around.

'Pasta again,' sighs my mother as she places a bowl of red macaroni in the centre of the table. Sticking out of the bowl is a huge ladle and gathered around it are twelve sets of hungry Sicilian eyes. My mother takes Nonna's plate first and ladles her a plateful of slippery, sauce-coated macaroni. Someone slides Nonna the cheese bowl and she dusts her plate with the *pecorino pepato* I had grated months before and that she had conserved in her freezer. My mother moves onto my father, Uncle Sam and Uncle Joe, then onto the children and finally to the women.

'*Buon Natale*,' says Nonna at the head of the table and holds up two, fat maca-roni spiked on her fork.

'*Buon Natale*,' we all call back and set to work on our red plates.

The tubes are al dente and the sauce is thick and heavy. Hidden in the layers of tomato is the taste of the *polpette* and steak that was browned in olive oil before it was lowered into the sauce to cook all the way through.

'Michele, pass the cheese will ya?' calls Uncle Joe, sitting to my right at the head of the table directly opposite Nonna. I reach out and slide it to him. Sarah reaches for the ladle and helps herself to another bowl.

'*Buono?*' Nonna asks her in Sicilian.

Sarah understands her instantly and nods her head. 'Very good,' she smiles.

'You just wait,' warns Auntie Fran, 'I'm telling you, once you start eating here you won't be able to say stop!'

'Michele, pass the wine will ya?' calls Uncle Joe. His hand is outstretched and it opens and closes in the direction of the wine bottle.

I reach out and slide it down to him.

'Who made these?' Uncle Sam asks, forking up the macaroni.

I've come to the end of mine and I can feel them starting to swell in my stomach. I need to leave room for second course and dessert.

'Nonna and I made them,' I reply.

'Who?'

'Me and Nonna.'

'You?'

'Yes,' I say slowly, 'and you ask me the same question every year.'

'What?'

'You ask me the same question every year.'

'Do I?'

'Aha.'

'Michele, pass the macaroni will ya?' calls Uncle Joe, opening and closing his hand again.

'Don't you ever sit next to anything?'

He just grins so I sigh and reach over to slide the bowl to him.

'Pippo, are the sausages ready?' Nonna asks.

'Ma, calm down,' Uncle Joe waves a broad palm at her, 'it's all under control.'

'Rosetta, you can start dressing the salads now,' Nonna says to my mother.

From her spot at the head of the table and with her eagle eye, Nonna keeps a tight rein on her kitchen and runs Christmas lunch like a German general.

'She trained with Rommel I think,' my mother says under her breath as she gets up and takes her place at the kitchen sink with the olive oil can. Uncle Joe forks up the remaining macaroni on his plate and goes outside to lay the last batch of sausages on the fire. I collect the red-rimmed bowls and smile as people are already starting to rub their stomachs with satisfaction. Ross reaches out and starts picking at the olives again.

When second course arrives we're all overheated from the macaroni, but somehow find a little more energy and a little more space for just a little bit more. Like all Sicilian meals, second course features the colour red. My mother sets the salads at the ends of the table. Ruby-red tomatoes and onion, and a bowl of lettuce slick with olive oil. In the centre she lays down a huge platter. Meatballs, square chunks of stringy skirt steak spiked with sharp cloves of garlic, round potatoes and slices of *falso magro*, all coated in the thick red pasta sauce. Uncle Joe bounds up the stairs and presents us all with golden roasted sausages. We all fall on second course as if the macaroni never existed.

'Pass the lettuce will ya.'

I roll my eyes, 'Joey "Passover", that's what we're going to call you from now on,' I say, and pass the lettuce.

I love the taste of the stringy steak with the crispness of the lettuce. I cut through my slice of *falso magro* and watch as the hardboiled egg falls away, then slice through the sausage and team a steaming piece of it with the cool tomato and onion salad. Ross breaks another bread roll in half and reaches for a hot sausage. We all sit in Nonna's kitchen, warm from the food and the weather. In this huge room, her long kitchen table fits all twelve of us snugly, elbow to elbow, thigh to thigh. Plates are shuffled and passed over, glasses are filled and emptied. From outside come the sounds of the same scene going on next door at Georgina's house and down the road at Great Uncle Charlie's. Some things from the old West End still remain, still survive and thrive.

We take a well-earned break between second course and dessert. The men have gone outside to sit in the concrete backyard and smoke. The children have gone into Nonna's lounge room to watch TV in airconditioned comfort, and the women are in the kitchen clearing the dishes and gossiping.

I take a seat on the top back step, halfway between the backyard and the kitchen. The macadamia nut tree in Rose's backyard that overhangs a corner of Nonna's is so old now that it no longer bears any fruit. When I was a child it used to drop nuts like rain on Nonna's backyard. They'd be everywhere and I'd collect them in a plastic ice cream tub. Nonno had a small hole in the concrete that was the perfect size for a nut. One by one he'd put them in there and with half a brick he'd crack them open and pass them to me to eat. The tree has been pruned all the way back and the only thing it drops now is a little bit of shade.

The feeling of Sicily is on me again. Maybe it's the sound of the language, or the feel of a full stomach, the warmth of the sun on the concrete and the pleasant sleepiness coming over me. It's the feel of Nonna's kitchen as well, I realise, the feel of this Sicilian kitchen. My most familiar feeling of all.

'Fran!' Nonna calls. 'You fu-coffey?' She grins and we all start laughing.

A slow smile spreads across Auntie Fran's face. 'Yeah Ma,' she waves a hand at Nonna, 'don't worry, I'll make it.'

And so begins dessert.

My fork slides down the side of my gelato. It's a triangular wedge of layered ice cream. Banana on the outside, then a layer of chocolate, then vanilla with multicoloured candied fruit, and at its narrowest point a liqueur-drenched piece of red sponge cake. It's our traditional Christmas dessert but for the first time in my life I'm not even remotely interested in it.

I look down the table to Nonna Anna who's sitting at its head. She's nibbling a forkful of gelato with her front two teeth so that her nose twitches like a mouse. Next to her is my mother who's rolling the gelato in her mouth, letting it melt along her tongue. One side of her face contorts and she squeezes her right eye shut. 'Oh, it's cold,' she says through gritted teeth.

Uncle Joe's sitting next to me and his round, olive face breaks into a grin. 'Hey Michele,' he nudges me, 'who am I?' he squints an eye, contorts his face and makes his whole body spasm.

'Ah shut up!' my mother says, as we all start laughing.

'God, I'm so full,' says Uncle Joe, hacking his gelato wedge with the side of his fork and making it disappear in five bites.

'Where did you get the gelato?' Uncle Sam turns and asks Auntie Gina.

'The Valley,' she replies coolly and brushes a hand through her perfect, honey-coloured hair.

'What?' Uncle Sam bellows down the table.

'The Valley!' Auntie Gina yells back.

'I'll have to get the phone number for that place.'

'You know that place has been there for thirty years and we have this conversation every Christmas,' Auntie Gina points out.

'What?'

'"Sammy Two Times"', I mumble, and Uncle Joe barks a laugh next to me.

'What?'

'Are you really hard of hearing or is it just an annoying habit?' I ask.

'What?'

'Will you just eat!' my mother snaps.

'You got any more?' Uncle Joe asks and rubs his stomach with a broad hand, 'ooohhhh, I'm so full.'

Auntie Gina and my mother roll their eyes but Uncle Joe just ignores them and continues.

'Next Christmas we're not having all this food. Next Christmas we're just going to have salads. You hear that Ma!' he yells down the table to Nonna. 'We can't keep eating like this! Look at me!' he slaps a hand against his stomach.

Nonna lowers her fork slowly and we all turn to her in silence. Her lips are smiling softly but her eyes are dead still.

'When I'm dead,' she says to her son, her voice cool and her eyes still, 'you can do whatever you want. But while I'm still alive, this is how it will be, because this is how it has always been. When I'm dead you can eat all the salads you like.' Nonna slides another piece of gelato into her mouth that sets her nose back to twitching.

'Ahh, you'd better live forever Ma!' says Auntie Fran from the other end of the table.

'Ohh, I can't eat anymore,' groans Uncle Joe, and scrapes his fork along his dessert plate collecting the last melted bits of his gelato.

'Well don't eat anymore!' Auntie Gina cries.

'What's the matter with you?' Ross asks and points at my plate.

'Nothing,' I start to mush my ice cream down with my fork.

'There's something seriously wrong when you don't eat ice cream,' my brother points out. I look up to find everyone staring at me. There's probably no good time to tell them, but at least now I have their complete attention and I can no longer ruin their appetite.

'I'm going back to Sicily,' I draw a deep, deep breath, 'for a little while.'

Silence descends and dark eyes are on me.

'What did she say?' Nonna asks my mother.

'I'm going back to Sicily,' I turn to Nonna and repeat myself in Sicilian, but

I know she understood me the first time in English.

Nonna's nut-brown eyes grow wide and her teeth start to grate against each other like she's chewing a mouthful of air.

'While I'm still alive you have to live here!' her heavy palm crashes down onto the table for emphasis and the silence grows deeper. I start to wonder what happened to 'whatever makes you happy dear', but this is a Sicilian family and we thrive on demands, passion and obsessive love.

'I'm going back to Sicily,' I say again, 'for a little while.'

This time I deliver each word slowly, in Sicilian, eye to eye and toe to toe with my Nonna. She just stares back at me with steel in her eyes.

'Not forever,' I say to her, 'but for a little while.'

'For how long?' she asks.

'I don't know.'

'Why?' my mother asks.

Because it's calling me, I want to say to her.

'For how long?' Nonna insists again.

Until Australia calls me back, I want to say to her. I know she will.

'Why?' my mother repeats.

I don't answer either of them, instead I just look up and smile.

The heavy stuff
Sugo

This is the heavy, full-bodied sauce we eat every Christmas. It's the sort of stuff that makes you want to lick your fingers and, like my brother's been doing of late, rub your stomach.

1 kg skirt steak, cut into 10–12 pieces
5–6 cloves garlic, peeled and halved
½ cup finely chopped flat-leaf parsley
olive oil, for cooking
4 potatoes, cut in half
1 quantity meatball mix (see page 66), formed into patties
2 quantities *sarsa semplice* (see page 11)

Stick the point of a knife into each piece of skirt steak and insert half a clove of garlic and a pinch of parsley.

In a frying pan heat some olive oil and, in batches, brown the potatoes, meatballs and skirt steak. When they're browned, reheat the *sarsa* and lower the potatoes, meatballs and skirt steak into the sauce. Cook, covered, on low heat until the meat has cooked all the way through (this should take no longer than an hour). Once cooked, remove the potatoes, meatballs and skirt steak from the sauce. Serve the sauce as first course with cooked spaghetti or macaroni, and serve the sauce-covered meat and potatoes as second course.

Serves 10–12

The Sicilian curse

'I don't understand,' Nonna wipes a broad palm over her face, 'we left there to come here. And now you want to go back?'

'Yes, but not forever,' I say. 'Just for a little while.' I add. Right now, that island is calling me. When this island calls me back, I will return. Australia will always be home, because home is where your memories are formed, the place where those perfect bubbles of the past are captured forever. I'm caught now, happily between my two islands, both perfect in their own way and both entirely my own. I don't have to choose one over the other, I just have to find a way to have them both.

Nothing is forever anymore, there are no great voyages to the other side of the world from which you never return. Nonna made the last great Sicilian voyage of immigration to the new world of Australia.

Immigration isn't a distant memory for me, it's still a living reality.

I feel a little like my mother's rag doll that dove overboard off the coast of North Africa.

I want to see how my immigration story ends.

ACKNOWLEDGEMENTS

My family have contributed the most to this book and I particularly acknowledge my mother's guiding and knowledgeable hand with the recipes.

I also want to acknowledge and thank Madonna Duffy for her encouragement and Fran Moore for taking on a new author.

Special thanks go to Julie Gibbs, Ingrid Ohlsson, Virginia Birch, Marina Messiha and everyone at Penguin for their joy, enthusiasm and assistance.

INDEX OF RECIPES

LIST OF FAMILY PHOTOGRAPHS

LANTERN

Published by the Penguin Group
Penguin Group (Australia)
250 Camberwell Road, Camberwell, Victoria 3124, Australia
(a division of Pearson Australia Group Pty Ltd)
Penguin Group (USA) Inc.
375 Hudson Street, New York, New York 10014, USA
Penguin Group (Canada)
90 Eglinton Avenue East, Suite 700, Toronto, Canada ON M4P 2Y3
(a division of Pearson Penguin Canada Inc.)
Penguin Books Ltd
80 Strand, London WC2R 0RL England
Penguin Ireland
25 St Stephen's Green, Dublin 2, Ireland
(a division of Penguin Books Ltd)
Penguin Books India Pvt Ltd
11 Community Centre, Panchsheel Park, New Delhi – 110 017, India
Penguin Group (NZ)
67 Apollo Drive, Rosedale, North Shore 0632, New Zealand
(a division of Pearson New Zealand Ltd)
Penguin Books (South Africa) (Pty) Ltd
24 Sturdee Avenue, Rosebank, Johannesburg 2196, South Africa

Penguin Books Ltd, Registered Offices: 80 Strand, London, WC2R 0RL, England

First published by Penguin Group (Australia), 2008

10 9 8 7 6 5 4 3 2 1

Design by Marina Messiha © Penguin Group (Australia)
Cover photography by Michele Di'Bartolo and Julie Gibbs
Internal photography by Simon Griffiths, Michele Di'Bartolo and Julie Gibbs (see picture credits below)
Author photograph by Ian Wallace
Typeset in 11/15pt Cochin by Post Pre-press Group, Brisbane, Queensland
Printed in China by 1010 Printing International Ltd.

National Library of Australia
Cataloguing-in-Publication data:

Di'Bartolo, Michele.

The Sicilian kitchen / author, Michele Di'Bartolo.

Camberwell, Vic. : Penguin Group Australia, 2008.

9781920989880 (hbk.)

Di'Bartolo, Michele–Travel–Italy–Sicily.
Cookery, Italian–Sicilian style.
Sicily (Italy)–Description and travel.

641.59458

penguin.com.au

Photographs on facing half-title page and pages iv, 9, 10, 23, 41, 47, 56, 61, 67, 72, 82, 146, 173 and 308 by Simon Griffiths. Photographs on pages iii, 1, 2, 18, 24, 28, 32, 64, 65, 96, 99, 100, 124, 130, 158, 163, 164, 174, 200, 210, 218, 223, 225, 253, 263, 264, 290, 303 and 311 by Michele Di'Bartolo. Photographs on front endpapers, back endpapers, pages vi–vii, 54, 74, 108–109, 115, 117, 118, 136–137, 143, 144–145, 151, 183, 189, 191, 194–195, 202–203, 207, 208, 214, 216–217, 226, 236–237, 247, 258, 260–261, 272, 279, 292–293, 304, 307 and facing page by Julie Gibbs.